# RECORDS OF CIVILIZATION

## SOURCES AND STUDIES

EDITED UNDER THE AUSPICES OF THE

DEPARTMENT OF HISTORY, COLUMBIA UNIVERSITY

NUMBER XXVII

# THE EDUCATION OF A CHRISTIAN PRINCE

# THE EDUCATION OF
# A CHRISTIAN PRINCE

BY

DESIDERIUS ERASMUS

TRANSLATED WITH AN INTRODUCTION
ON ERASMUS AND ON ANCIENT AND
MEDIEVAL POLITICAL THOUGHT

BY

LESTER K. BORN

NEW YORK: MORNINGSIDE HEIGHTS
COLUMBIA UNIVERSITY PRESS
M·C·M·XXXVI

FOREIGN AGENTS

OXFORD UNIVERSITY PRESS
HUMPHREY MILFORD, AMEN HOUSE
LONDON, E.C.4, ENGLAND

KWANG HSUEH PUBLISHING HOUSE
140 PEKING ROAD
SHANGHAI, CHINA

MARUZEN COMPANY, LTD.
6 NIHONBASHI, TORI-NICHOME
TOKYO, JAPAN

OXFORD UNIVERSITY PRESS
B. I. BUILDING, NICOL ROAD
BOMBAY, INDIA

To
T. K. B.

God gives not Kings the stile of *Gods* in vaine,
For on his Throne his Scepter doe they swey:
And as their subjects ought them to obey,
So Kings should feare and serve their God againe:
If then ye would enjoy a happie raigne,
Observe the Statutes of your heavenly King,
And from his Law, make all your Lawes to spring:
Since his Lieutenant here ye should remain,
Reward the just, be steadfast, true, and plaine,
Represse the proud, maintayning aye the right,
Walke alwayes so, as ever in his sight,
Who guardes the godly, plaguing the prophane:
   And so ye shall in Princely vertues shine,
   Resembling right your mightie King Divine.

> JAMES I OF ENGLAND, *Basilikon Doron*,
> prefatory sonnet.

# PREFACE

This volume makes available for the first time a complete
English translation of the *Institutio principis Christiani* of
Erasmus. The study was first begun some nine years ago and
was essentially finished in 1932. After several prolonged delays
it is now ready in this year which marks the four hundredth an-
niversary of the greatest humanist's death in the body, of his
continued life in influence and inspiration. The work embraced
in the volume represents a sincere effort to illuminate the text
with notes and introduction of nature and proportion adequate
for the purpose intended. The tremendous force of tradition, in
which the best of classical literature and learning occupied the
dominant place for over two thousand years, is unescapable.
Erasmus interpreted the problems of his day directly or indirectly with the equipment of his classical learning. Whether
many of this present day realize it or not, not a few current
problems are identical in nature with those of past generations.
They are, accordingly, capable of solution (and are being at
least partially solved) on the same basis. For this reason the
classical background of Erasmus's political theories has been
presented in detail. The quantity of material is great. Discussion of points which in themselves have attracted attention in
many separate studies has, of necessity, been reduced to a minimum, so that the factual evidence, completely documented,
could be displayed to an extent considerably greater than is
usual. No doubt the opinions of readers will differ upon the
satisfactoriness of the compromise attempted. In the words of
St. Augustine, "those who think I have said too much, and those
who think I have said too little, I ask to forgive me."

The translation was made from the 1540 edition of Froben
and was checked against the edition of LeClerc published in
1706. The partial translation of the *Institutio* by Corbett I

had before me as I made my own rendering of the second half
of the treatise. The points in which my version differs from
his are, in the main, minor and largely in connection with
what appear to me to be omissions on the part of Corbett.
My translation is probably the more literal. The study of
Geldner (*Die Staatsauffassung des Erasmus . . .*), which I
did not see until I had completed the first writing of my own
introduction, is especially important for the relation between
Erasmus and the Netherlands. The only work which to my
knowledge is at all similar in nature to the present study is
that by Bagdat (*La "Querela pacis" d'Érasme . . .*), who has
translated and discussed the *Complaint of Peace*, but without
reference to the classical background of its author. De Iongh's
dissertation (*Erasmus' Denkbeelden over Staat en Regeering*)
is a careful discussion of Erasmus's ideas, with a long chapter
on their relation to the period. The bibliography appended to
the present volume is "selective" only to the extent that it
includes nothing not actually cited or quoted. It seemed unnec-
essary and out of place to repeat the extensive bibliographies
of literature on Erasmus that have already been many times
published. Sufficient information is given for the accurate iden-
tification of each item included. An attempt has been made to
combine accuracy with brevity.

I am happy to make various acknowledgments at this time.
Professor David P. Barrows, of the University of California,
first aroused my interest in Erasmus and in other ways did
for me more than he himself may have realized. The editors
of the *Political Science Quarterly*, the *American Journal of
Philology*, the *Revue belge de philologie et d'histoire*, and
*Speculum*, and the manager of the University of Chicago
Press (for the *Journal of Modern History*) have kindly
granted permission to use material from my articles which
had already appeared in their respective periodicals. My
former assistant, Agnes Knight, has generously allowed me to
make free use of the materials in her thesis on the classical
sources of the *Institutio*. The Board of Trustees of the George
Washington University has advanced the cost of publication

of this volume so that it might appear at this time. Professor
John Dickinson has made a number of constructive criticisms
on the content of the book, and Professor Austin P. Evans has
been most painstaking, patient and constructive in his several
readings of the manuscript. My wife has helped me greatly
with the reading of the proofs and the preparation of the index.

L. K. B.

WASHINGTON, D. C.
  June 1, 1936

# CONTENTS

## Introduction

## Text

# INTRODUCTION

History is the school of princes; from it they learn the mistakes of the past centuries and how to avoid them, and thus to develop a system and follow it step by step. Only those who have best figured out their course of action can surpass those who act less logically than they. — Frederick the Great, *Histoire de mon temps*, Pref.

# I

## THE POLITICAL THEORIES OF ERASMUS

During the last two decades many volumes have appeared
that deal with the period of the Renaissance and the Reformation. In these works Erasmus has claimed his place, and in
some of them his politico-ethical ideas have been discussed, but
largely from a general historical point of view rather than
with specific interest in his contribution to political theory.
Prior to these recent contributions, Erasmus was almost entirely neglected except by his biographers.[1]

The dominating place occupied by Erasmus at the turn of
the sixteenth century gave him a unique position. He really
faced in two directions: by all his training and humanistic
learning, his heart was of the Middle Ages; but his mind was
of the modern world. By drawing upon his vast resources,
Erasmus brought to bear on the critical problems of his day
many a timely truth that foreshadowed theories and principles
that were to be formulated and elaborated at a later date. The
first years of the sixteenth century, in which all of Erasmus's
political works were written, were filled with the struggle of

---

[1] Gumplowitz, *Geschichte der Staatstheorien* (Innsbruck, 1926), and Dunning,
*History of Political Theories*, II (New York, 1905), do not even mention Erasmus. Janet, *Histoire politique dans ses rapports avec la morale* (4th ed., Paris,
1913); Münch, *Gedanken über Fürstenerziehung aus alter und neuer Zeit*
(Munich, 1909), give brief summaries. The most complete studies are those
of Elise Constantinescu Bagdat, *La "Querela pacis" d'Érasme*, (diss., Paris,
1924), which analyzes most of his political doctrines, and that of Ferdinand
Geldner, "Die Staatsauffassung und Fürstenlehre des Erasmus von Rotterdam,"
*Hist. Stud.*, Hft. 191 (Berlin, 1930), which devotes much of its attention to the
relation of Erasmus's political ideas to those current in the Netherlands of his
day. There is a good bibliography of recent material, published and unpublished, in Germany. The *Institutio principis christiani* was studied in some
detail by Enthoven, "Ueber die Institutio principis christiani des Erasmus,"
*Neue Jahrb. für das klass. Altertum*, XXIV (1909), 312-29, with special attention
to its influence. See also Adriana W. de Iongh, *Erasmus' denkbeelden over staat
en regeering*, Amsterdam, 1927. None of these works is definitive.

the still new national monarchies, with the development of
trade and world expansion (both of which received their stim-
uli from the spirit of nationality and yet offered the greatest
opportunities for its transformation into the conception of
empire), while intellectually the time was ripe for a critical
judgment of history and society. It is accordingly not surprising that the Dutch scholar spent part of his time and thought
in a frank study of current problems.

What is surprising is the prominence of certain ideas, in
some cases borrowed bodily from antiquity, in others of more
recent conception, which Erasmus helped to crystallize by
directing them to the attention of the leading figures of the
day: the Emperor Charles V,[2] Henry VIII of England,[3] and
Ferdinand of Spain,[4] all of whom were molding the political
fate of modern Europe as Erasmus was destined to mold that
of the new intellectual world.[5]

The ideas of Erasmus on politics are intimately involved in
his theories of ethics. We find references to his ideas and
ideals of political theory in many places, with a consequent
strange blending of the practical and the idealistic.[6] These
ideas may be didactically set forth, or may be glossed over with
satire or jest, but whatever Erasmus says is worth noting.

The earliest work of Erasmus that we can associate with
politico-ethical ideas is a long letter entitled *Epistula exhorta-
toria ad capessendam virtutem* [7] addressed to Adolph, prince
of Veere (then a very young boy), in 1498. This letter was

[2] Erasmus dedicated the *Institutio* to him early in 1516.

[3] Erasmus sent him a copy of the *Institutio* in 1517; cf. Allen, *Opus epistularum Desiderii Erasmi* (Oxford, 1906-), Ep. 657, lines 46-68.

[4] In 1518 Erasmus reworked the *Institutio* for Ferdinand; cf. Allen, Ep.
853, lines 63 to end.

[5] Geldner, *op. cit.*, p. 54, stresses this same point: "Erasmus suchte aber die
Gunst der Mächtigen nicht nur im engen persönlichen Interesse; seine weitreich-
enden Reformpläne konnte er nur mit Hilfe der Herren der Welt durchset-
zen. . ."

[6] Geldner, *op. cit.*, 148-50, has also noted this point and cites, as a very good
illustrative example, Erasmus's theory that a prince not in favor with his people
should resign. Erasmus apparently did not foresee chaos as the logical practical
result of his ideally satisfactory suggestion.

[7] *Opera omnia* (Leyden, 1703-6), V, 65; cf. Allen, Ep. 93, introductory note
and selections.

included in the first edition of the *Lucubratiunculae* at Antwerp in February, 1503, and reprinted with that collection in seven editions in eleven years, usually under the title, *Exhortatio ad virtutem*, or *Oratio de virtute amplectenda*.

In 1500 were first published the *Adagiorum collectanea*, or *Adages*, dedicated to Lord Montjoy, Erasmus's first real patron and long-continued staunch friend and supporter. In his commentaries upon the innumerable quotations and phrases from ancient and modern authors which are contained in this work, Erasmus often expressed his feelings on war, peace, ethics, and other allied subjects. The collection was expanded in 1506 and later. In 1513 a new revised edition was issued by Froben, marking the first association of that famous printer with Erasmus.[8] In 1521 an *Epitome* appeared, which was much prized for its convenience and consequently very widely used.[9] Sixty-two editions, of one sort or another, appeared during the lifetime of Erasmus, and many others have since been issued.[10] The influence of such a work can hardly be overestimated.

As its full title [11] and prefatory letter to Nicholas Ruistre [12] show, the first real political work, the *Panegyricus*, was written for Prince Philip, on the occasion of his safe return (1503) from his expedition to Spain. From the "Epilogue" to the work we learn that it was delivered orally to the young prince by Erasmus himself on the Feast of the Epiphany, 1504, in the Ducal Palace at Brussels in the presence of many distinguished personages. As might have been supposed, Erasmus was immediately assailed with criticisms for his fulsome praise

[8] Allen, Ep. 269.

[9] Cf. the letter of Vives to Henry VIII (Allen, Ep. 1204, Introd.).

[10] My references to the editions of the various works of Erasmus are from the *Bibliotheca Erasmiana, Répertoire des œuvres d'Érasme, Ire série, Liste sommaire et provisoire des diverses éditions de ses œuvres* (Ghent, 1893). For some of the works, a more complete description appears in the *Bibliotheca Belgica*, 2me série (Ghent, 1891-), s.v. Erasmus.

[11] *Ad illustrissimum principem Phillipum, archiducem Austriae . . . de triumphali profectione Hispaniensi deque foelici eiusdem in patriam reditu gratulatorius panegyricus. Conscriptus ac eidem principi exhibitus a Desyderio Erasmo Roterdamo. . . .*

[12] Allen, Ep. 179.

of the prince, and charged with flattery. In fact this irksome charge was so strong that in a letter to his intimate friend, John Desmarais, who had been inquiring about the first edition of the *Panegyricus*, Erasmus took occasion to deliver himself of a long *apologia pro panegyricis*,[13] as it were, in which he defended himself by analogy with the ancients —Callisthenes, Lysias, Isocrates, St. Paul, Pliny, and St. Augustine. Here Erasmus not only develops his thesis that "no other way of correcting a prince is as efficacious as offering the pattern of a truly good prince under the guise of flattery to them, for thus do you present virtues and disparage faults in such manner that you seem to urge them to the former while restraining them from the latter," [14] but also reveals his general attitude toward political ethics and his close acquaintance with the best ancient literature of this *genre*.

Whatever others may have thought concerning Erasmus's deserts in the case, the prince did not forget him, but rewarded him with a cash gift [15] and offered him the opportunity of joining his establishment.[16] The former (always acceptable to, and almost always needed by, Erasmus) was accepted; the latter, declined. Shortly after its delivery[17] at the court, the first edition of the *Panegyricus* appeared at Antwerp, and was frequently reprinted, with certain revisions.

Six years later, in 1510, after his return from Italy,[18] whence he had set out in July, 1509, Erasmus wrote the *Moriae encomium*, or *Praise of Folly*, while he was a guest in the home of Thomas More, to whom he dedicated the work. The date

[13] Allen, Ep. 180; the letter occupies 5 pages in Allen's edition (189 lines). Cf. an expression of the same ideas six years earlier in Ep. 93.

[14] Allen, Ep. 179, lines 42-45; cf. Ep. 180, lines 39-44, and *passim*. Quotations from the works of Erasmus not available in English are given in my own translation; so also are those from Dio Chrysostom, the Panegyrici Latini, Martin of Bracara, Smaragdus, Peter Damiani, and Thomas Aquinas. Standard translations have been used wherever possible, so that readers who care to follow up a theme at greater length than space here permits may do so without confusion.

[15] Allen, Ep. 179, lines 13-16, and introductory note in which Allen quotes from the records of Philip's exchequer an expenditure of 50 livres that must refer to Erasmus.

[16] *Ibid.*

[17] Allen, Ep. 180, lines 181-89; Ep. 179, lines 2-3.

[18] Allen, Ep. 222.

of the dedicatory epistle which is only "June 9th" cannot therefore refer to a year earlier than 1510.\According to Allen's argument, based on a letter by Erasmus [19] in which he states that the *Praise of Folly* was reprinted several times within a few months, and on the sheer likelihood of the situation, the work was not published in 1510, but was withheld until 1511.[20] Countless other editions appeared, many in the lifetime of Erasmus, in spite of the criticism which he knew would come upon him for having written "a playful booklet too light to become a theologian, too caustic to befit Christian meekness," [21] in which he had unmercifully exposed the wrongdoings of the clergy in particular and of society in general.

The *Institutio principis Christiani*, which is described and analyzed in detail in the next chapter, was written in 1516. The following year there first appeared, in separate pamphlet form, the little treatise *Dulce bellum inexpertis*, which was an expansion of a letter written to Antony Bergin, abbot of St. Bertin, in March 14, 1514. In its larger form this strong plea for peace and arbitration had been included in the 1515 edition of the *Adages* (No. 3001), and in addition to being reissued with that popular work in its later forms, it was one of the most frequently published of the short works of Erasmus. In the same year, the *Scarabaeus quaerit aquilam*, also formerly a part of the *Adages*, was published separately. This, too, was many times reissued. The *Sileni Alcibiades*, another of the *Adages*, was first separately published in the same year.

But 1517 is best remembered in connection with Erasmus because of the *Querela pacis*, or *Complaint of Peace*, which was written shortly after he had been invited to the court of Philip,[22] upon the suggestion of John Le Sauvage, the chancellor, when the peace conference of Cambrai (which took place March, 1517) was being arranged. The *Querela pacis* was dedicated to Philip, bishop of Utrecht.[23] The first edition

[19] Allen, Ep. 337, lines 139-41.

[20] Cf. Allen, Ep. 222, for a complete discussion of this point; see also *Bib. Eras.* for the dates of the editions.

[21] Allen, Ep. 222, lines 26-27.

[22] Allen, Ep. I, pp. 18-19, lines 29-33; Ep. 370, line 18 note.

[23] For details of the dedication, its reception, etc., see Allen, Ep. 603 (the

of the work by Froben was delayed, so Erasmus had a manuscript copy sent to the bishop on October 5, 1517; the edition appeared in December, and others soon followed at frequent intervals.

The next work of Erasmus that contains important political doctrines is not primarily a political work. The *Familiarium colloquiorum formulae*, or the *Familiar Colloquies*, as they are usually called, were first composed for private use in 1497,[24] and first published (without Erasmus's knowledge or permission) by Beatus Rhenanus in 1518.[25] Erasmus seems to have countered with an authorized edition of his own in 1519.[26] This edition was revised and enlarged in 1522,[27] and again in 1524.[28] This latter, apparently, is the work as we have it, for it "had already grown to the size of a real volume." [29] The frankness of the language in this series of conversations intended for the education of young gentlemen had frequently to be defended.[30]

Twelve years later, in 1530, the *Utilissima consultatio de bello Turcis inferendo* (*A Valued Discussion on* [*the Subject of*] *War against the Turks*) was written and dedicated to John Rinck, jurist, in the hope that in this fashion Erasmus might "stimulate his abilities [to action] so that, from the texts of the law in which he enjoyed so great a reputation, he might bring about better conditions." [31] Although cast in the form of a letter, the work is really an essay, as Erasmus himself realizes, on the evils and folly of waging wars against the Turks on flimsy pretexts. Erasmus's utter disapproval of the warlike policy of the age is clearly shown in the opening lines of the treatise: "All monarchs are cut from the same cloth. Some are busied with collecting the sinews of war; some, with

---

dedicatory epistle), introd.; for the most complete treatment of the work and its place in Erasmus's political writings, see Elise Constantinescu Bagdat, *op. cit.* The various chapters are really essays upon Erasmus's political philosophy in relation to his environment, with some attention to his predecessors.

[24] Allen, Ep. 56; Ep. 130, lines 92-93.      [27] Allen, Ep. 1262.
[25] Allen, Ep. 56, Introd.; Ep. 130.      [28] Allen, Ep. 1476.
[26] Allen, Ep. 909 and 1041.      [29] *Ibid.*, line 15.
[30] Cf. the Preface to the Reader in the edition of 1526.
[31] From the "Epilogue," *Opera*, V, 368.

leaders and machines; but hardly any are planning for the betterment of human life, which is the [ultimate] source of everything else and pertains with equal importance to all alike." So forceful was this polemic that in the very year of its appearance it was issued four times — at Basle, Cologne, Paris, and Vienna — although this was the year in which the emperor Charles V was raising his own armies to fight the Turks.

The *Apophthegmata*, or, as the secondary title reads, *Lepide dicta principum, philosophorum* . . ., was originally issued in six books in March, 1531, and later expanded into eight books, its final form.[32] As Erasmus points out in his dedicatory epistle of Feb. 28, 1531, to young Prince William (whose tutor, incidentally, was the learned Conrad Heresbach) his collection is based primarily on that which Plutarch had made for the young emperor Trajan, with additions from the newly issued collections of Filefo and Raphael Regius, and many additions that had been culled from his own wide reading. Among the observations — often pointed and sound — on the value of certain Greek and Latin authors and their methods, Erasmus expresses his own ideas on the value of such collections of maxims. "From the best authors I have gathered together what the Greeks call *Apophthegmata*, i.e., maxims, because I could see no type of argument better suited for presentation to a prince, especially one so young. . . . For in him who is born to rule, virtue must from the outset be developed [33] . . . By handsome studies character is developed, is made more vigorous for supporting its burdens, and is rendered more agreeable to all human customs." [34] As might be expected, the *Apophthegmata* were widely read; they went through thirteen editions in the remaining five years of their author's life, and many more after that.[35]

[32] It occupies cols. 93-380 in *Opera*, IV.

[33] *Opera*, IV, cols. 87-88.

[34] *Ibid.*, cols. 91-92.

[35] There is extant a copy of the Leyden, 1541, edition with marginal notes in the hand of Martin Luther. See Preserved Smith, *Erasmus* (New York, 1923), p. 408, n. 6.

With the exception of the *Epistles*, the works just described embrace essentially all that Erasmus wrote of a political nature. In them the "social contract" theory of Hobbes, Locke, and Rousseau is clearly foreshadowed; the economic factors of society and statecraft, which were perhaps the latest to be evaluated by theorists,[36] are definitely recognized in the midst of all the unrest; the evils of hereditary succession, with those of state alliances, in the day when Charles V ruled Burgundy, Germany, Spain, and part of Italy, are unflinchingly revealed; the curse of aggressive wars [37] is set forth, and the germ of international law, later to be developed by Grotius, is present.

Because of his proximity to the Middle Ages, Erasmus did not differentiate clearly between the separate functions of the state administration, especially in the case of the legislative, judicial, and executive departments; but he emphasized the need of distributing power and responsibility. It remained for his younger contemporary, Bodin, to declare that the judicial power should not rest solely in the hands of the reigning prince. But, in general, Erasmus had the same conception of the state as that of our contemporary theorists.[38] He recognized its responsibilities to maintain order, to protect life and property, to determine legal relations, liabilities, and contracts, to define crime, to establish punishments and administer justice, to outline the political duties and responsibilities of citizens and confirm their rights and privileges, and to enter into and maintain foreign relations.[39]

All nature, Erasmus tells us, feels the need of unison and society. Nature includes the inanimate objects, the plants, and the animals.

Animals destitute of reason, live with their own kind in a state of so-

[36] E. R. A. Seligman, *Principles of Economics* (New York, 1905), p. 30.

[37] The treatise *Utilissima consultatio de bello Turcis inferendo* was sent to the emperor at the time he was involved in his attacks on the Turks as a result of his connection with the wars in Italy.

[38] W. W. Willoughby, *An Examination of the Nature of the State* (New York, 1896), p. 4, defines the state as "a community of people socially united; a political machinery, termed a government, and administered by a corps of officials termed a magistracy; a body of rules or maxims, written or unwritten, determining the scope of this public authority and the manner of its exercise."

[39] Woodrow Wilson, *The State* (Boston, 1918), *passim*.

cial amity. Elephants herd together; sheep and swine feed in flocks; cranes and crows take their flight in troops; storks have their public meetings to consult previously to their emigration and feed their parents when unable to feed themselves; dolphins defend each other by mutual assistance; and everybody knows that both ants and bees have respectively established, by general agreement, a little friendly community.[40]

Man, then, surely should be a social creature. From birth human beings are mutually dependent.[41] The real basis of society is the proper fitting of each one into his own peculiar sphere.[42] Yet man is now the most discordant of the animals; hence it would seem that the original state of nature were best.

Among the several kinds of living Creatures . . . they thrive best that understand no more than what Nature taught them. What is more prosperous or wonderful than the Bee? And though they have not the same judgment of sense as other Bodies have, yet wherein hath Architecture gone beyond their building of Houses? What Philosopher ever founded the like Republique? Where as the Horse, that comes so near man in understanding is therefore so familiar with him, is also partaker of his misery. . . . In the Battel, while he contends for Victory, he's cut down himself, and, together with his Rider, "lies biting the earth": not to mention those strong Bits, sharp Spurrs, close Stables, Arms, Blows, Rider, and briefly, all that slavery he willingly submits to, while, imitating those men of Valour, he so eagerly strives to be reveng'd of the Enemy.[43]

This expression of opinion, occurring as it does in the *Praise of Folly*, must not be taken at its face value. It is charged with satire and castigation. But after all this is removed, the basic idea seems to remain.

Since, however, we do live in a modern society, there must be a form of unity, law, and order. Erasmus takes for granted that this form is to be monarchy, although a limited monarchy, for he says that the prince was made for the good of

[40] *The Complaint of Peace* (first American edition, Boston, 1813), p. 12. In subsequent references to this and other works of Erasmus, the citation will be by title and page of the edition first given. References have been made from the English translations, wherever possible, for greater convenience of those who may wish to pursue the matter further.

[41] *Ibid.*, pp. 15-16.

[42] *The Praise of Folly* (translated by John Wilson, 1668; reprinted London, 1913), p. 38.

[43] *Ibid.*, pp. 66-67; cf. pp. 62-66.

the commonwealth, not the commonwealth for the good of the prince.[44] Furthermore, the prince is subject to the law and assumes responsibilities equal to his honors when he takes up the reins of government.[45] Provided he rules in such a way as will help and augment the public prosperity, the individual who occupies the throne at any time is of relative inconsequence.[46] Since according to the present scheme it is not possible to choose the prince, it is of prime importance to perfect the person already set over the country.[47] The selection of the tutor to accomplish this task is a very grave matter; his responsibilities are tremendous.[48]

In several places Erasmus gives us a picture of the ideal prince.[49] One of them is found in the *Praise of Folly.*

Whoever did but truly weigh with himself how great a burden lies upon his shoulders that would truly discharge the duty of a Prince . . . would consider that he that takes a Scepter in his hand should manage the Publik, not his Private Interest; study nothing but the common good; and not in the least go contrary to those Laws whereof himself is both the Author and Exactor: that he is to take an account of the good or evil administration of all his magistrates and subordinate Officers; that, though he is but one, all men's Eyes are upon him, and in his power it is, either like a good Planet to give life and safety to mankind by his harmless influence, or like a fatal Comet to send mischief and destruction: that the vices of other men are not alike felt, nor so generally communicated; and that a Prince stands in that place that his least deviation from the Rule of Honesty and Honour reaches farther than himself, and opens a gap to many men's ruine.[50]

[44] *The Colloquies* (translated by N. Bailey, 1725; reprinted in 3 vols., London, 1900), "Courtesy in Saluting," I, 38. Cf. *Utilissima consultatio de bello Turcis inferendo*, in *Opera* (Leyden, 1706) V, 366F, on limited monarchy.

[45] *Panegyricus*, in *Opera*, IV, 530C-D.

[46] *Complaint of Peace*, p. 37.

[47] *Aut regem aut fatuum nasci oportere*, in *Opera* (Leyden, 1706) II, 109E-F. All subsequent references to this and other selections from the *Adages* will be cited by page reference only. This title, and other titles equally long, will be arbitrarily shortened for the sake of convenience.

[48] *Ibid.*, II, 110A-111F.

[49] In the *Aut regem*, II, 108F-109A, we have the "organic analogy" clearly stated. This is emphasized in the *Institutio*. The adage *Aut regem* is really a "prospectus" of the *Institutio*.

[50] *Praise of Folly*, pp. 138-39. Cf. *Coll.*, "Beggars' Dialogue," II, 162; *ibid.*, "The Fabulous Feast," p. 172; *Paneg.*, IV, 509B-D; *ibid.*, p. 547C-D; *Aut regem*, II, 106A; *ibid.*, p. 108D-E; p. 109D. The difference between a prince and a tyrant is demonstrated, *ibid.*, p. 109B-D. Cf. *ibid.*, pp. 106E-107E for

Among the various qualities necessary for the good prince are wisdom and integrity,[51] continence and clemency,[52] devotion to his people,[53] self-restraint,[54] interest in truth and liberty,[55] freedom from the vices of cruelty and pride,[56] and the careful avoidance of flatterers.[57] The prince should be like God in his manners and qualities.[58] He should learn from association with wise men.[59] The prince should realize that it is his vices of pompous display and extravagant banquets, games, gambling, and other forms of amusements that waste the funds of the treasury.[60] He should know, too, that his best defense against his enemies lies in the loyalty and love of his people.[61] One of the best ways for the prince to come to know his people (and to be known in turn), and as a result to have an intimate knowledge of the places and conditions with which he will have to deal, is to travel throughout his realm.[62] Foreign travel should not be indulged in, because affairs at home are not satisfactorily administered when the prince is away.[63]

The prince should be a practical man as well as a philosopher.[64] Yet he should be careful not to attempt too much, and so go beyond the province of human attainment.[65] His main task is to strive to leave the state in better condition than it was when he first received it.[66] Real prosperity depends upon

the same point with fuller examples. Cf. also *Sileni*, II, 773F-774A; *Scarabaeus*, II, 871A-872F; *ibid.*, p. 873D.

[51] *Coll.*, "The Unequal Marriage," III, 67-68.

[52] *Paneg.*, IV, 539C-D; cf. *Scarabaeus*, II, 880B.

[53] *Ibid.*, p. 526E-F; cf. *ibid.*, p. 541B.

[54] *Ibid.*, p. 527A-C; cf. *ibid.*, p. 530E.

[55] *Ibid.*, p. 527E.

[56] *Ibid.*, p. 527E; cf. *Scarabaeus*, II, 872E-F.

[57] *Ibid.*, pp. 529F-530A; cf. *Praise of Folly*, p. 72; *Paneg.*, IV, 528B; *Aut regem*, II, 110E-111F; *Sileni*, II, 781A.

[58] *Sileni*, II, 777C.     [59] *Sapientes*, II, 849D-E.

[60] *Utilissima consultatio de bello Turcis inferendo*, V, 363C-D; cf. *Scarabaeus*, II, 872E-F.

[61] *Paneg.*, IV, 535D; cf. *Complaint of Peace*, p. 73, where Erasmus says that those princes are most secure who are ready to abdicate if the people demand it. Cf. *Scarabaeus*, II, 870E-F, where he says that the good prince, like the queen bee, has no sting; *ibid.*, pp. 872F-875F, where he shows that wicked princes have no friends.

[62] *Ibid.*, p. 521B-E.     [64] *Praise of Folly*, pp. 45-48.

[63] *Complaint of Peace*, p. 54.     [65] *Ibid.*, p. 68.

[66] *Coll.*, "The Old Men's Dialogue," II, 78. The *Institutio* repeatedly em-

the common people, and this the prince should not forget.[67]
On this the prosperity of the prince depends.[68] In short, the
prince should realize that good deeds are the best means of
acquiring and maintaining a good reputation.[69] The prince
should always keep this in mind because he is readily imitated
by all of his people.[70]

Erasmus believes that state marriage alliances [71] and hereditary succession are the causes of many evils. Something should
be done, he believes, so that ruling princes can provide for
their children within their own realm; if it seems essential to
ally with a neighboring princely house, then all hope of succession should be cut off at the time of the marriage.[72]

Erasmus also has some definite ideas on the subject of law.
In his colloquy called *The Fish-Eaters*, the dialogue of a
butcher and a fishmonger, the two characters debate the justice of forbidding meat on one day per week, and in the course
of their argument they arrive at a discussion of the origin of
divine law. They decide that mankind has thrown off all reverence for God and is living as unrestrainedly as if He did not
exist. For that reason there were created the bars of the law,
and the bridles of threat and precept, to bring men to know
themselves.[73] Further on in the same dialogue, the butcher

---

phasizes this. *Respublica virum docet,* II, 1023B, states that no one is fit to rule
until he has had practical training. See also *Aut regem,* II, 109D-F, for the
same idea. But, whoever the person is to whom the power has been given, he
must be obeyed by those who gave it: *Principi obtemperandum in omnibus,* II,
1202B-C; in fact, it is often better to bear with an evil prince than chance a
worse one: *Sileni,* II, 781D.

[67] *Complaint of Peace,* p. 40; cf. *Sileni,* II, 775D: "They call the function of
a prince dominion, when in truth the part of a prince is nothing else than the
administration of matters common to all."

[68] *Ibid.,* p. 51: "Let a king think himself great in proportion as his people are
good; let him estimate his own happiness by the happiness of those whom he
governs; let him deem himself glorious, in proportion as his subjects are free;
rich, if the public are rich; and flourishing, if he can but keep the community
flourishing, in consequence of uninterrupted peace."

[69] *Coll.,* "The Lover of Glory," III, 169-70; cf. *Sileni,* II, 780E.

[70] *Paneg.,* IV, 531E; cf. *Aut regem,* II, 107F; *Princeps indiligens,* II, 941D.

[71] *Complaint of Peace,* p. 37; cf. *Sileni,* II, 775D-E.

[72] *Complaint of Peace,* p. 50 and pp. 53-54.

[73] *Coll.,* "The Fish-Eaters," II, 257. Cf. Grotius, *De iure belli et pacis,* I, 1,
10: "Natural law is the dictate of right reason which points out that a given
act, because of its opposition to or conformity with man's rational nature, is

advances the idea that there is a difference between human and divine law.

Divine Laws are immutable, unless such as are of that Kind that they seem to be given only for a Time, for the Sake of Signification and Coercion. . . . And then again, as to human Laws; there are sometimes unjust, foolish, and hurtful Laws made, and therefore either abrogated by the Authority of Superiors, or by the universal Neglect of the People: But there is nothing such in the Divine Laws. Again, a human Law ceases of itself, when the Causes for which it was made cease. . . . Add to this, that a human Law is no Law, unless it be approved by the Consent of those who are to use it. A divine Law can't be dispensed with nor abrogated; altho' indeed, *Moses* being about to make a Law, required the Consent of the People; but this was not done because it was necessary, but that he might render them the more criminal in not keeping it. For, indeed, it is an impudent Thing to break a Law that you gave your Approbation to the making of.[74]

War, of course, was hateful to Erasmus,[75] and his unceasing invectives against it together with a plea for the better appreciation of ethics and true religion as he saw it, are among his outstanding thoughts. In his *Dulce bellum inexpertis*, Erasmus marshals forth a host of arguments on the general subject of aggressiveness. Especially is he opposed to empire, "of which there was never none yet in any nation, but it was gotten with the great shedding of mans' blood." [76] In *The Fish-Eaters*, again, the fishmonger, who is explaining what he would do if he were emperor at that time, delivers a magnanimous and idealistic speech on the attainment of peace and the renunciation of territorial aggrandizement.

I would immediately take upon me a Vow of Peace, and publish a Truce throughout my Dominions. . . . Were I Emperor, I would without Delay, thus treat with the King of *France*: "My Brother, some evil Spirit has set this War on foot between you and me; nor do we fight for our Lives, but our Dominions. You, as to your Part, have behaved yourself as a stout and valiant Warrior. But Fortune has been on my

---

either morally wrong or morally necessary, and accordingly forbidden or commended by God, the author of nature."

[74] *Coll.*, "The Fish-Eaters," II, 284-85.

[75] *Sileni*, II, 776D-777B.

[76] *Erasmus against War* (reprint of first English translation [1533-34]; introduction by J. W. Mackail, Boston, 1907), p. 22; cf. *Sileni*, II, 776D; *ibid.*, 780C-E.

Side, and of a King made you a Captive. What has been your Lot, may be mine, and your mishap admonishes all our human Condition. We have experienced that this Way of Contention has been detrimental to both of us; let us engage one another after a different Manner. I give you your Life, and restore you your Liberty, and instead of an Enemy take you for my Friend. Let all past Animosities be forgotten, you are at free Liberty to return into your own Dominions, enjoy what is your own, be a good Neighbor, and for the future let this be the only Contention, which shall out-do the other in Offices of Fidelity and Friendship; nor let us vie one with another, which shall govern the largest Dominions, but who shall govern his own with the greatest Justice and Goodness. In the former Conflict I have bore away the Prize of Fortune, but in this he that gets the better, shall gain far more Glory. As for me, the Fame of this Clemency will get more true Glory than if I had added all *France* to my Dominion." [77]

Treaties and leagues are opposed by Erasmus because of the trouble which they bring. He opposes leagues because they throw into jeopardy so many peoples, merely to secure for some one prince a relatively unimportant advantage.[78] Treaties he inveighs against because all too often wars arise out of the infringement of some small clause in the treaty,[79] while the spirit of the whole is neglected.

When we come to examine the evidence which Erasmus advanced against war, and his remedies for it, we should realize, more than in any other connection, the position of esteem and intimacy, already alluded to, which Erasmus held at the great courts of Europe — those of England, France, and the Empire; not to mention his relations with the academic centers and the papal see.[80]

Erasmus held that the wise prince is the one who prevents war by his wisdom rather than the one who wins it by his skill.[81] But wars (which usually arise from some private mo-

---

[77] *Coll.*, "The Fish-Eaters," II, 266-67.

[78] *Erasmus against War*, p. 49; cf. *Sileni*, II, 775D-E. In the *Principes inter se noti*, II, 933A-B, Erasmus says that princes fight openly, while they agree privately; the whole combat is merely a scheme to strengthen their powers.

[79] *Complaint of Peace*, p. 37.

[80] Erasmus's works as a whole show this, but a few specific references to his letters written to, or about, princes may be of interest. F. M. Nichols, *The Epistles of Erasmus* (London and New York, 1901-18), II, 77, 84, 114-15, 145, 185, 189, 244-47, 271, 314, 374, 404, 410, 433-34, 512, 538-39, 544; III, 44, 46, 287, 305, 367.      [81] *Paneg.*, IV, 538E. Cf. *ibid.*, p. 534B-F.

tives of the prince) [82] should be employed only as a last resort [83] and to repel invasion.[84] The people, who bear the
brunt of war and its afflictions, should be the ones to declare
it by "full and unanimous consent," not the prince alone, or his
minister, or a group of men.[85] It is the people who suffer from
the effects of war, and not the prince. "The largest part of
the evil falls upon landholders, husbandmen, tradesmen, man-
ufacturers, whom, perhaps, the war does not in the least
concern, and who never furnished the slightest cause for a national rupture."[86] There are two rewards of war, glory and
extension of territory; [87] the evil consequences are almost
legion,[88] among them, that ubiquitous evil of mankind, graft.[89]

[82] *Complaint of Peace*, p. 61. Cf. *Utilissima consultatio de bello Turcis inferendo*, V, 353B, 363E-F; *Erasmus against War*, p. 53; and *Principes inter se
noti*, II, 933A.

[83] *Utilissima consultatio de bello Turcis inferendo*, V, 353D-F.

[84] *Complaint of Peace*, p. 58. Cf. *ibid.*, pp. 61-62, where Erasmus says that
"racial hatred" which is so much in evidence is based on mere names only; and
*ibid.*, p. 61, for war propaganda. "When kings can find no cause . . . as, indeed,
they seldom can, then they set their wits to work to invent some fictitious, but
plausible, occasions for a rupture. They will make use of the names of foreign
people in order to feed the popular odium till it becomes ripe for war, and
thirsts for the blood of the outlandish nation, whose very name is rendered a
cause of hostility. This weakness and folly of the very lowest classes of the
people, the grandees increase by artful insinuations, watchwords, and nick-
names, cunningly thrown out in debates, pamphlets, and journals." See also
Nichols, III, 289-90, on "war measures," which recall those of 1917, four centuries later. Those who stay at home are to avoid luxuries in their households
and to be sparing in their expenses and pleasures that the men at the front
may receive all possible support. Such men as "are detained at home by necessary business" must coöperate in this to the fullest extent.

[85] *Complaint of Peace*, p. 55.

[86] *Ibid.*, p. 52; cf. Nichols, II, 121-25.

[87] *Paneg.*, IV, 538F.

[88] *Complaint of Peace*, pp. 66-67. Cf. *ibid.*, pp. 10-11; *Praise of Folly*, pp. 42-
43; Nichols, II, 48, 122, 191, 560; *Sileni*, II, 776D-777B; *Paneg.*, IV, 536B-538D,
on the blessings of peace and the losses of war; *Coll.*, "Courtesy in Saluting," I,
43; *ibid.*, "The Old Men's Dialogue," II, 89; *ibid.*, "The Lying-in Woman," II.
187; *ibid.*, "Charon," III, 46. *Coll.*, "The Soldier and Carthusian," I, 276-85, is
a complete dialogue devoted to this subject. It shows the folly of young men who
run off to the wars; the manners and ways of soldiers; the effect upon their
morality; the constant dangers of their everyday life — all for a mere pittance.

[89] *Complaint of Peace*, pp. 70-71. Erasmus has been enumerating the great
financial expenditures which war necessitates. He concludes by saying, "In this
cursory computation of your expense, for that I am chiefly considering, and the
gain that accrues from victory, I do not reckon the vast sums that stick to the
fingers of commissioners, contractors, generals, admirals, and captains, which
is certainly a great part of the whole."

By contrast, there are the multifarious blessings of peace. The first step toward peace, Erasmus says, is the desire for it.[90] In a letter to Wolfgang Capito he writes: ". . . At the present moment I could almost wish to be young again, for no other reason but this, that I anticipate the near approach of a golden age; so clearly do we see the minds of princes, as if changed by inspiration, devoting all their energies to the pursuit of peace." [91]

Erasmus's inborn aversion to tumult and strife was so strong that he advocated "peace at any price." The best expression of this doctrine is found in the *Querela pacis*:

There are occasions when, if peace can be had in no other way, it must be purchased. It can scarcely be purchased too dearly, if you take into account how much treasure you must inevitably expend in war, and what is of infinitely greater consequence than treasure, how many of the people's lives you save by peace. Though the cost be great, yet war would certainly cost more; besides, what is above all price, the blood of men, the blood of your own fellow citizens and subjects, whose lives you are bound by every tie of duty to preserve instead of lavishing away in prosecuting schemes of false policy and cruel, selfish, villainous ambition. Only form a fair estimate of the quantity of mischief and misery of every kind and degree which you escape and the sum of happiness you preserve in all the walks of private life, among all the tender relations of parents, husbands, children, among those whose poverty alone makes them soldiers, the wretched instruments of involuntary bloodshed; form but this estimate, and you will never repent the highest price you can pay for peace.[92]

The joyous results of peace, the flourishing prosperity of the land; the cities in good order; the productive cultivation of the farm lands; the enforcement of good laws; the advancement of the arts, sciences, and education; the uplift of human society, justify any sacrifices, in Erasmus's opinion, to save them.[93]

But Erasmus was not an idle dreamer. In spite of his seclu-

[90] *Complaint of Peace*, p. 60: "Upon the whole it must be said, that the first and most important step towards peace, is sincerely to desire it. They who once love peace in their hearts, will eagerly seize every opportunity of establishing or recovering it."

[91] Nichols, II, 506.    [92] *Complaint of Peace*, p. 56.

[93] *Ibid.*, p. 66.

sion as a scholar he had a practical association with the world of princes, nobles, and lords spiritual.[94] He advocated advanced ideas, yet he realized that they could only be brought into fruition by the united and genuine sympathy of the reigning princes. The initial impetus to reform could be given by a man of letters; the will to change could alone accomplish the end.[95]

Erasmus's most concrete remedy to end war is his proposal of international arbitration. This he made in March, 1514, in a letter to Anthony Bergen, abbot of St. Bertin, in which he decried the ravaging destructions of war.

But you will say, that the rights of sovereigns must be maintained. It is not for me to speak inadvisedly about the acts of princes. I only know this, that *summum jus*, extreme right, is often *summa injuria*, extreme wrong; there are princes who first decide what they want and then look out for a title with which to cloak their proceedings. . . .

But suppose there is a real dispute, to whom some sovereignty belongs, where is there the need of bloodshed? It is not a question concerning a nation's welfare, but only whether it is bound to call this or that personage its sovereign. There are Popes, there are Bishops, there are wise and honorable men, by whom such small matters may be settled, without sowing the seeds of war upon war, and throwing things divine and human alike into confusion. It is the proper function of the Roman Pontiff, of the Cardinals, of Bishops, and of Abbots to compose the quarrels of Christian princes, to exert their authority in this field, and show how far the reverence of their office prevails.[96]

These suggestions were made to end a specific strife. Just two years later Erasmus set forth the same proposal in formal and general terms in the *Institutio principis Christiani*, and in the year after that he again advocated arbitration in the *Com-*

---

[94] Erasmus was not a man of the people, as was his contemporary and later controversialist Martin Luther; nor did he have an intimate feeling for the people. His concern for them (which was not unqualified) seems rather to be in the attitude of one who sees from a position aloof, and not that of one who has been a fellow-sufferer. By his very nature and constitution he was removed from the coarser phases of life and unable to endure or to tolerate them. His attitude extended even to the medium of his expression. He wrote only in Latin, while all about him were the flourishing pens of Luther, More, Colet, Melanchthon, Budé, Machiavelli, who, at least part of the time, used the vernacular in order to reach even the meanest of the people. See also n. 5.

[95] Cf. *Complaint of Peace*, p. 50, on some remedies against war.

[96] Nichols, II, 123.

*plaint of Peace.* Even in this bloodless method of settling differences, the human equation must be considered; and this Erasmus understood. But he maintained that, even if the arbiters were corrupt, the evil suffered as a result of a biased decision would be far less than if there had been "recourse to arms, to the irrational and doubtful decision of war." [97]

Erasmus has been called a coward. It is true that this unpleasant epithet is usually fastened upon him as a result of his position — or lack of position — with regard to the Reformation. But the arguments advanced to justify it are not limited to the sphere of religion; they purport to be based upon his general attitudes.

Erasmus was essentially a critic and an intellectual, not a militant leader. Steeped in the atmosphere and life of classical antiquity as he was, he came to feel that his life was one of mental, not physical, activity; of concern with finer things, not with force. By his very nature he fits into this plan. As he himself says, "I cannot help execrating strife, I cannot help loving peace and concord." [98] T. M. Lindsay in his *History of the Reformation*,[99] has given a word picture which provides the key, I feel, to most that Erasmus says and does:

> Every line of the clearly cut face suggests demure sarcasm — the thin lips closely pressed together, the half-closed eyelids, and the keen glance of the scarcely seen blue eyes. The head is intellectual, but there is nothing masculine about the portrait [he is describing one of the Holbeins]. . . . The dainty hands, which Holbein drew so often, and the general primness of his appearance, suggest a descent from a long line of maiden aunts. The keen intelligence was enclosed in a sickly body, whose frailty made constant demands on the soul it imprisoned.

[97] *Complaint of Peace*, pp. 48-49. Cf. Nichols, II, 450, for the plans for the peace conference at Cambrai in 1517. As Preserved Smith has pointed out (*Erasmus* [New York, 1923], p. 199), "these suggestions were too far ahead of the time to bear immediate fruit." But Erasmus's place in this cause seems now to be claiming its due attention; cf. James Bryce, *International Relations* (New York, 1922), Lecture I, "International Relations in the Past," p. 18: "The incessant wars of the fifteenth century suggested to the great Erasmus the need for some concerted efforts to secure peace, and those of you who have not seen it may be advised to read a little book of his, published in the early sixteenth century and quite recently reprinted [probably the reprint of the 1802(?) translation, at London in 1917], called *The Complaint of Peace*. . . ."

[98] Allen, Ep. 1342, lines 999-1000.

[99] Vol. I (New York, 1906), 177.

We must consider one more factor which was long neglected until modern psychology learned to understand it. The circumstance of Erasmus's birth was not a happy one. Most of us would perhaps not support unqualifiedly the latest study of Erasmus from this point of view,[100] but at least it may help us to understand, if not to overlook, some of his apparently weaker sides.

The more one becomes versed in following out the mental processes of Erasmus the more convinced he becomes that there were two Erasmuses — one the literary, and the other the purely personal; and the difficulty arises in having always to distinguish between the two. As a *litterateur* he was perhaps the greatest, broadest, and most catholic writer of his age; as a man he was narrow, carping, and selfish. . . . Call this a temperamental defect, or a constitutional weakness, or what you will; but any skilful neurologist can recognize therein the earmarks of neurasthenia. And surely never was any boy more exposed to the causes which make for neurasthenia — the pre-natal anxiety of his mother, due to her uncertain relations with his father, the early loss of his parents, mental overwork, lack of exercise from sedentary occupation, unfavorable psychic influences due to the uncertainty of his future — all these were well calculated to undermine his nervous poise and lessen his emotional control.[101]

Erasmus was *not* essentially weak, if we judge him in his proper sphere, with the proper background and surrounding historical events. What man without the courage of his convictions, without the force of right, as he saw it, would have consistently stood for the principles that Erasmus maintained during the thirty turbulent years in which his political writings occurred? [102] These thirty years saw the creation of a new Holy Roman emperor, crowned by the pope; the unceasing and personal warfare between the emperor and Francis I of France; the Protestant Reformation and its unhappy accompaniment, the Peasants' Revolt; the defection of England

---

[100] J. J. Mangan, *Life, Character and Influence of Desiderius Erasmus of Rotterdam* . . . (New York, 1927).

[101] *Ibid.*, pp. 37-38. In my quotation of this interesting point, I do not overlook the important fact that the attitude of the sixteenth and twentieth centuries toward illegitimacy is hardly comparable.

[102] Geldner's view coincides in general with mine; e.g., "seine [i.e., Charles the Fifth] vorwaltenden Staatsprinzipien sind im Fürstenspiegel des Erasmus verurteilt" (*op. cit.*, p. 144).

from the papal authority and the foundation of the Anglican Church; the war against the Ottoman Turks who were dominating the Mediterranean and occupying most of the Balkans; the new social and economic life of Europe as a result of the discovery of the New World; the inevitable changes in art, science, and literature that must keep pace with changing society.

Perhaps some discrepancies can be found in minor points of Erasmus's teachings from one end of the span to the other, but no basic principle is even slightly altered. The idea of a limited monarchy, under a good, intelligent, God-fearing prince, himself subject to the laws, in a state where peace and harmony reign over good economic conditions, is seen in the *Panegyricus*, which was dedicated to the grandson of the reigning emperor, Maximilian I. The same general ideas appear very strikingly in the *Institutio*, which he dedicated twelve years later to Charles I of Spain (then only sixteen years of age) who was later to become Emperor Charles V, and whose life was destined to exemplify the very antitheses of nearly all Erasmus's teachings, in which he, Erasmus, nevertheless persisted.[103] His ideas of peace, especially, were summed up in the *Complaint of Peace*, which was written by court command

---

[103] Erasmus was not unaware of Charles's faults, or of the discrepancies between his actions and the suggestions which Erasmus had repeatedly pointed out to him. See Allen, Epp. 1403 and 1597; and Geldner, *op. cit.*, pp. 145-46, who points out, among other pertinent matters, the fact that the works of Erasmus were not included in the lists of recommended readings prepared by Charles for his sons.

I am happy to see that Dr. James Brown Scott, whose work was published after my chapter was written, completely supports my thesis here. "It is often said by those who seem to begrudge Erasmus his place in the sun that he prostrated himself before the great and the mighty; that he flattered them for his selfish purposes; and that he was sincere only in his own behalf. This is a grave charge against a priest who, as we have said, was offered a bishopric by his Prince, to whom he had addressed the tractate on the *Christian Prince*, in appreciation of the appointment as counsellor, and whose 'worldliness' may be appraised by his refusal of a cardinal's hat, with a prospect of the Vatican in sight. None but an enemy could maintain that the comment on the measures which a good Prince should take was only calculated to curry favour with the mighty, and especially Charles. . . . The conclusion which Erasmus draws . . . could not have been pleasing to a lad [Charles V] to whom the consent of the people meant little." — *The Spanish Origin of International Law* . . . (Oxford, 1934), pp. 45-46.

in 1517, just when the emperor was making war with Francis I; and in his *Valued Discussion on [the Subject of] War against the Turks* in 1530, which by its very subject was directed primarily against the emperor. All these works maintain his original theses.[104]

Perhaps Erasmus's friendships, or at least acquaintance-ships, with so many princes, lay and secular, so many kings and popes, can be adduced to show that he was adept at straddling political fences and so managed to keep in the good graces of all. Is it not rather a mark of his great power, intellectual and moral, that in spite of his teachings, in spite of the fact that he is known to have been on good terms with Charles V and Philip I, he still retained the patronage of Henry VIII of England, of Francis I of France, and had complete freedom of association with the scholars of those opposing countries? More, Colet, Budé, Vives, Melanchthon, Luther were all close to him. With the latter he broke, naturally enough, for they

---

[104] The doctrines of some of the *Adages*, such as *Aut regem aut fatuum nasci oportere*, the *Scarabaeus*, the *Sileni Alcibiades*, and the *Dulce bellum inexpertis*, the *Frons occipitio prior*, the *Principi obtemperandum in omnibus*, the *Principes inter se noti*, and the *Princeps indiligens*, all support the same views.

Erasmus's ideas have suffered varying interpretations (see also n. 107). Gettell, *History of Political Thought* (New York, 1924), p. 167, has one line: "Erasmus wrote on the folly of hereditary monarchy and the value of representative institutions." Preserved Smith, *The Age of the Reformation* (New York, 1920), p. 592, says: "Still more noteworthy than his moral postulates is Erasmus's preference for the republican form of government. . . . In his *Adages* he interpreted the spirit of the ancients in a way most disparaging to monarchy. . . . It is not too much to regard it as one of the main sources of the republican current of thought throughout the century." With this view, of course, we must agree without reservation, if by "republican" Professor Smith means "government in which the people have a voice." See the next chapter for Erasmus's theory of the state. I find no direct reference to government without royalty (cf. *Opera*, IV, 602), and also none by implication, in anything by Erasmus that I have read. His opinions of the utter inadequacy of the common people for anything of importance are classic; e.g., *Aut regem* . . ., in *Opera*, II, 108 C: "[it is best] to scorn the things which the rable admires and to hold opinions far different from those of the multitude"; and the *Institutio*, in *Opera*, IV, 564: "It is fruitless to attempt advice on the theory of government until you have freed the prince's mind from those most common and yet most false opinions of the common people;" *ibid.*, 566: "The great mass of people are swayed by false opinions. . . ." Even Thomas More's *Utopia* has a ruler, who though nowhere named by any title, is obviously not a regularly elected magistrate. Geldner's pithy observation, based on a sound interpretation of Erasmus's character and his works, is worth adding here. "Erasmus war in der Theorie Demokrat, Aristocrat aus Neigung, und der Wirklichkeit gegenüber Monarchist" (*op. cit.*, p. 88).

were not kindred spirits in the final essence. The great mind of Erasmus and his intellectual prowess and courage in the world in which he moved — not the "Modern Europe" in which his physical body lived — enabled him to transcend hostile national boundaries. His position as a citizen of the world [105] enabled him to view impersonally the seething pot of Europe.

Erasmus has been called a carping critic, who himself, rather than the times, was out of joint; who did not try to adjust himself; who offered no original solutions to current problems save to recall the Golden Age of Greece and Rome. If we may anticipate the findings of Chapter IV on the ancient sources of Erasmus we can readily state that great originality in political thinking was not his contribution.[106] In this connection I was once asked the question, "Would the political theories of Erasmus be worth reading, if someone other than

[105] Erasmus lived least of all in the country of his birth (although "Erasmus of Rotterdam" has made his birthplace famous), preferring to spend most of his time in France, Italy, England, Germany, or Switzerland. Geldner, *op. cit.*, pp. 44-63, in his discussion of the personality of Erasmus (who realized his own weaknesses, e.g., Allen, Ep. I, p. 30), suggests that the main reason why Erasmus remained physically aloof from his native land was his dislike for the manners of the people (pp. 47-48). Geldner believes, however, that the laws, practices, and history of the Netherlands had a deep influence upon Erasmus's outlook, and consequently upon the written expression of his ideas (pp. 140-53). In view of the wealth of precedent in antiquity for almost all that Erasmus discussed, whether as examples of evil practices to be avoided, or beneficial reforms to be instituted, and in view of Erasmus's detailed acquaintance with these practices through their sponsors or other sources, it seems to me difficult to agree with Geldner in the extent to which he attributes the influence of contemporary Netherlands (Burgundy) on Erasmus. E.g., from the evidence presented (pp. 141-44) one could well agree with Geldner that "many ideas which Erasmus presented had had a long continued use in the Netherlands" (p. 140), but might hesitate to agree that "consciously or unconsciously the state of Burgundy was constantly in the background" (p. 142), in spite of such specific matters as references to civil war, criticisms of court practices, and an apparent familiarity with the laws and customs of the Netherlands (p. 143). On this point, see also Enthoven, "Erasmus Weltbürger oder Patriot?", *Neue Jahrb. f. das klass. Altertum*, XXIX (1912), 205-15. A. W. de Iongh, *op. cit.*, treats systematically the general reflection of Erasmus upon monarchs and their duties (chap. i, pp. 1-50), the prince as an individual, and his education (chap. ii, pp. 50-91), the organization of the state, its problems and functions (chap. iii, pp. 92-134), and the conclusion on Erasmus's composite picture (chap. iv, pp. 135-94), ". . . een beeld, samengesteld uit tallooze kleine trekjes, die Erasmus aan de werkelijke vorsten van zijn tijd ontleend heeft" (p. 193).

[106] Cf. above, p. 10, for matter in Erasmus that anticipated later principles and doctrines. See below, chap. vi, for his relation to the Middle Ages.

Erasmus had written them?" The answer is "Yes, if written by someone of Erasmus's power, age, and reputation." In other words, the mere fact that Erasmus did not originate — in fact could not have originated — most of the doctrines he expounded in no way militates against his importance in the world of political theory.[107] The important point is that he did appreciate the need of reform in church and state, and from his own highly sensitive point of view, most keenly in the hearts of his fellow men. This reform he sought whole-heartedly and unceasingly to accomplish through the means that he knew and understood, the application and development of critical insight and the power of humane letters.

[107] It seems to me untenable to hold that because Erasmus was not allied with the Protestant Reformation under Luther, the Catholic Reformation under such scholarly popes as Paul III, the Calvinistic and Zwinglian movements in Switzerland, or the Anglican Reform in England, he should be given only a passing reference or omitted entirely. J. W. Allen (*A History of Political Thought in the Sixteenth Century*, New York, 1928) takes up the great movements in Germany, France, England, and Italy, with no place for scholars not allied with one of the great causes; Erasmus is dismissed with three citations by name, while his works (except the *Institutio*, which is mentioned by name once in a footnote about Thomas Elyot's *The Gouvernour*) are not mentioned in the text or bibliography. The principles that Erasmus fought for all have common ground somewhere in the various tenets of the several movements. His influence in the very center of the maelstrom of Europe could not have been utterly ineffectual.

# II

## THE EDUCATION OF A CHRISTIAN PRINCE

In the first chapter we examined the political ideas of Erasmus and considered the general influence and nature of his writings in which those ideas were put forth, leaving for separate examination, however, his most formal treatise on political theory, the *Education of a Christian Prince.*

Early in the year 1515 proposals had been made to Erasmus to join the court of Prince Charles [1] (the future Charles V), and his actual appointment and assumption of office probably took place at the end of that year or on the first day of January, 1516.[2] This particular treatise, *The Education of a Christian Prince*, was prepared during this period and was intended from the first for the young prince (then only sixteen years of age). The exact date of composition is somewhat doubtful, due to a conflict of evidence in the letters of Erasmus himself. He first mentions the treatise in a letter to Domenico Grimani [3] dated at London in the spring of 1515, where he tells us that he is busy with this little treatise which he intends for Prince Charles. In a letter to Martin Dorp written toward the end of May we find practically the same news.[4] Hence it would seem that the treatise was begun prior to the appointment of Erasmus as councilor at the court. However, in a letter (the *Catalogus lucubrationum*) to John Botzheim, dated at Basel, January 30, 1523,[5] he tells us that he did not give the work to Prince Charles until after he had been appointed and was actually at the court. Therefore, he continued, the benefice was not in the nature of a "plum" that he had plucked, but

---

[1] Allen, Ep. 370, n. 18.
[2] *Ibid.*; cf. also Ep. 392, lines 15-18.
[3] *Ibid.*, Ep. 334, lines 170-72.
[4] *Ibid.*, Ep. 337, lines 88-89 and introd.
[5] *Ibid.*, Ep. 1, p. 19, lines 24-33; and p. 44, lines 2-6.

rather the treatise was his means of returning the favor conferred upon him by the prince.[6] At all events, we know that the work was in the hands of the printer by May 12, 1516,[7] but on the first of June Erasmus, "although very anxious to present it to the prince," had to leave Basel before its completion.[8] On June 17, John Froben, the Basel printer and friend of Erasmus, informed him that the *Institutio* was off the press.[9] The treatise is therefore contemporaneous with the more famous *Utopia* (1516) of Thomas More and Machiavelli's *Il principe* (1513, first printed in 1532).

The number of editions called for in a few years would seem to indicate the ready reception of this book, an acceptance that justified Thomas More's expectations of it. More wrote to Erasmus, "You have done well in writing on the instruction of a Christian prince. How I wish Christian princes would follow good instructions. Everything is upset by their mad follies. I am very desirous of having this book, for I am sure that like everything else of yours, it will turn out perfect." [10]

[6] In his letter to Henry VIII of England, dated at Antwerp on September 9, 1517, Erasmus says that since he had become one of the councilors of the prince his prime object should be to make available the sources of all admonitions (*consilia*) ; hence he wrote the *Institutio*. In the light of the letters to Grimani and Dorp, this is not incongruous with the Botzheim letter of six years later, for here Erasmus does not specifically state that he *wrote* the treatise after entering upon his duties. Allen suggests (Ep. 370, n. 18) that Erasmus was offered the position in May and did not actually begin until January 1, 1516. In that case, the matter is probably settled, since Erasmus would consider himself one of the court once he had been named. Cf. also Bagdat, *op. cit.*, pp. 2-12. Enthoven, "Ueber die Institutio principis Christiani des Erasmus" in *Neue Jahrb. für das klass. Alter.*, XXIV (1909), 312, seems to have confused his information when he says, "Auf der Wunsch des burgundischen Kanzlers Joannes Silvagius und zum Dank für seine Ernennung . . . verfasste Erasmus . . . die Institutio." John le Sauvage requested Erasmus to undertake the matter contained in the *Querela pacis* (Allen, I, p. 19, line 2) : "Itaque iussu Ioannis Sylvagii scripsi Pacis querelam." Cf. Bagdat, *op. cit.*, p. 7: "Cet ouvrage [*l'Institutio*] . . . avait été certainement demandé à Érasme par le Chancelier le Sauvage. Érasme a dû être, en tout cas, vivement encouragé à l'écrire." However, Allen, Ep. 410, does not bear this out as stated ; and Nichols, *Epistles of Erasmus*, II, 250 and 263, makes no comment to that end.

[7] Allen, Ep. 407, line 5. *Bibliotheca Erasmiana, répertoire des oeuvres d'Érasme*, 1^re série, p. 111, shows two editions in 1515 — one at Venice and one at Louvain. It is hard to believe there is not an error in those dates.

[8] Allen, Ep. 410, lines 3-5; cf. Ep. 416, lines 10-11.

[9] Allen, Ep. 419, lines 4-6. Cf. Nichols, *op. cit.*, II, 249.

[10] Allen, Ep. 423, lines 21-25. Cf. Ep. 421, lines 88-90, where Erasmus tells of the frankness with which he has treated all subjects.

*40 editions*
*16 translations*
*Eng. latest 1921*

There were three editions from Froben in 1516; another at Louvain in that same year; and others by Froben in 1518 and 1519.[11] There were also other editions in 1523 and 1525. In all, there have been some forty editions of this work, of which eighteen complete editions and several translations were issued during the remaining twenty years of Erasmus's life.[12] Of the sixteen translations of the treatise, the latest is in English and issued in 1921.[13]

But we are not dependent upon numerical data alone for our knowledge of the reception and distribution of this work. Colet had it in England at once, and Erasmus himself sent a copy to Henry VIII in 1517.[14] That Budé knew of it in France in the year of its publication is clear.[15] Whether Budé wrote his treatise *De l'institution du prince* in the same year or later is still open to some question. It was not published until 1546, six years after his death. It has been suggested that Budé withheld its publication because he "did not wish his less impressive vernacular piece to come into critical comparison" with that of Erasmus.[16] On December 13, 1517, Count Friederich II of Bavaria laid down a course of study for his nephew, Prince Philip. In this he prescribed that the young man should read the *Institutio* or a comparable work for three hours every day.[17] In 1518

[11] Cf. *ibid.*, Ep. 393, introd.; and Ep. 801, lines 17-20.

[12] *Bibliotheca Erasmiana*, 1re série, pp. 111-112. We should be careful not to estimate the size of old editions by the number of volumes in our modern editions.

[13] This is the first English version, and is a translation of the second half of the treatise done by P. Corbett, in the *Grotius Society Publications. Texts for Students of International Relations*, No. 1 (London, 1921), pp. 63.

[14] Allen, Ep. 657, lines 46-68; cf. Ep. 658.

[15] *Ibid.*, Ep. 421, lines 88-89.

[16] Woodward, *Education in the Age of the Renaissance* (Cambridge, 1906), p. 132. Enthoven, *op. cit.*, p. 314, refers to this as a positive statement. Triwunatz (*Guillaume Budé's De l'institution du Prince*, Erlangen, 1903) believes it was written in 1516 and withheld for the reason given above. He explains the similarities of the works of Erasmus and Budé as borrowing on the part of Erasmus; this seems to me (and to others) untenable. Geldner, *op. cit.*, p. 157, n. 7, holds with Delaruelle (*Guillaume Budé: les origenes, les debuts, les idées maitresses*, Paris, 1907, p. 210) that Budé did not write until 1519, that he did so then at the request of Francis I, who could read no Latin, for a digest of the ideas of Erasmus. As the work was therefore purely a command production intended for the king alone, it naturally was not published.

[17] *Monumenta Germaniae paedagogica*, XIX, 256-57. "Item nach dreyen

Erasmus reworked the treatise for presentation to Prince Ferdinand,[18] who seems (if we can believe Erasmus) to have kept it constantly with him.[19] Thomas Elyot, in *The Boke Named the Governour*, written and published in 1531 and dedicated to the king, drew a great deal upon Erasmus. He especially recommends the use of this little treatise by the most excellent doctor Erasmus, saying that "there never was boke written in latine that in so lytle a portion contained of sentence, eloquence & vertuous exhortation a more compendious abundance." [20] In the middle of this same century Sebastian Cocceius at Schwäbische Halle employed the *Institutio* in the training of Prince Eberhard of Württemberg.[21] About this same time Catharine de'Medici had a French paraphrase made for the use of her sons. In 1584 William V of Bavaria, when prescribing in detail the studies for his sons Maximilian and Philip (but more especially in laying down the instructions for their tutors) very probably had the principles of the *Institutio* consciously or unconsciously in mind.[22]

The last edition, except that of the *Opera omnia* (1703-6), was published at Leyden in 1641; and the last translation for two centuries was that in Swedish in 1721. From that point on we have a break of tangible evidence until the present day.

What was the cause of the long neglect of the *Institutio*? The treatise was didactic in purpose and for this reason might have had a more limited appeal. The *Complaint of Peace*, written shortly thereafter, has a much more general appeal; the *Colloquies* and the *Praise of Folly*, especially, have more gen-

---

Uren sol her Jörg seinen gnadn ein pros, als Erasmus Rotherdamium de Instituendo principe oder ainen andern auctorem, der seinen gnaden am dienstlichsten und nützlichsten ist, machen, dieselben seinen gnaden exponiren und verteutschen" (p. 257).

[18] Allen, Ep. 853, lines 63-end.

[19] *Ibid.*, Ep. 943, lines 23-24. Cf. Epp. 917; 970, lines 22-25; 1009, lines 45-51; and 1323, lines 3-5. This appears to be the last mention of the work by Erasmus himself.

[20] 1880 edition, p. 95.

[21] *Mitteilung d. Geschichte f. deutsche Erziehungs- und Schulgeschichte*, XV (1905), 109.

[22] *Mon. Germ. paed.*, XIV, xlix, n. 5, where the editor especially comments on certain passages; and pp. 39-47.

eral interest and his *Adages* have always been popular.[23] In
these works, wedged in among extraneous matter and disguised
under jest or satire is much that after proper sifting can be
taken seriously. The popular guise of these works probably
played a large share in overshadowing the more formal *Institutio*.[24] Furthermore, the *Institutio* is full of platitudes,
repetitions, and miscellanies that at first seem to detract. But
we must not forget that Erasmus was writing for his own day,
drew his comparisons from that same period, and reinforced
his ideas by constant references to classical antiquity in true
humanistic fashion.[25]

Let us now look at the work in detail. Erasmus begins as
follows:

When a prince is to be chosen by election, it is not at all appropriate
to look to the images of his forefathers; to consider his physical appearance. . . . Seek a nature staid, in no way rash, and not so excitable that
there is danger of his developing into a tyrant under the license of good
fortune and casting aside all regard for advisers and counselors. Yet have
a care that he be not so weak that he be turned now this way and now
that, by whomsoever he meets. Consider also his experience and his age

[23] Erasmus's influence was also exerted through his translations of Plutarch
and Isocrates.

[24] Cf. Enthoven, *op. cit.*, p. 314, who holds about the same view. "Eine Er-
klärung dieser Tatsache dürfte nicht sowohl im Inhalt der Scrift, im Übermass
der von Erasmus gestellten Forderungen als in ihrer wenig glücklichen Form
zu suchen sein. . . . Anstatt einer übersichtlichen und logisch geordneten Dar-
stellung [finden wir] meist nur eine lose Aneinanderreihung von Merksprüchen
und Aphorismen."

The view of Dr. James Brown Scott is a much finer one. "The chapters are
difficult to summarize, for they are in themselves a summary of the matured
views of Erasmus on the great question before Europe: how the princelings of
the day could become enlightened rulers. Then, too, the difficulty is enhanced
by the fact that we are dealing with a masterpiece of the world's literature,
in which every phrase has an artistic value. But it is more than a work of art;
it is the work of an internationalist, who from his closet expressed the views
which the statesman should follow in his cabinet. Within the compass of a few
pages we may only hope to show the reader of to-day why he should read this
tractate of more than four centuries ago, for if it were read and its counsel
pondered and accepted, the world would be better than it is, and indeed better
than it ever has been." — *The Spanish Origin of International Law* . . . (Oxford,
1934), p. 35. The complete summary and appreciation occupies pp. 33-47.

[25] Cf. chap. iv on "The Ancient Sources of Erasmus;" also Enthoven, *op. cit.*,
p. 315, n. 1; and Smith, *op. cit.*, p. 196.

— not so severe as to be entirely out of sympathy with the frivolity nor so impetuous as to be carried away by flights of fancy.[26]

Erasmus then brings in the familiar figure of the ship of state and points out that in its guidance, just as in actual navigation, the helmsman should be one eminently fitted; the one idea that should motivate a prince in his official acts — the good of the state — should move the people in their selection of a prince.[27] This theme continually recurs.

When the usual practice of hereditary rule prevails, then the hope of a good prince rests upon the choice of his tutor; for "nothing remains so deeply and tenaciously rooted as those things learned in the first years."[28] This tutor must not only instill in the young prince the basis of all moral principles but must also keep him away from undesirable associates who will corrupt or flatter him.[29] Furthermore, he must be such a one that the young man will love him and yet be obedient to all he prescribes.[30] This tutor should seek the young prince's natural bents and develop him along those lines.[31] But any ideas or tastes incongruous with his future position should be carefully stamped out. "It is fruitless to attempt advice on the theory of government until you have freed the prince's mind from those most common, and yet most truly false, opinions of the common people."[32] This the tutor should never cease to have in mind, adapting his method to the years of his pupil, for there is no one who cannot be brought around eventually. Part of this training should be accomplished by reference to simple analogies such as the social life of bees and ants.

The principles of Christian dogma should be inculcated from the first and kept continually in the fore. No one can be a real prince, we are told, who is not also a philosopher; and a philosopher and true Christian are one and the same in fact.[33] Especially does Erasmus stress the fact that adher-

---

[26] *Opera* (1703-6 edition), IV, 562. All succeeding references to the *Institutio* will be to the same edition; hence only the page number (i.e., alternate column numbers) will be given.

[27] *Ibid.*, p. 562.    [28] *Ibid.*, p. 562.    [29] *Ibid.*, p. 562.

[30] *Ibid.*, p. 562.    [31] *Ibid.*, p. 564.    [32] *Ibid.*, p. 564.

[33] *Ibid.*, p. 566.

ence to Christian principles applies to prince and subject with
equal force. Here we have the seeds of the ethical idea which
continues throughout the treatise. Erasmus now engages in a
long discussion of the "true good," the baseness of worldly
wealth, the common ways of the populace, the aim of magnanimity on the part of the prince, the nature of nobility, the
symbolism of the princely insignia,[34] the true meaning of
Christianity, and concludes with the responsibilities of the
prince.[35]

The prince must not indulge himself but remember that he
is the model for his people and that an evil in which he indulges is made manifold among his subjects. "The common people are unruly by nature, and magistrates are easily corrupted
through avarice or ambition. There is just one blessed stay in
this tide of evils — the unsullied character of the prince. If he
too is overcome by foolish ideas and base desires, what last
ray of hope is there for the commonwealth?"[36] This very
naturally brings Erasmus to the comparison of a good and a
bad prince, which occupies six pages of the treatise.

The wicked prince he compares with the various beasts, and
points out their counterparts in the ancient empires. The tyrant
he shows in contrast to a king as one who conducts his rule
only for his own advantage. "There is the same difference
between a good prince and a tyrant as there is between a kindly
father and a harsh master."[37] He then gives the usual picture
of the wicked prince as a rapacious beast, loathsome in all
details.[38] After concluding this description with a series of
references to the wicked rulers of biblical times, by way of
contrast Erasmus begins his picture of the good prince also
with quotations from the Bible. With these as his text, he
further develops the idea of the unity of Christian ethics and
ruling authority, and he has recourse to the familiar figure of
the state as one big family of which the prince should be

[34] *Ibid.,* p. 566.        [35] *Ibid.,* p. 568.        [36] *Ibid.,* p. 570.
[37] *Ibid.,* p. 572.
[38] *Ibid.,* p. 572. Cf. Bagdat, *op. cit.,* p. 84: "Ce tableau du Tyran peut sem-
bler de nos jours exagéré, il ne l'était nullement du temps d'Érasme."

the benign *paterfamilias*.[39] This brings him to a discussion of the best kind of state.

Although there are many types of state, it is the consensus of nearly all wise thinking men, that the best form is monarchy. This is according to the example of God that the sum of all things be placed in one individual, but in such a way that, following God's example, he surpasses all others in his wisdom and goodness, and, wanting nothing, may desire only to help his state. But if conditions were otherwise, that would be the worst form of state. Whosoever would fight it then would be the best man. If a prince be found complete in all good qualities, then a pure and absolute monarchy is the thing. (If that could only be! I fear it is too great a thing even to hope for.) If an average prince (as the affairs of men go now) is found, it will be better to have a limited monarchy checked and lessened by aristocracy and democracy. Then there is no chance for tyranny to creep in, but just as the elements in nature balance each other, so will the state hold together under similar control. If a prince has the interests of the state at heart his power is not checked on this account, so it will be adjudged, but rather helped. If his attitude is otherwise, however, it is expedient that the state break and turn aside the violence of a single man.[40]

After comparing the relation of the state with the prince to that of the body with the mind, Erasmus again has recourse to the divine. Here he sounds the note of his controversy with Luther concerning free will eight years later. He says: "God gave the angels and men free will so that He would not be ruling over bondsmen, and so that He might glorify and add further grandeur to His kingdom. Who, now, would swell with pride because he rules over men cowed down by fear like so many cattle?" [41] To the objection that he is lessening the power and prerogatives of the prince by all this restraint, he answers that no prince really rules unless over free men; no good prince ever requires anything that would not be freely given without compulsion.[42] This is all summarized in the outline of the duties of the prince and pointed by an idea that is typical of Erasmus's principles. "All other men take great

[39] *Ibid.*, p. 574.

[40] *Ibid.*, p. 576. This is the most detailed and formal statement of Erasmus's political doctrines; its importance can hardly be overestimated. Cf. the opening lines of the *Institutio*, and the discussion *supra*, on p. 23.

[41] *Ibid.*, p. 578.        [42] *Ibid.*, p. 580.

pains to get previous knowledge of the profession which they follow. How much more care should the prince take to get an early knowledge of the theory of government!" [43] In conclusion he adds another idea, only too idealistic for his day. "As the painter gets pleasure from a picture beautifully executed, and the farmer, the truck-gardener, the smith all get pleasure from their work, what should bring more enjoyment to the prince than the contemplation of his country improved and more flourishing as a result of his efforts?" [44]

Again and again Erasmus points out that the exalted position of the prince makes manifold demands upon his mind, his ability, his character, and his honor, above those upon the common people. "In the case of a private citizen it is perhaps quite enough to have a good mind, since he is directed by the laws. . . . But in the case of the prince, it is of little help to have been endowed with a good mind . . . if there is not also present wisdom which points the way to gain that which the prince desires." [45] After further deliberation on the same theme, Erasmus comes to his second chapter, which deals with "The Avoiding of Flatterers."

Flattery is subtly presented to the prince in many ways; [46] even the laws which give him great authority and imply his superiority to them flatter him. [47] Next follows a list of recommended readings, which include in the order named, the *Proverbs of Solomon, Ecclesiasticus,* the *Book of Wisdom,* and then the *Gospels.* These are to be followed by Plutarch's *Moralia,* supplemented by Seneca, "whose writings are wonderfully stimulating and excite one with enthusiasm for a life of moral integrity." The *Politics* of Aristotle and the *Offices* of Cicero should be read in excerpts. "But Plato is the most venerable source of these things," in the opinion of Erasmus. Of the historians, for example, Herodotus and Xenophon, Erasmus's recommendation is qualified, for they tell much which is not to be inculcated in the mind of the Christian prince. [48]

[43] *Ibid.,* p. 580.  [44] *Ibid.,* p. 582.  [45] *Ibid.,* p. 582.
[46] *Ibid.,* p. 586.  [47] *Ibid.,* p. 588.  [48] *Ibid.,* p. 588.

With the next section on "The Arts of Peace" we come to the more technical part of the treatise. Erasmus begins it thus: "Although the writers of antiquity divided the whole theory of government into two sections, war and peace, the first and most important objective is to instruct the prince how to rule wisely during times of peace in which he should strive his utmost to preclude any future need for war." [49] Under this heading come the love of a prince for his subjects, and the reciprocal faith and loyalty that it engenders. The prince should first know his own kingdom thoroughly by travel and by the study of history and geography, so that he can understand its problems.

At this point Erasmus anticipates his later chapter on state marriages by saying that the prince should be one who was born and raised in his own country, "for the ties of birth and country, and a mutual spirit of understanding, as it were, have a great deal to do with establishing a feeling of good will." [50] The prince should stay within the borders of his kingdom [51] (not wander all over the world as Ulysses did),[52] governing his people with kindliness and clemency, keeping his household of the same tenor as himself. Erasmus advocates a policy of conservatism, saying that all innovation by its very nature is dangerous and should be resorted to only if a great good is to be gained thereby.

The next point has a distinctly modern touch. "A prince who is about to assume control of the state must be advised at once that the main hope of a state lies in the proper education of its youth. . . . As a result of this scheme of things there will be no need of many laws or punishments, for the people will of their own free will follow the course of right." [53] If, however, the people should somehow prove untractable the prince should never cease his efforts to win them over gradually.

[49] *Ibid.*, 590.   [50] *Ibid.*, p. 590.

[51] *Ibid.*, p. 592. Cf. Enthoven, *op. cit.*, p. 325: "Wenn wir uns aber erinnern, dass Albrecht II. nie persönlich in den Reichslanden gewesen ist, dass Friederich III. 27 Jahre lang, von 1444 bis 1471, sich niemals im Reiche hat blicken lassen, so wird der Warnung des Erasmus ihre Berechtigung nicht abgesprochen werden können."

[52] *Opera*, IV, p. 604.   [53] *Ibid.*, p. 592.

The next chapter deals with "Tributes and Taxes." Erasmus believes the old proverb that parsimony is a great source of revenue and advises that all extravagant expenditures which serve the sensual pleasures of the prince and court should be curtailed.[54] Since some taxes will be necessary, the staples needed by the average man should be lightly taxed, while the burden should be borne by those who enjoy the luxuries of silks, spices, and precious stones from the Orient. To this Erasmus appends a word on the coinage and the stability which must be maintained in it.

Under the caption "Beneficences of the Prince," we are first told that the staunch supporters of the state should be rewarded,[55] and that no privileges should be permitted to the court circle which are not deemed proper for the people as a whole. This is a sign of equity and justice. Erasmus believes that a prince's first duty is to his own people, but (following Plato) he advocates especial care and consideration of foreigners, for they are entirely dependent upon the good will of the ruler.

To the chapter "On Enacting and Emending Laws," Erasmus devotes his greatest attention.[56]

The best laws under the best prince make a city (*civitas*) or a kingdom most fortunate. The most felicitous condition exists when the prince is obeyed by everyone, the prince himself obeys the laws, the laws go back to the fundamental principles of equity and honesty, with no other aim than the advancement of the commonwealth.[57]

In framing the laws several things must be kept in mind. Laws should be just, fair, and directed to the common good with a corrective as well as a punitive purpose.[58] The main purpose of a prince is to prevent crime and misdeeds rather than to punish derelictions once committed. This aim is to be accomplished through an educational program accustoming the people by example and precept to the principles of right and wrong, and by administration of the existing laws through prudent and honorable officials.[59] Only as a last resort should

[54] *Ibid.*, p. 594.
[55] *Ibid.*, p. 596.
[56] *Ibid.*, pp. 596-602.
[57] *Ibid.*, p. 596.
[58] *Ibid.*, p. 598.
[59] *Ibid.*, p. 598.

the incorrigible be sacrificed by the law, and then only to save the remaining members of society.

In attacking the sources of offenses against society, Erasmus first strikes against idleness, through which most of the evil in every state is created.[60] The prince should therefore always be on guard to keep the idle element among his courtiers down to the minimum and should either force them to be busy or else banish them from the country.[61] He would also include under his ban itinerant priests, street peddlers, money lenders, brokers, procurers, and those keepers and wardens of large estates that cater to the idle pleasures. He also believes that the monasteries and colleges are sources of discontent.

As remedies, Erasmus suggests a practical education for the sons of the idle rich and sumptuary laws enforcing frugality. He also advocates a severity of the law in proportion to the station of the offender, arguing that it is worse for an official to do wrong than for a commoner, and for a man of rank than for one of lowly place.[62]

Laws should not be promiscuously enacted, or once enacted, repeatedly changed and amended. However, if the exigency for which the law was created no longer exists, the law should be removed from the statute books.[63] Furthermore, the abuse of laws which have been established by long custom is not to be tolerated. By way of example Erasmus tells us that the customs laws, which were originally for the protection of the traveler and interstate merchant, are in his day entirely devoid of any idea of protection, although the tax remains. The laws should obviously be binding with equal force on everyone — a rule which is too often not observed.[64]

The prince should be very careful in dealing with a charge of *lèse-majesté*, remembering that it is a mark of a weak character to take vengeance for personal criticisms.[65] That man is really guilty of treason who diminishes that in which lies the true greatness of the prince; that is, his qualities of character and the affairs of his people that are prospering

[60] *Ibid.*, p. 598.     [61] *Ibid.*, p. 598.     [62] *Ibid.*, p. 598.

[63] *Ibid.*, p. 600.     [64] *Ibid.*, p. 600.     [65] *Ibid.*, p. 600.

through his wisdom.[66] The state (*res publica*) will be a state even if there be no prince; but there can be no prince without a state. Therefore, Erasmus concludes, "What is that which alone makes a prince if it is not the consent of his subjects?"[67]

After dealing with the diversified topics outlined above, Erasmus concludes as follows: that the laws should be as few as possible; that they be as just as possible; that they have a view to the welfare of the state; and that they be thoroughly familiar to the people.[68]

Under "Magistrates and Their Functions" Erasmus clearly states that it is not enough merely to have appointed the magistrates, even granted that they were selected from the older men of reputable character, but the prince must see to it that they carry out their duties properly.[69] Here Erasmus ends by recurring again to the organic analogy:

The parts of the mind are not all equal in importance; some control, others obey. The body only obeys. As the prince is the most important part of the state he ought to know most and be farthest divorced from all gross passions. And closest to him will be the magistrates who obey in part, and rule in part, for they obey the prince and rule the common people. Therefore the prosperity of the state is closely associated with the honest creation of the magistrates. . . .[70]

The next chapter deals with "Treaties." In Erasmus's view, great abundance of treaties is an outward recognition of poor faith, for true faith, he says, will stand without a written agreement. He takes this opportunity to speak on his favorite theme of pacifism, saying: "A treaty is usually prepared to set an end to war, but at the present time an agreement that starts a war is called a treaty. These alliances are nothing but war measures; and wherever the situation looks best, there treaties are arranged."[71] Granted that a treaty has been made, then every effort should be made to keep it. Infringements of some small clauses are not to be seized upon as an excuse for declaring the whole instrument null and void.[72] Especially is faith to be kept with the neighboring states, for if they are

[66] *Ibid.*, p. 600.      [67] *Ibid.*, p. 602.      [68] *Ibid.*, p. 602.
[69] *Ibid.*, p. 602.      [70] *Ibid.*, p. 602.      [71] *Ibid.*, p. 604.
[72] *Ibid.*, p. 604.

wrought up they can do a great deal of harm; while if they are friendly, they are a big help, and without mutual business relations a state cannot exist.[73] The prince should know and understand the characteristics of all peoples, and on the basis of this knowledge, as well as on a consideration of geographical location, he should enter upon treaties with other states. The friendship of some peoples is hardly more bearable than enmity, and others are widely separated by mountains, seas, or plains.

"The Marriage Alliances of Princes" are all-important, Erasmus tells us. "For my part," he says, "I should think that it would be by far most beneficial to the state if the marriage alliances of princes were confined within the limits of their own kingdoms, or if they had to go beyond their own boundaries, with only their nearest neighbors." [74] State marriages are more often arranged to suit the vanity of the ruling princes than for the good of the state. "The prince's wife should be selected from among all women for her integrity, modesty, and wisdom . . . and be such a one as will bear him children worthy of their parents and the state (*patria*)." [75] Continuing this last idea, Erasmus says that it is not probable that children born of mixed parentage will have unalloyed affection for their future kingdom, or that the people will fully accept them as their own.[76] As to the argument that peace is promoted by these alliances, Erasmus answers that when the matter of succession arises there is usually a war among the claimants and their respective houses, due to the long intermingling of ruling lines. His ethical sensibilities prompt him to bring in a question which is probably unique. How about the young girls themselves, who are sent off to far-away places to marry princes they have never seen — men who differ from them in language, manners, and characteristics? He recognized the hopelessness of his position due to long-established custom, but "deemed it best to give his advice in case things turned out beyond his hopes." [77]

[73] *Ibid.*, p. 604.     [74] *Ibid.*, p. 604.     [75] *Ibid.*, p. 604.
[76] *Ibid.*, p. 604.     [77] *Ibid.*, p. 606.

The responsibilities of the prince, as pointed out in "The Occupations of the Prince in Peace," are numerous and are based upon ethics.[78] He is to take part in public affairs, always conducting himself in such a manner that he does some good by his very presence. If the prince thinks that this is beneath his dignity, let him remember that even the greatest princes of antiquity did not scorn to take an active part in public administration. "A good *paterfamilias* is never at a loss for something to do in his own home. Is a prince without anything to to do in so vast a domain?"[79] The prince should enact laws; amend poor ones; repeal evil ones; punish corrupt magistrates; lighten the burdens on the poor; rid the country of brigands; and foster internal concord among the people. In addition, he should travel about his domain, beautify it by the erection of public buildings, help its economic and social conditions by the construction of bridges, churches, aqueducts, by draining swamps, digging canals, and scientifically directing the use of farm land.[80] His main object should be not the extension of his domain, but rather the betterment of it. If a prince will do these things for the progressive improvement of his state, he will at the same time be warding off the negative causes which reduce its welfare.

In the final chapter, "On Beginning War," Erasmus brings out formally his pacifistic ideas which show through all his works, and which he had already set forth in part twelve years before in the *Panegyric* to Philip.

Although a prince ought nowhere to be precipitate in his plans, there is no place for him to be more deliberate and circumspect than in the matter of going to war. Some evils come from one source, and others from another, but from war comes the shipwreck of all that is good, and from it likewise the sea of all calamities pours out.[81]

Consequently, war should be used only as a last resort; and once engaged upon, should be concluded as swiftly as possible, with the least bloodshed and suffering to the people. The prince should consider beforehand the worries, the trials, the

78 *Ibid.*, p. 606.      79 *Ibid.*, p. 606.      80 *Ibid.*, p. 606.
81 *Ibid.*, p. 608.

expense, and the after effects — the increase of depravity along with the sorrows and misfortunes of those left behind.[82] The prince should learn his lessons not at the expense of loss and disaster to his people, but by sage counsel with himself, and from the costly examples of others.

Erasmus's next argument is based on religious grounds. He says he will not attempt to decide whether war is ever justifiable, but will merely give some references. St. Augustine, St. Bernard, and others of the church fathers believed that there were just occasions for war. But — what of the teachings of the apostles and of Christ himself! They never sanction war, and is their authority inferior to that of the fathers?

In Erasmus's opinion, most wars are begun to avenge some personal wrong to the prince.[83] He seems to feel that real rights should be maintained, although care should be taken to see that a clear conception of them is secured. Then, "if a disagreement arises between princes, why not go to arbiters? There are plenty of bishops, abbots, and learned men, reliable magistrates by whose judgment the matter could better be settled than by such slaughter, spoliation, and calamity to the world." [84] After this suggestion of arbitration, Erasmus returns to the ethico-religious argument, pointing out what a disgrace it is for Christian peoples to be fighting without end among themselves. As it is now,

every Angle hates the Gaul, and every Gaul the Angle for no other reason than that he is an Angle. The Irishman, just because he is an Irishman, hates the Briton; the Italian hates the German . . . and so on through the list. District hates district; city hates city. Why do these stupid names do more to divide us than the common name of Christ to unite us? [85]

But, Erasmus says, he has elsewhere written extensively on the evils of war and should not repeat himself here.[86] Therefore he will add just one thing more. Christian princes should cast aside all feigned pretexts and excuses and earnestly work for the extinction of war, which has so long persisted among Christians. "If, after common counsel, we should carry out our

[82] *Ibid.*, p. 608.          [83] *Ibid.*, p. 610.          [84] *Ibid.*, p. 610.
[85] *Ibid.*, p. 610.          [86] *Ibid.*, p. 610.

common task, even those things which are purely personal to each one would be more prosperous. Now, even that for which alone we are fighting, is lost." [87]

Erasmus concludes the treatise with his plea to Prince Charles that he, at least, keep his kingdom free from all the sullying taints of war and tumult:

I pray that Christ, who is all good and supreme, may continue to bless your worthy efforts. He gave you a kingdom untainted with blood. He would have it always so. He rejoices to be called the Prince of Peace. May you do the same, that by your goodness and your wisdom at last there may be a respite from this maddest of mad wars. The memory of the misfortunes we have passed through will also commend peace to us, and the calamities of earlier times will render twofold the favor of your kindness. [88]

The *Institutio* was written when Erasmus was fifty years old and the recognized intellectual leader of Europe. It represents his mature and richest thought. It embodies his chief hopes for the Christian world — peace, harmony, true religion, education, and prosperity. Various permutations of these same ideas are found in many other places in works of Erasmus, as we have seen, but with very few exceptions [89] nothing is encountered with respect to political philosophy which is not included in the *Institutio*.

Janet has said that the *Institutio* "est un bon traité de morale; mais ce n'est pas un traité politique." [90] With the first idea we can readily agree. But is the *Institutio* not a political treatise? If we are correct in pointing out that only four ideas of political theory are found in other works of Erasmus that are not also found in this, and if we are further correct in attaching considerable political importance to the content of these other works, then it must follow that this formal exposition of the views of Erasmus at the height of his

[87] *Ibid.*, p. 612.        [88] *Ibid.*, p. 612.

[89] E.g., *Complaint of Peace*, p. 80, the true majesty of a prince is in his ability to avoid war; *Praise of Folly* (Bailey's trans., 1900 edition), pp. 34-35, the true basis of society consists of everyone's being in his right place; *idem.*, pp. 68-70, the "back to nature" idea; and *Colloquies* (Bailey's trans., 1900 edition), II, 257, the origin of law.

[90] *Op. cit.* (3d ed.), I, 105. Cf. also Erasmus's prefatory letter to Charles (Allen, Ep. 393).

career is likewise an important document in the history of political theory. In addition to its many precepts, which are probably responsible for the criticisms directed against it,[91] the *Institutio* has many references to contemporary matters in its discussion of the corruption of the laws and the law courts, the mal-functioning of the customs service, the monetary system, the difficulties of safe and convenient travel, the organization of the armies, the recommended program of road making, and sanitary engineering. In the light of all these matters the *Institutio* deserves more detailed attention than has hitherto been accorded to it.

[91] In this connection we should remember that Erasmus borrowed the idea of his treatise from Isocrates (who had addressed the first of this *genre* that we have in classical times to Nicocles, king of Cyprus), as he tells us in his prefatory letter. Isocrates justifies the commonplaces of his treatise in these words: "And do not be surprised that in what I have said there are many things which you know as well as I. This is not from inadvertence on my part, for I have realized all along that among so great a multitude both of mankind in general and their rulers there are some who have uttered one or another of these precepts, some who have heard them, some who have observed other people put them into practice, and some who are carrying them out in their own lives. But the truth is that in discourses of this sort we should not seek novelties, for in these discourses it is not possible to say what is paradoxical or outside the circle of accepted belief; but, rather, we should regard that man as the most accomplished in this field who can collect the greatest number of ideas scattered among the thoughts of all the rest and present them in the best form" (40-41). The translation is that of G. Norlin in the "Loeb Classical Library," *Isocrates*, I (New York, 1928).

# III

## ANCIENT THEORIES OF STATECRAFT

In this present chapter it is our purpose to examine in detail all of the great influential treatises on princeship in classical antiquity and many other examples, whether specifically *genre* essays or parts of larger works, so that we may have a complete background upon which to study and illuminate the treatise of Erasmus, the *raison d'être* of this volume. The task presents several obvious difficulties which, in the opinion of the reader, may or may not have been satisfactorily met. It seemed absolutely essential to set forth in great detail, carefully documented, the factual evidence in all cases, even at the expense of curtailing thereby prolonged discussions of the points raised. Too many books have been written, albeit by competent authorities, which contain too much of the modern writer and too little of the original. By arranging the material according to a biographico-chronological system (as we have also done in the chapter on the Middle Ages) the force of tradition, the effect of contemporary events, the development of ideas should be as nearly as possible self-evident. In some centuries the material is much more abundant than in others; for this there are two possible explanations, of which the first is usually the correct one: the political stimulus of the particular period may have caused more political works to be produced, or fate may have preserved more of them for us through the ages. At all events, no important or relevant material has been knowingly excluded from consideration.[1]

Man has long lived in a state of organized society, and for

[1] The fragmentary material of the third-second century B.C. has not been given in detail as it is available in the work of Goodenough (see p. 60 n. 175) and is amply represented by the two writers discussed in this chapter. It is not our purpose to present a complete bibliographical list of *specula principis* in antiquity or later times.

a great space of time that state has been predominately mon-archical. Once the principle of monarchy is thoroughly estab-lished in a reasonably stable society, it is not surprising that philosophic thinkers should concern themselves with the rights, powers, duties, responsibilities, and personal qualifications of those destined to occupy the supreme position of king, whether that position be elective or hereditary, limited or absolute. It is quite natural that we of western civilization should place the inception of that thought in the Golden Age of Greece.[2] Unlike most of the great original contributions of Greece this *genre* did not, for obvious reasons, appear in the fifth century when Athenian democracy was at its zenith, but in the mid-fourth century, when men's minds were inevitably directed toward political thinking and especially toward kingship, for which the rising power of Macedon was the inspiration.[3] In Rome we meet a similar situation. Quite naturally early Rome, which was republican long before the earliest extant literature was created, has left us no essays on kingship. But in the Alexandrian period, under Hellenistic influence, abstract think-ing began, and contact with surrounding states developed the germ that was to blossom forth so fully under the Empire.

It is inconceivable, even if we were without the specific ac-knowledgments of indebtedness in many places, that so many writers dealing with the same general theme could be inde-pendent one of the other. Several things make dependence indisputable. The most obvious is the exact paralleling of certain topics in exactly similar circumstances; next, we occa-sionally have specific quotations; and lastly we have as a guide the several schools of philosophy represented by the writers. Given those facts, plus the logical hypothesis that essays on the same general subject (all highly ethical in tone) cannot but have much in common, we conclude at once that originality is not one of the prime essentials of a good treatise on the education of a prince. In fact, Christianity, which did not exert

[2] Cf. chap. v, note 2, for references to oriental and other early political phil-osophies.

[3] Of course I do not overlook the references in Homer, in the gnomic poets (Hesiod, Theognis, Phocylides), and in Herodotus, III, 80, 81, 82..

a manifest influence until quite late in our period, is the only really new element since the earliest times. Of course we do not mean to preclude some degree of originality in minor points. The specific relationships between several writers have usually been indicated at the appropriate places. It is in the Middle Ages, discussed in Chapter V, that many new elements appear. But a reading of this and the following chapter should clearly manifest one conclusion: many so-called "modern" ideas are merely reversions to the basic ideas of Greco-Roman antiquity which in many cases were engulfed in the vortex of the Middle Ages only to appear again in our own day.[4]

## ISOCRATES, 436-338 B. C.

With Isocrates we begin the long succession of philosophers, educators, and rulers who wrote treatises on the specific subject of prince training, or general treatises on ethics or statecraft in which there are references of sufficient number and importance to demand their consideration along with specific examples of this *genre*. Isocrates's treatise, *To Nicocles*, was sent to the young king of Cyprus probably shortly after his succession to the throne upon the death of his father, Evagoras, in 374 B. C. This short treatise sets forth the duties and responsibilities of a prince to his people. It was followed a few years later [5] by another, *Nicocles or the Cyprians*, which

---

[4] For a general discussion of ancient theories of statecraft see, *inter alios*, R. von Pöhlmann, *Geschichte der sozialen Frage und des Sozialismus in der antiken Welt* (3d ed., 2 vols., Munich, 1925), who in many instances relates the problems to those of the modern world; and J. Kärst, *Studien zur Entwickelung und theoretischen Begründung der Monarchie im Altertum* (Munich, 1898). Those readers who may wish to pursue the study of ancient mirrors of princes should consult the histories of Greek and Latin literature, Christ, Wm.-Schmid, Wm.-Stählin, O., *Geschichte der griechischen Literatur* (6th ed., Munich, 1912-24), Croiset, A. and M., *Histoire de la littérature grecque* (Paris, 1914-29), Schanz, M., *Geschichte der römischen Literatur* (Munich, 1927-), Krumbacher, K., *Byzantinische Literaturgeschichte* (2d ed., Munich, 1897), Manitius, M., *Geschichte der lateinischen Literatur des Mittelalters* (Munich, 1911-31), and the indispensable bibliographical works, Bursian's *Jahresbericht über die Fortschritte der klassichen Altertumswissenschaft* (including the *Bibliotheca philologica classica*), and Marouzeau, J., *Dix années de bibliographie classique*, 1914-24 (Paris, 1927-), continued as *L'Année philologique*.

[5] Cf. chap. 63 of the treatise, and Jebb, *Attic Orators*, II, 86, in which the date is placed between 372 and 365 B. C.

may well have been written at the request of the king. In this, Isocrates, writing in the person of Nicocles, sets forth the duties of the people to their king; Chapters 29-47, however, deal with the obligations of Nicocles himself.[6] The Evagoras, a biography of the king by that name, contains passing references to politics, as do many of the orations, but none are cited here since they are not germane to our purpose.

After the opening chapter of To Nicocles in which he remarks that advice on kingship should be the most acceptable gift from a friend, Isocrates proceeds to say that "the office of king is . . . the most important of human functions and demands the greatest wisdom." [7] Isocrates accepts monarchy as the best form of government without question.

> It is said that even the gods are ruled by Zeus as king. If the saying is true, it is clear that the gods also prefer this regime; but if, on the other hand, no one knows the truth about this matter, and we by our own conjecture have simply supposed it to be so, it is a proof that we all hold monarchy in the highest esteem; for we should never have said that the gods live under it if we did not believe it to be far superior to all other governments.[8]

The duty of a king is to relieve the state in time of distress, to enlarge it when small, to be energetic and intelligent in all public acts.[9] In return for this thoughtful care, the people are to obey the laws and commands of the ruler, to be virtuous in their conduct, to rear their children in proper manners, to be mild and peaceful.[10] The prince should love his people and his country [11] and take care to rule in such a way that his govern-

---

[6] The latest text of the works of Isocrates is that of Drerup, Isocratis opera omnia (Leipzig, 1906-), which is not yet complete. Numerous translations of all or part of his works have been made, among which the handiest for general reference is that by G. Norlin in the "Loeb Classical Library" (3 vols., New York, 1928-). Cf. also Blass, Die attische Beredsamkeit (Leipzig, 1868-80), II, 1-304; Jebb, Attic Orators (London, 1876), II, 1-260. On Isocrates's political ideas in general see G. Mathieu, Les Idées politiques d'Isocrate (Diss., Paris, 1925), especially chap. xiv, "Isocrate et la philosophie politique de son temps."

[7] 6. All direct quotations are from the translation of Norlin; all references are to the To Nicocles unless preceded by a "C" (The Cyprians).

[8] C 26. Cf. C 14-26, which is the general discussion on monarchy.

[9] 9-11; cf. C 32.

[10] C 48-62.

[11] 15.

ment is acceptable to the people.[12] Education [13] for his task is
the best security of a prince's position; it insures peace and
happiness for ruler and subject alike.[14]

All governments last longest if they serve the masses; [15]
it is better to rule as wisely as possible than to try to extend
the kingdom.[16] Laws no longer appropriate should be
changed; [17] cases should be settled by the courts as quickly as
possible.[18] No outrages should be allowed; the good should be
rewarded.[19] Let the people respect the prince for his fairness.[20]
He should never act in anger; [21] he should always be careful to
govern himself and his desires,[22] so that his self-control may
be an example to the people, for they imitate the prince in all
matters.[23]

The prince should watch his morals and actions, careful
always to be cautious and dignified; [24] value the truth; [25] worship God; [26] act in a manner appropriate to the circumstances
at hand.[27] He should be chary of extending his own friendship
and should select his friends with great care,[28] remembering
that his truest defense is loyal friends.[29] He should surpass
all in virtue,[30] emulate the well educated, and be conversant
with good literature, remembering that wisdom is better than
fortune.[31] He should have only one wife, of station equal to
his own, who will bear him children worthy to represent his
house.[32]

Princes frequently lack real advice, for people habitually
flatter royalty.[33] But the good prince should know that criti-

[12] 15.
[13] The gnomic poets, Hesiod (7th cent.), Theognis (6th cent.), and Phocylides (6th cent.) should be read for the moral precepts embodied in their
works (43).

| | | |
|---|---|---|
| [14] 8. | [15] 15-16; cf. C 30-47. | [16] 25-26. |
| [17] 17. | [18] 17. | [19] 16. |
| [20] 23; C 31-35. | [21] 23. | [22] 29; C 36-37. |
| [23] 31. | [24] 34. | [25] 22. |
| [26] 20. | [27] 37. | [28] 27. |
| [29] 21. | [30] 11; C 30, 38. | |

[31] 30. Isocrates is careful to point out that there can be no absolute standard on
many of these points: ". . . we ought not to test all the virtues in the same set
of conditions, but should test justice when a man is in want, temperance when
he is in power, continence when he is in the prime of youth." (C 44.)

[32] C 40-42.        [33] 4.

cism is better than flattery;[34] in fact "a good counsellor is the most useful and the most princely of all possessions."[35] The evils and responsibilities of ruling are equal to the glory;[36] in their youth and inexperience private citizens are protected by the laws, but a prince is not so protected.[37] He should be careful to rule the city as he would control his own private estate;[38] he should be magnificent on public occasions.[39] He should remember to keep strictly attentive to the main affairs at hand, not to be confused or misled by minor details, and not to judge a matter by the pleasure of his choice, but by its inherent worth.[40] In choosing assistants for any of his tasks, he should remember that they act only in his name, and that he is responsible for them.[41] It is better to live in honor than to live in shame,[42] and when his time has come, to prefer to leave behind him as a memorial, images of his character rather than of his body.[43]

## XENOPHON, ?430-?354 B. C.

Contemporary with Isocrates for the earlier part of his life was Xenophon, an historian and philosopher whom we shall now consider. From among his several works only the *Cyropaedia*, or *Education of Cyrus*, the *Memorabilia*, the *Agesilaus*, the *Hiero*, and the *Oeconomicus* concern us. The first of these, in eight books, is a biographico-romantic story of Cyrus, the king of Persia, in which he is presented in many ways as the ideal prince.[44] The date of publication is uncertain, but it is generally agreed to be later than 364 B. C. The second is the biography of the late King Agesilaus, in which Xenophon emphasizes the political interests and military achievements of the king. It was probably written in 361-60 B. C., the year of the king's death. The *Hiero* is an imaginary dialogue between Hiero of Syracuse and the poet Simonides of Ceos, on the subject of a ruler's obligations. The date of its composition

---

[34] 28.   [35] 53.   [36] 5.   [37] 3.   [38] 19.
[39] 19.   [40] 50.   [41] 27.   [42] 36.   [43] 36.

[44] Xenophon was not the first to do this in connection with Cyrus, for Antisthenes, the founder of the Cynic school, is reported in Diogenes VI, 16, to have written a dialogue, *Cyrus or On Kingship*. This same Antisthenes wrote another dialogue of the same *genre*, *Archelaus or On Kingship*, of a moral tone.

has been placed between 383 and 359 B. C., but cannot be definitely established. The *Oeconomicus* is a small work that continues the material of the *Memorabilia*; it must have been
written later than 384 B. C., the date of publication of the
*Memorabilia*.[45]

"Government of men with their consent and in accordance
with the laws of the state is kingship; while government of
unwilling subjects, not controlled by laws, but imposed by the
will of the ruler, is despotism." [46] The ruler should remember
that nothing is better for men than order,[47] and that a "king is
chosen not to take good care of himself, but for the good of
those who have chosen him." [48] The prince should be like a
shepherd to his people,[49] or like a father to his children.[50] He
should first of all know himself,[51] for no one should rule unless
he is better than his subjects.[52] A clear proof of a ruler's goodness is the support of the people in time of danger.[53]

Justice and virtue are wisdom; those who love the one, act
according to the other.[54] The ruler is obeyed readily when he
obviously displays wisdom superior to that of the common
people.[55] He should always be self-controlled, temperate,[56]
take little sleep, and have great physical endurance; [57] be courageous, wise, patriotic, and dignified at all times.[58] By his own
virtues, the good prince will be an example to all.[59] If the

[45] The most recent complete text of Xenophon is that by E. C. Marchant,
*Xenophontis opera omnia* (Oxford, 1900-) ; the best translation is that by W.
Miller, *Cyropaedia* in the "Loeb Classical Library," 2 vols. (London, 1914) ; and
E. C. Marchant, *Economicus*, and *Scripta minora*, both in "Loeb Classical Library" (London, 1923 and 1925). On his political importance see W. W. Willoughby, *The Political Theories of the Ancient World* (New York, 1903), chap.
x; P. A. R. Janet, *Histoire de la science politique dans ses rapports avec la
morale* (2d ed., Paris, 1872), I, 132-35.

[46] *Mem.* IV. 6. 12.     [47] *Oec.* 8. 3.     [48] *Mem.* III. 2. 3.

[49] *Cyr.* VIII. 2. 14; *Mem.* III. 2. 1-3.

[50] *Cyr.* VIII. 1. 1; *Ages.* 7. 3.

[51] *Cyr.* VII. 2. 20.                    [52] *Cyr.* VIII. 1. 37.

[53] *Oec.* 4. 19.                         [54] *Mem.* III. 9. 5; cf. *Cyr.* I. 6. 22.

[55] *Cyr.* I. 6. 21.                       [56] *Cyr.* VIII. 1. 32.

[57] *Mem.* II. 1. 3 and 6; *Cyr.* I. 6. 25; *Ages.* 5. 1-3. Cf. *Cyr.* I. 6. 8, where
Cyrus discourses disapprovingly of the customs of the Medes which are contrary
to this ideal.

[58] *Ages.* 8. 3-8.

[59] *Ages.* 10. 2; cf. *Oec.* 21. 2-8, *Ages.* 11. 1-16, which is a recapitulation of
all the good qualities of a ruler.

prince himself obeys the laws, who else would object to doing so? [60] There is no better way to inspire a desire for the good and desirable than by setting the example.[61] Absolute obedience marks the recognition of a good ruler.[62]

Because of his heavy responsibilities [63] a good prince has far fewer pleasures than the average man.[64] He suffers much from flatterers; [65] he can never be sure that he has genuine affection shown him,[66] although to be loved by others is the greatest blessing.[67] He is always open to danger [68] and can really trust no one,[69] but must fear all brave men if he is a despotic ruler, however good.[70] To win willing obedience is a gift more divine than human.[71] The prince should be seen frequently and be readily accessible to all.[72] He should reward the good.[73] He should be just in financial transactions,[74] respectful toward religion,[75] kind to prisoners of war.[76]

The prince is responsible to the state for its needs and its provisions.[77] A busy commercial life in the state gives little room for idleness and vice.[78] If the common good demands it, the prince should not hesitate to give freely of his private fortune.[79] Only good can result from keeping the wealth of the citizens employed.[80] If a good prince needs financial help from his people, they will not fail him.[81] "Enrich your friends, for so you will enrich yourself. Exalt the state, for so you will deck yourself with power. . . . Account the fatherland your estate, the citizens your comrades. . ." [82]

[60] *Ages.* 7. 2.
[61] *Cyr.* VIII. 1. 21; cf. *ibid.*, VII. 5. 85; VIII. 7. 23.
[62] *Oec.* 4. 19; cf. *Mem.* III. 3. 9.
[63] *Hiero* 2. 6; 8. 8-10.
[64] *Hiero* 1. 8; cf. 4. 6-8.       [65] *Hiero* 1. 15.
[66] *Hiero* 1. 37, 38.       [67] *Hiero* 3. 1, 2; cf. *Cyr.* I. 6. 24.
[68] *Hiero* 2. 8; cf. 10. 4-8.       [69] *Hiero* 4. 1-5; 6. 4-16.
[70] *Hiero* 5. 1-4.       [71] *Oec.* 21. 12.
[72] *Ages.* 9. 1, 2. This is the opposite of the Persian practice (*Ages.* 1. 9).
[73] *Cyr.* VIII. 2. 10. ". . . a great ruler should delegate to others the task of punishing those who require to be coerced, and should reserve to himself the privilege of awarding the prizes," for censure brings ill-will to those who make it, while praise gains favor (*Hiero* 9. 3).
[74] *Ages.* 4. 1-6.       [75] *Ages.* 3. 2.       [76] *Ages.* 1. 21-22.
[77] *Mem.* II. 1. 8-9.       [78] *Hiero* 9. 8.       [79] *Hiero* 11. 1-2.
[80] *Hiero* 11. 4.       [81] *Cyr.* VIII. 2. 15-19.       [82] *Hiero* 11. 13-14.

## PLATO, 427-347 B. C.

In Plato, the younger contemporary of Isocrates, the famous pupil of Socrates, and founder of the Academic school of philosophy, we meet the intellect whose influence directly or indirectly was to mold the course of political thought in the western world more than any other influence, Christianity not excepted, until the ascendency of Aristotle in the thirteenth century A. D. Plato did not write a specific treatise on our subject, but the germ ideas of nearly all subsequent essays of this *genre* are contained in his famous works, the *Republic* and the *Laws*. The *Republic*, in ten books, was probably finished between 380 and 370 B. C. (the date is very difficult to fix with accuracy) and represented the labors of many years. The *Laws*, in twelve books, was the last effort of the writer, and was left unfinished, to be published only after its author's death. Some of Plato's political ideas are also found in his other works; e.g., in *The Statesman*, a short treatise written about 364 B. C.[83] Plato thrice went to Sicily as a brain-trust of one at the court of Dionysius the Elder (388) and of his son (367 and 361). Unfortunately his relations with the tyrants were most unsatisfactory and he was unable to put his theories to practical test.

Of the five types of states — monarchy, timocracy, oligarchy, democracy, tyranny — Plato tells us that monarchy is the best and most felicitous, while tyranny is the worst.[84]

[83] The best text of Plato's works is that of J. Burnet, *Platonis opera* (5 vols., Oxford, 1900-07); the classic translation of the works of Plato is still that by B. Jowett, *The Dialogues of Plato* (3d ed., 5 vols., Oxford, 1892); the *Laws* is also translated by R. G. Bury in the "Loeb Classical Library" (2 vols., New York, 1926); and the *Republic* by Paul Shorey, in the "Loeb Classical Library" (New York, 1930-35). It is impossible to cite even a portion of the many works dealing with Plato's political influence, but the following handy references, with their bibliographies, may prove suggestive. E. Barker, *The Political Thought of Plato and Aristotle* (London, 1906); Janet, *op. cit.*, I, 104-76; Willoughby, *op. cit.*, pp. 88-130; Dunning, *A History of Political Theories, Ancient and Mediaeval* (2d ed., New York, 1923), chap. ii.

[84] *Rep.* IX. 580. Cf. the detailed discussion of this point in *The Statesman*, 291-303. The references in Plato are cited according to the scheme followed by Jowett: the work, book, and page reference in the edition of Stephanus (found in the margins of Jowett's translations). The translations quoted are not always Jowett's.

This is true because in a monarchy the one single ruler can make his decisions readily, lead at once for others to follow, and by setting a perfect example of efficiency and goodness [85] help his subjects. But under such a scheme (monarchy) the native characteristics and ideas of the ruler are of the utmost importance. First of all, the ideal prince must cherish only the truth,[86] and then he must be temperate, just, and careful, but withal, possessed of courage and the ability to act.[87] He should also be quick to learn,[88] self-controlled,[89] gentle,[90] possessed of a good memory,[91] a sound training, and years of experience.[92] Furthermore, the ruler of the state should be tested for physical and mental endurance under severe strain, for he must be able to bear such crises equitably.[93] The prince is to order his life and actions on those of God.[94] The prince who remains watchful at night is a great

[85] *Laws* IV. 711; cf. *ibid.*, IV. 713 and III. 699. Cf. *Rep.* VIII. 547, 548.

[86] *Rep.* VI. 506, 484.

[87] *States.* 311; *Rep.* II. 376; *id.* VI. 487. " 'You are aware,' I replied, 'that quick intelligence, memory, sagacity, cleverness, and similar qualities, do not often grow together, and that persons who possess them and are at the same time high spirited and magnanimous are not so constituted by nature as to live orderly and in a peaceful and settled manner; they are driven any way by their impulses and all solid principle goes out of them. . . . On the other hand, those steadfast natures which can better be depended upon, which in a battle are impregnable to fear and immovable, are equally immovable when there is anything to be learned; they are always in a torpid state, and are apt to yawn and go to sleep over any intellectual toil' " (*Rep.* VI. 503).

[88] *Rep.* VI. 487.

[89] *Laws* I. 626; *Rep.* IV. 441. "Give me the State under a monarchy; and let the monarch be young and possessed by nature of a good memory, quick intelligence, courage, and nobility of manner; and let that quality which we formerly mentioned [temperance] as the necessary accompaniment of all the parts of virtue, attend now also on our monarch's soul if the rest of his qualities are to be of any value" (*Laws* IV. 709-10).

[90] *Rep.* III. 410.

[91] *Rep.* VI. 486.

[92] *Rep.* VI. 487. "You must contrive for your future rulers another and a better life than that of a ruler, and then you may have a well-ordered State; for only in the State which offers this, will they rule who are truly rich, not in silver and gold, but in virtue and wisdom, which are the true blessings of life. Whereas if they go to the administration of public affairs, poor and hungering after their own private advantage, thinking that hence they are to snatch the chief good, order there can never be; for they will be fighting about office, and the civil and domestic broils which thus arise will be the ruin of the rulers themselves and of the whole State" (*Rep.* VII. 521).

[93] *Rep.* VI. 503.       [94] *Laws* IV. 716.

defense against evildoers.[95] The function of the prince is a noble one.[96]

Plato, among others, presents to us the famous parable of the pilot and the ship of state. It is true that in the passage whence the comparison is taken, the pilot meant is not one ruler but the people, and the storm represents the politicians, but as he himself says at the end of his remarks, "You will hardly need . . . to hear the interpretation of the figure, which describes the true philosopher in relation to the state." [97] He likewise makes the equally familiar comparison of a good ruler and a reliable physician who prescribes, not for his own good, but for the good of his patient.[98]

Until philosophers are kings, or the kings and princes of this world have the spirit and power of philosophy, and political greatness and wisdom meet in one, and those commoner natures who pursue either to the exclusion of the other are compelled to stand aside, cities will never have rest from their evils — no, nor the human race, as I believe — and then only will this State have a possibility of life and behold the light of day.[99]

The good prince is likewise the shepherd of his people.[100]

By contrast with the good prince, Plato shows us the tyrant.[101] He is either the master or slave of the others; he never realizes true freedom or true friendship.[102] This type comes into being when a leader becomes filled with uncontrolled lusts and desires, when his means are insufficient for his supposed needs.[103] It is not hard for a tyrant to change the modes and manners of a state, because by his example, as in the case of a good ruler, people follow his actions.[104] The essence of a tyrant's power is disorder; when he has stirred up sufficient confusion and uprising against established government, he

---

[95] *Laws* VI. 758.          [96] *States.* 261.

[97] *Rep.* VI. 488-89. Cf. the elaborate development of this point in *States.* 276-77, and the long discussion following it, *ibid.*, 297-99.

[98] *Laws* IV. 720.

[99] *Rep.* V. 473. Cf. also *Rep.* VI. 499 and I. 347. Plato disapproves of the situation permitted by Cyrus, king of the Persians, who allowed his children (future rulers) to be raised by indulgent nurses who yielded to their every whim and so spoiled them (*Laws* III. 695).

[100] *States.* 267; cf. *ibid.*, 272-74.          [101] *States.* 276.

[102] *Rep.* IX. 576.          [103] *Rep.* IX. 572-4; cf. *ibid.*, VIII. 569.

[104] *Laws* IV. 711.

appears as the leader of the people. This same principle holds also when he has gained the throne — by keeping wars going, he is the only leader capable of directing the people's welfare.[105] It is the task of the tyrant to seek out and guard against all high-minded, wise, and influential men, for they are his enemies.[106] The life of the tyrant is fraught with worry, for "he has to be master of others when he is not master of himself; he is like a diseased or paralytic man who is compelled to pass his life, not in retirement, but fighting and combating with other men." [107] The tyrant lives furthest removed from true pleasure and the philosophers, while the king is the nearest to them.[108]

As we should expect, Plato has much to say regarding education.[109] Power and capacity for learning exists in the soul, its development must take place in the body.[110] Therefore, education of the child is of great importance since the training received during the formative years may affect the later life very materially.[111] Knowledge should not be acquired under compulsion; [112] the child should be drawn to those subjects of which he needs mastery in later manhood.[113] A gifted mind, uneducated, becomes bad; [114] one naturally gifted and flattered in his development is prone to scorn real effort in seeking knowledge.[115] Justice and gentleness, as opposed to rudeness and unsociability, mark the philosopher from the untrained man.[116] "The simple and moderate desires which follow reason and are under the guidance of mind and true opinion, are to be found only in a few, and those the best born and best edu-

---

[105] *Rep*. VIII. 567.          [106] *Rep*. VIII. 567.
[107] *Rep*. IX. 579. Cf. *Rep*. IX. 580; IX. 588.
[108] *Rep*. IX. 587.
[109] This topic and others of a similar nature connected with statecraft in general, rather than the education of a prince alone, are examined in detail in the sections devoted to such writers as Plato, Aristotle, Seneca, Plutarch, and St. Augustine, for they all exercised great influence upon subsequent writers. Erasmus's own treatise devotes considerable space to these matters of statecraft.
[110] *Rep*. VII. 518.          [111] *Rep*. II. 377.          [112] *Rep*. VII. 536-37.
[113] *Laws* I. 643. Women should also be carefully educated (*Laws* VII. 805).
[114] *Rep*. VI. 491.
[115] *Rep*. VI. 494; cf. *Laws* III. 691.
[116] *Rep*. VI. 486.

cated." [117] The true lover of learning will be absorbed in the delights of the spirit and free from sensual pleasure.[118] Of the three classes of men — lovers of wisdom, lovers of honor, lovers of gain — only the first class is truly happy.[119] By his famous story of the cave, Plato points out the enlightenment, or the opposite, of our natures.[120] When the philosopher-rulers have been educated they are to return to this cave, and by their superior training, see the realities beyond the apparent shadows, and guide the remaining people in their blindness.[121]

In connection with law and the courts, Plato tells us that the best laws and the best constitutions of states are realized only when supreme power is coincidental with the highest wisdom and self-control.[122] The rulers should be subject to this law.[123] Only a tyrant acts contrary to law and custom.[124] The ruler should deviate from the established law only when he is sure such action will do the most good.[125] However, the young men are not to question the authority of the law.[126] Men should leave as much as possible to general education rather than try to set up rules of conduct, procedure, and business by law in all its detail.[127] The prince will supervise this education himself

---

[117] *Rep.* IV. 431. "The disposition of the mass of mankind is exactly the opposite of this; when they desire, they desire without limit, and when they can make moderate gains, they prefer to gain insatiably" (*Laws* XI. 918). Plato outlines a course of study in *Rep.* VI. 498.

[118] *Rep.* VI. 485.          [119] *Rep.* IX. 581-82.

[120] "Let me show in a figure how far our nature is enlightened or unenlightened: — Behold! human beings living in an underground den, which has a mouth open towards the light and reaching all along the den; here they have been from childhood and have their legs and necks chained so that they cannot move, and can only see before them, being prevented by the chains from turning round their heads. Above and behind them a fire is blazing at a distance, and between the fire and the prisoners there is a raised way; and you will see, if you look, a low wall built along the way, like a screen which marionette players have in front of them, over which they show the puppets. . . . And do you see, I said, men passing along the wall carrying all sorts of vessels . . . made of wood and stone and various materials, which appear over the wall? . . . they see only their own shadows, or the shadows of one another, which the fire throws on the opposite wall of the cave." (*Rep.* VII. 514-15.)

[121] *Rep.* VII. 519.          [122] *Laws* IV. 712.          [123] *Laws* IV. 715.
[124] *States.* 301.          [125] *States.* 300.          [126] *Laws* I. 634.

[127] *Rep.* IV. 425-26. The rule of law is good, but if a good prince can be found, his will, over the laws, is even better, for he is possessed of personal judgment; laws alone can only be general in their application, with no power of discrimination (*States.* 293-95).

in order to insure its adequacy.[128] Those in charge of the law should hold office not before their fiftieth year.[129] Laws should be admonitory as well as punitive.[130] While mercy is in general to be extended to wrongdoers, flagrant offenders should be severely dealt with.[131] Incorrigibles in wickedness should pay the death penalty.[132] Laws should be changed when new needs arise.[133]

We may perhaps add a miscellaneous group of ideas here, all of which have a bearing upon later political thinking. The ruler of the state must see that riches and poverty are not extreme, for they engender idleness and mischief.[134] On this same principle all beggars should be barred from the state.[135] The ruler will encourage poets and other writers to treat of valorous, good, and temperate themes, to glorify the virtuous and decry the wicked.[136] There shall be no remuneration for service to the state.[137]

Civil war is the worst of all evils;[138] other wars are of questionable good.[139] Expansion is dangerous: "So long as the city, as it increases, continues to be one, so far it may increase, but no further."[140] It is best to enact war legislation for peace, rather than peace legislation for war.[141]

## ARISTOTLE, 384-322 B. C.

Aristotle, the pupil of Plato and tutor of Alexander the Great, comes next in importance as well as in time. We are here concerned with only one of his four hundred works, the *Politics*, which he wrote in eight books as a continuation of the matter just reached at the end of the *Nicomachean Ethics*, and which he must have issued between 338 and 332 B. C.[142] The

---

[128] *States.* 308.
[129] *Laws* VI. 755.  [130] *Laws* IX. 862-63.  [131] *Laws* IX. 862.
[132] *Rep.* III. 409. Judges should be older men who have had the opportunity to study life, and appreciate causes of evil (*Rep.* III. 409).
[133] *States.* 296.  [134] *Rep.* IV. 421.  [135] *Laws* XI. 936.
[136] *Laws* II. 655, 659-60; cf. *Rep.* X. 606.  [137] *Laws* XII. 955.
[138] *Laws* I. 629, *Rep.* V. 470. All was peace and harmony in the Golden Age (*States.* 271).
[139] *Rep.* V. 470-71.  [140] *Rep.* IV. 423.  [141] *Laws* I. 628.
[142] The best text of the *Politics* is that of O. Immisch, *Aristotelis politica* (3d ed., Leipzig, 1929); the most elaborate translation of Aristotle's works is that

*Politics,* for many years lost to the western world, when found
again in the thirteenth century completely eclipsed all other
literature in its influence upon the time.

"Monarchies . . . are royal in so far as the monarch rules
according to law over willing subjects; but they are tyrannical
in so far as he is despotic and rules according to his own
fancy," [143] for tyranny is arbitrary power which is responsible
to no one. The same principle would be applicable in oligarchies: the ruling class should not be the enemies of the common
people, but should rule for their mutual good.[144] Any change
of government that may be needed should be readily acceptable to the people, for all changes, at best, bring confusion.[145]

It is clear then that a state is not a mere society, having a common
place, established for the prevention of mutual crime and for the sake
of exchange. These are conditions without which a state cannot exist;
but all of them together do not constitute a state, which is a community
of families and aggregations of families in well-being, for the sake of a
perfect and self-sufficing life.[146]

The prince should be virtuous and a rational thinker; [147] he
should be chosen for leadership because of his personal conduct and mode of life.[148] Virtue must be practiced to be permanent.[149] The worthy man, willy-nilly, should be selected for
office: [150] "When a whole family, or some individual, happens
to be so preëminent in virtue as to surpass all others, then it is
just that they should be the royal family and supreme over all,
or that this one citizen should be king of the whole nation." [151]
Only a man who surpasses all others has a right to absolute
power; [152] no one should rule others until he has learned to
obey.[153] When such a person of preëminent capabilities is found
in a state, he should no longer be part of the state, for it would
be wrong to judge him by the standards of others. But he

edited by W. D. Ross, *The Works of Aristotle* (11 vols., 1908-31) ; the *Politics*
has also been translated by H. Rackham, in the "Loeb Classical Library" (New
York, 1932). On the political ideas of Aristotle see E. Barker, *op. cit.*; I. A. Loos,
"The Political Philosophy of Aristotle," *Annals Amer. Acad. Polit. and Soc. Sci.*,
X (1897), 313-33; Janet, *op. cit.*, I, 177-255; Dunning, *op. cit.*, chap. iii.

[143] IV. 10; cf. III. 14.     [144] V. 9.     [145] IV. 1.

[146] III. 9.     [147] I. 13.     [148] II. 9.     [149] VIII. 1.

[150] II. 9.     [151] III. 17.     [152] VII. 30.     [153] III. 4.

should not be banished; he should be put at the head of the state.[154]

The state should be ruled for the essential good of the ruled, just as in the case of household management, or in the case of medicine, or physical education, which are practiced for the good they bring, not to the physician or the trainers, but to the people under their care.[155] Just as each person is happy in proportion to his virtue and wisdom,[156] so the best state is that which is morally best.[157] That state is safest which has an even distribution of wealth;[158] monarchy is primarily affected by internal disturbances — quarrels within the ruling house or attempted tyranny.[159] But revolutions may be caused by insolence and avarice, unequal distribution of honors, predominance of certain individuals, fear, contempt, intrigue, carelessness by which disloyal people can occupy high office, neglect of small matters, racial differences, incompatible points of view,[160] and widespread poverty.[161]

Aristotle points out, as does Plato, that as monarchy, aristocracy, and democracy in a good state are desirable in the order named, so, in a bad state, they are bad in the same order: tyranny, oligarchy, and democracy.[162] The tyrant helps to secure his position by stirring up distrust of each other among his citizens, removing their power, and reducing their positions generally; he must allow no common gatherings where plans could be made, no means of confidence or independent courage among his people; he must lay heavy taxes upon them.[163] The only true salvation of tyranny is to maintain an appearance of monarchy; the people should be honored and treated equitably.[164] Tyrannies are mainly attacked because of hatred and contempt.[165] If a tyrant assumes the qualities of virtue and

---

[154] III. 13. "Mankind will not say that such a one is to be expelled or exiled; on the other hand, he ought not to be a subject — that would be as if mankind should claim to rule over Zeus, dividing his offices among them. The only alternative is that all should joyfully obey such a ruler, according to what seems to be the order of nature, and that men like him should be kings in their state for life" (III. 13).

[155] III. 6.    [156] VII. 1; cf. IV. 11 = *Eth.* VII. 13.

[157] VII. 1.    [158] IV. 11.    [159] V. 10.    [160] V. 10.    [161] II. 6.

[162] IV. 1. Aristotle develops this point also in V. 10.

[163] V. 11.    [164] V. 11.    [165] V. 10.

rules as a king "his rule will of necessity be nobler and happier, because he will rule over better men whose spirits are not crushed, over men to whom he himself is not an object of hatred, and of whom he is not afraid." [166]

Although the good ruler must have some force with which to uphold the law,[167] yet "the laws when good should be supreme." [168] But good laws, if not obeyed, do not make a good state.[169] Even when established, laws should not be unalterable but should be corrected when out of date; however, this is in itself a problem, for all such changes cause confusion and breed disregard for the law.[170] Education is the soundest foundation for any state; [171] early impressions are strong and lasting.[172] Wars of conquest are not desirable or felicitous; [173] much of the attention devoted to affairs military should be diverted to peace-time measures.[174]

## DIOTOGENES AND PSEUDO-ECPHANTUS, ?3D CENT. B. C.

Of Diotogenes nothing is known except from several fragments of two works, *On Piety* and *On Kingship*, both of which are preserved by Stobaeus (*c.* 6th cent. A. D.) in his *Anthology* in four books, of which the fourth is devoted to political matters. Stobaeus has also preserved, among many other interesting selections from authors now lost, three fragments of another work, entitled *On Kingship*, which is attributed to Ecphantus but which from the nature of the political philosophy can only be of a later period. Professor E. R. Goodenough has clearly shown that both Diotogenes and the Pseudo-Ecphantus must be Hellenistic, that is, in the period including the third and second centuries B. C.[175]

---

[166] V. 11.          [167] III. 15.          [168] III. 11.          [169] IV. 8.

[170] II. 8. Aristotle states that all administration should be so arranged by law that no magistrate gains thereby (V. 8).

[171] V. 9.          [172] VII. 17.          [173] VII. 14.          [174] VII. 14.

[175] E. R. Goodenough, "The Political Philosophy of Hellenistic Kingship," *Yale Classical Studies*, I (1928), 55-102; especially 64-77, 83-89. His stimulating article cites a good many other writers of the same *genre*, and deals especially with the philosophic conception of the Hellenistic king and the possible origin of such ideas. The fragments of Diotogenes and Ecphantus are translated by Goodenough, *loc. cit.* The latest text of Stobaeus is that by Wachsmuth and Hense, *Anthologia*, Leipzig, 1884-1912. The fragments are found in IV. 7. 61, 62; and IV. 7. 63, 64, 65.

There can be no justice without law. The king is law; therefore he must be just. He should be self-controlled, be different from the common people, have virtue as his ultimate goal, learn to rule himself before he attempts to rule others, and be eager for wealth in so far as it is needed for good uses. He should set an example to his people by his own goodness; he should be gracious, equitable, merciful, and just, for injustice is the worst possible sin. "Justice is a good shared in common between the rulers and the ruled and is accordingly the harmonizing principle in the political community." The greatest pleasure of the prince should come from his good and great deeds. His main task is to bring about harmony in the state.

The good prince should look like a king and command respect by his outward appearance as well as by his character. He has several important functions, among which are military leadership and just civil administration. He must thoroughly understand his task in order to maintain his position satisfactorily. He must follow the laws himself, help the needy, and not be a burden to his people. The really good prince is like the skillful pilot of a ship, or the successful physician in healing the sick, for he guides and aids his people in time of distress. The king should be in his state what God is in the universe. "Now the king bears the same relation to the state as God to the world . . . for the state, made as it is by a harmonizing together of many different elements, is an imitation of the order and harmony of the world. . . ." [176]

Ecphantus believes the prince must be just, self-restrained, intelligent, for the prince is the highest among men, having been fashioned by God after His own likeness. Nothing in the world is without a ruler. There must be harmony and understanding between the prince and his subjects; fear diminishes good will. The prince, like God in Heaven, is self-sufficient; he is the earthly counterpart of God. "He who rules in accordance with virtue is called, and is, king, for he has the same love and communion with his subjects as God has with the universe and the things in it. . . ."

[176] All the material in these two paragraphs is found in IV. 7. 61, 62; that in the following one, from IV. 7. 64, 65.

## POLYBIUS, ?205-123 B. C.

The famous historian Polybius wrote his *History of Rome* after a long sojourn at the city itself, and several later visits, during all of which he formed intimate friendships with the great Roman leaders of the period. There he also developed a great appreciation for the real greatness of Rome and her institutions. Accordingly it is not surprising that in his history of the world to his own day, in forty books, he should discuss in detail, with the thoroughness and ability of a true historian, the political institutions of the Roman state. These ideas are found primarily in his well-known sixth book, of which copious fragments remain.[177] The ideas on princes, in discussing a republic, are necessarily few.

"It is by no means every monarchy which we can call straight off a kingship, but only that which is voluntarily accepted by the subjects and in which they are governed rather by an appeal to their reason than by fear and force." [178] In the opinion of Polybius, monarchy develops into kingship only after the principles of justice, goodness, and forethought are added to those of might and power.[179] Duty is coexistent with, and practically the same as, justice.[180] Fortitude and temperance are also valuable.[181] Those who realize this are allowed by their people to found a ruling house, with hereditary rulers, for it is believed that from such an environment would come the young man who would be most apt to continue the rule in the same fashion.[182] Where the people have the right or opportunity to elect their king, such a one as just described should be their choice.[183] Under a good prince the people always obey, for they have nothing to fear.[184]

Early princes, once the hereditary principle was established, allowed themselves beautiful palaces and luxurious food and clothing. This caused envy and trouble. The result was ty-

---

[177] The latest text of Polybius is that by Th. Buettner-Wobst, *Polybii historiae*, 5 vols. (Leipzig, 1882-1904); there is a good translation by W. R. Paton, in the "Loeb Classical Library," 6 vols. (New York, 1922-27). Cf. Willoughby, *op. cit.*, chap. xviii.

[178] VI. 4.  [179] VI. 5.  [180] VI. 6.  [181] VI. 48.
[182] VI. 7.  [183] VI. 7.  [184] VI. 6.

ranny.[185] This naturally causes Polybius to discourse on the several usual types of states — six in all: monarchy, aristocracy, and democracy, with their perverted counterparts,[186] and also to expound, as Plato does, the cycle in which they develop each from the other.[187] His conclusion is, that since states decay for two causes, internal and external,[188] the best way to prevent internal dissolution of the state is a composite of the three good types,[189] for then the executive power (prince) is checked by the legislative and advisory (senate), and the people are assured a fair and just part in the conduct of public affairs.[190] Such a constitution was that of Lycurgus in Sparta, and most notably that of Rome.[191] This Polybius considered the ideal existent state,[192] for good laws and customs make a state good.[193]

## CICERO, 106-43 B. C.

Cicero is the first of the Romans who has left for us his philosophy of statecraft. We find these ideas primarily in the *Republic*, which after a hazardous descent through the ages is extant only in part,[194] in the *Laws*, and in the *Offices*.[195] The first was composed probably between 54 and 51 B. C., in six books. The second, which is a sequel to the *Republic*, was perhaps written intermittently between 52 and 45 B. C.; of this only three books (we know that at least five were written) survive. Both the *Republic* and the *Laws* depend primarily upon the corresponding works of Plato. As the title suggests, the *Offices*, in three books, is not connected directly with political theory but with ethics in general; it was composed about 44 B. C.[196]

[185] VI. 7.       [186] VI. 3, 4.      [187] VI. 8, 9.      [188] VI. 57.
[189] VI. 3.      [190] VI. 10.      [191] VI. 11.      [192] VI. 18.

[193] VI. 46. Among the great states of the past Polybius declares Sparta to have been the best (VI. 48-50), while the Athenian democracy is likened to a ship's crew without a pilot (VI. 44).

[194] It must be kept in mind, in considering the material of this treatise as a background for the Middle Ages and the Renaissance, that, except for the *Somnium Scipionis* in Book VI, and miscellaneous quotations, largely in Augustine's *City of God*, the *Republic* was lost until 1820.

[195] I give the usual name for this work out of deference to custom; the correct translation of the Latin title, *De officiis*, is *On Duty*.

[196] The latest text of the *Republic* is by K. Ziegler (Leipzig, 1915); and of the *Laws*, by G. Sichirollo (Padua, 1885); the best translations are those of

Cicero, like those before him and practically everyone succeeding him for nearly two thousand years, believed that monarchy is the best form of government, "but only so long as it
retains its true character. But it does that only when the safety,
equal rights, and tranquillity of the citizens are guarded by the
life-long authority, the justice, and the perfect wisdom of a
single ruler." [197] In the earlier history of Rome, only men of
high moral integrity were selected for the kingship, so that
the people would have a just rule.[198] The state should be governed for the benefit of the common people, not the ruler.[199]
The prince should be solicitous for the greatest good of his
people and should watch over them as a father over his children.[200] It is not enough for this chosen ruler merely to possess
virtue, he must practice it.[201] The man who rules best has himself learned how to obey in the past.[202] The highest glory a
prince can attain comes from the affection, confidence, and
esteem of his people.[203] This he can readily gain by seeing that
no private citizen loses any of his personal or property rights
through action of the state.[204]

It is interesting to find Cicero, the statesman, the lawyer,
the scholar (who wrote these essays after his political power
was doomed) saying that the life of a statesman is more
deserving of praise than is the quiet studious life devoted even
to the noblest arts.[205] Man can be the greatest help or greatest
hindrance to man.[206] A man possessed of the qualities essential
for a good ruler should put aside all thoughts of personal
convenience and devote himself to state life.[207] The state has

C. W. Keyes, in the "Loeb Classical Library" (New York, 1928) ; G. H. Sabine
and S. B. Smith, *On the Commonwealth* (Ohio State University Press, 1929)
with elaborate introduction on the sources and political philosophy of the
treatise. W. Miller, *Cicero: De officiis* in the "Loeb Classical Library" (New
York, 1913). On Cicero's political philosophy see *inter alios*, F. Cauer, *Ciceros
politisches Denken* (Berlin, 1903) ; T. Petersson, *Cicero* (Berkeley, 1920), chap.
xiii, pp. 443-61 ; Janet, *op. cit.*, I, 256-85 ; Willoughby, *op. cit.*, chap. xix.

[197] *Rep.* II. 23. 43; cf. I. 35. 54, 55.

[198] *Off.* II. 12. 41.      [199] *Off.* I. 25. 85.      [200] *Rep.* II. 26. 47.

[201] *Rep.* I. 2. 2. In his *Ep. ad Fam.* I. 9. 12, Cicero tells us that "as the
princes are wont to be in a state, so are all the rest of the people."

[202] *Laws* III. 2. 5.      [203] *Off.* II. 9. 31.      [204] *Off.* II. 21. 72.

[205] *Rep.* III. 3. 6; *Off.* I. 21. 70.      [206] *Off.* II. 5. 17.

[207] *Off.* I. 21. 72.

given men advantages so that it may claim for itself the greater part of their wisdom, talents, and courage.[208]

It is by various motives that people are led to submit to another's authority and power: they may be influenced (1) by good will; (2) by gratitude for generous favours conferred upon them; (3) by the eminence of that other's social position or by the hope that their submission will turn to their own account; (4) by fear that they may be compelled perforce to submit; (5) they may be captivated by the hope of gifts of money and by liberal promises; or, finally, (6) they may be bribed with money. . . . But of all motives, none is better adapted to secure influence and hold it fast than love; nothing is more foreign to that end than fear. For Ennius says admirably: "Whom they fear they hate. And whom one hates, one hopes to see him dead." [209]

Good will is won for princes primarily through their good deeds, good reputation, kindness, justice, honor, generosity, and affability.[210] Justice [211] is especially to be cultivated and maintained, for if justice and wisdom are combined, there is really nothing that cannot be accomplished by the ruler and the state.[212] "The noblest use [of virtue] is the government of the state," [213] for there really is no other occupation which so closely approaches the duties of the gods as the beneficial rule of a state.[214] There can be no nobler motive in life than the desire to be a ruler, so that one may maintain the supremacy of good and prevent the usurpation of power by the wicked.[215]

An approximation to the organic analogy is found in Cicero. He says that the mind is comparable to the kingdom, and reason, to the king.[216] Whoever believes that matters should be governed by his own convenience, not by virtue, cannot value friendship or justice.[217] The young man should learn by

---

[208] *Rep.* I. 4. 8.      [209] *Off.* II. 6. 21 — 7. 23.

[210] *Off.* II. 9. 32, 33. "The command of confidence can be secured on two conditions: (1) if people think us possessed of practical wisdom combined with a sense of justice. . . [for] (2) confidence is reposed in men who are just and true — that is, good men — on the definite assumption that their characters admit of no suspicion of dishonesty or wrongdoing. And so we believe that it is perfectly safe to entrust our lives, our fortunes, and our children to their care" (*Off.* II. 9. 33).

[211] *Off.* II. 11. 38.      [212] *Off.* II. 12. 42.      [213] *Rep.* I. 2. 2.

[214] *Rep.* I. 7. 12 ; cf. I. 20. 33.      [215] *Rep.* I. 5. 9.

[216] *Rep.* I. 38. 60 ; cf. III. 25. 38.      [217] *Off.* I. 2. 5.

association with his elders.[218] The ultimate good is the conquest of the body by the mind, the attainment of pure goodness.[219] The leader of the state "should be given almost no other duties than this one (for it comprises most of the others) — of improving and examining himself continually, urging others to imitate him, and furnishing in himself, as it were, a mirror to his fellow-citizens by reason of the supreme excellence of his life and character." [220] If princes do evil by their own acts, it is in reality a manifold evil, for everything they do is imitated by their subjects.[221]

The ruler is the speaking law; the law, the silent ruler.[222] Therefore, the ruler must make especial effort to become thoroughly conversant with the law and with its origins:

> But he should not allow his time constantly to be taken up with consultations or by reading and writing on these subjects . . . he must be fully conversant with justice in its highest aspects, for without that no one can be just; and he must not be ignorant of the civil law, but his knowledge of it should be like the pilot's knowledge of the stars, or a physician's knowledge of physics; for each uses his knowledge in his own art, but does not allow it to keep him from his own special duties.[223]

## SENECA, ?4 B. C. — A. D. 65

Seneca, the philosopher, poet, and tutor of the emperor Nero, unlike Cicero, did not write a formal treatise on statecraft, but did write what is essentially the first Latin "mirror of a prince" in his *De clementia* for Nero. In that and in his philosophic works, especially *On Anger* (*De ira*), and the *Moral Epistles*, which alone are considered here, he sets forth many ethical principles to which subsequent writers for many centuries were heavily indebted.[224] The *De ira*, in three books, was written after A. D. 41, although the exact date cannot be determined. The *De clementia*, in three books also, of which

218 *Off.* I. 34. 122.    219 *Laws* I. 23. 60.    220 *Rep.* II. 42. 69.    221 *Laws* III. 14. 31.

222 *Laws* III. 1. 2. Cicero defines "law" as follows: "Law is the highest reason, implanted in Nature, which commands what ought to be done and forbids the opposite. This reason, when firmly fixed and fully developed in the human mind, is Law" (*Laws* I. 6. 18, 19). On this subject see my paper, "Animate Law in the *Republic* and *Laws* of Cicero," *T. A. P. A.*, LXIV (1933), 128-37.

223 *Rep.* V. 3. 5.

224 The best available text of Seneca's *Moral Epistles* is that of O. Henze

only the first and part of the second are preserved, was probably written in A. D. 55 or 56, shortly after Nero, to whom it was dedicated, became emperor. *The Moral Epistles*, in twenty-two books, of which twenty are extant, appeared in final collection after A. D. 62.

As we might expect, early in the *De clementia* Seneca gives us his portrait of a prince:

He whose care embraces all, who, while guarding here with greater vigilance, there with less, yet fosters each and every part of the state as a portion of himself; who is inclined to the milder course even if it would profit him to punish, showing thus how loath he is to turn his hand to harsh correction; whose mind is free from all hostility, from all brutality; who so covets the approbation of his countrymen upon his acts as ruler that he wields his power with mildness and for their good; who thinks himself aboundingly happy if he can make the public sharers in his own good fortune; who is affable in speech, easy of approach and access, lovable in countenance, who most of all wins the affection of the masses, well-disposed to just petitions and even to the unjust not harsh — such a one the whole state loves, defends, and reveres.[225]

Nature herself first conceived the idea of king, as we can readily see from the life of the bees and other creatures. It is noteworthy that the queen bee alone has no sting.[226] The essential difference between a prince and a tyrant is that the former acts only on reason and out of necessity, while the latter serves his own pleasure.[227] The prince and tyrant differ not in name only but in deed.[228] The prince should be different from the common people.[229] Here we approach the organic analogy again: the soul rules the body as king or tyrant, depending upon which has the controlling power, reason, or

---

(Leipzig, 2d ed., 1914) ; of *De clementia*, by C. Hosius (Leipzig, 1900) ; of *De ira*, by E. Hermes (Leipzig, 1905). The *De ira* and *De clementia* are translated by J. W. Basore, in "Loeb Classical Library" (New York, 1928) ; the *Moral Epistles* are translated by R. M. Gummere, in the "Loeb Classical Library," 3 vols. (New York, 1917-25).

[225] *Clem.* I. 13. 4, 5.

[226] *Clem.* I. 19. 2, 3. Cf. Verg. *Geor.* IV. 150-78; the ancients referred to the "king-bee," which makes the analogy even closer. See T. Hudson-Williams, "King Bees and Queen Bees," *Class. Rev.* XLIX (1935), 2-4, who shows that the opinion of the ancient writers is not as consistent as is commonly supposed.

[227] *Clem.* I. 11. 4.    [228] *Clem.* I. 12. 1.    [229] *Ep.* 25. 7.

emotion.[230] The good prince, for whom the people silently pray, should so act that all may know that he belongs to the state, not the state to him.[231] No prince can be safe when nothing is safe from the prince.[232] A prince should wish to act toward his subjects, as he would wish the gods to be to him.[233]

The title "Father of His Country" is given to a prince so that he may realize his position toward his people;[234] the truly wise consider the office of ruler a duty.[235] A peaceable and kind prince can always trust his attendants.[236] The good prince should imitate the gods,[237] for they cannot do harm;[238] and he should remember that cruel anger is unseemly, for by it he descends below the level of his people.[239] He should be merciful,[240] slow to take vengence,[241] and quiet of speech.[242] Flattery, especially in early years, should be guarded against.[243] Since we cannot control our past, including our ancestry, glorious or humble as the case may be, our present condition, which we can control, is all that makes us virtuous or otherwise. The noble prince is entitled to that designation only on the basis of his character, not his ancestry.[244] He who bears himself in a godlike manner, who is kind and good ranks next to the gods;[245] it is not hard to be good.[246] A high-thinking rational mind should be cultivated,[247] for, by common agreement, in the Golden Age the rulers were wise.[248]

The tyrant has more worries than any other person, for he fears both men and gods, yet cannot turn back in his course because of his previous acts.[249] If the tyrant does maintain his

[230] *Ep.* 114. 3.　　[231] *Clem.* I. 19. 7, 8.　　[232] *Clem.* I. 19. 5.
[233] *Clem.* I. 7. 1.　　[234] *Clem.* I. 14. 2.　　[235] *Ep.* 90. 5.
[236] *Clem.* I. 13. 1.　　[237] *Ep.* 95. 2.　　[238] *Ep.* 95. 3.
[239] *Clem.* I. 5. 4. In *De ira* II. 23. 3, Seneca praises Alexander and Caesar for not yielding to anger when sorely tempted.
[240] *Clem.* I. 3. 3; II. 3. 2. Mercy is not only the glory of a ruler, but his greatest protection (*Clem.* I. 11. 4; cf. *ibid.*, I. 3. 3).
[241] *Clem.* I. 20. 3.
[242] *Clem.* I. 8. 1. "Pray, let us see to it, my dear Lucilius, that our lives, like jewels of great price, be noteworthy not because of their width but because of their weight. Let us measure them by their performance, not by their duration" (*Ep.* 93. 2. 5).
[243] *Ira* II. 21. 7, 8.　　[244] *Ep.* 44. 3, 4.　　[245] *Clem.* I. 19. 9.
[246] *Ira* II. 13. 1, 2.　　[247] *Ep.* 124. 3.　　[248] *Ep.* 90. 5; cf. *Ep.* 5, *passim.*
[249] *Clem.* I. 13. 2.

rule, and keep his realm intact, there is still no peace, harmony, happiness, or order anywhere.[250] The prince should remember "full many he must fear whom many fear." [251] If the tyrant's life can only be preserved by constant bloodshed among his citizens, his life is not worth living.[252]

Seneca, of course, mentions education and the laws. A careful check should be made to prevent freedom of development in the mind from becoming insolence.[253] The teachers should be men who practice their own good doctrines in their daily lives.[254] The early period of education is extremely important, for it is easy to train the young mind but hard to curb faults that have once become deep-rooted.[255] Laws were not needed until the vices of men made them necessary.[256] As the physician applies simple remedies at first, and only resorts to heroic measures as a last resort, so punishment should be graded to the offense: [257]

These three aims, which the law has had in view, should be kept in view also by the prince: either to reform the man that is punished, or by punishing him to make the rest better, or by removing bad men to let the rest live in greater security. . . . Good morals are established in the state and vice is wiped out if a prince is patient with vice, not as if he approved of it, but as if unwillingly and with great pain he had to resort to chastisement. The very mercifulness of the ruler makes men shrink from doing wrong; the punishment which a kindly man decrees seems all the more severe.[258]

Punishment should be meted out, as far as possible, as a corrective for the future rather than as punishment for the past.[259] By this system the laws can really be constructive.[260]

## SUETONIUS, 1ST-2D CENT. A. D.

Suetonius, the secretary of Hadrian, is best known for his

[250] *Clem.* I. 26. 2.
[251] *Ira* II. 11. 3. Quoted from Laberius (in Ribbeck, *Com. Rom. Frag.* 126).
[252] *Ep.* 93. 2-5; cf. *Clem.* I. 9. 6. Seneca decries war in general: "We check manslaughter and isolated murders; but what of war and the much-vaunted crime of slaughtering whole peoples?" (*Ep.* 95. 30; cf. also *Ep.* 94. 64-71).
[253] *Ira* II. 21. 3.      [254] *Ep.* 52. 8, 9; cf. *ibid.*, 3.
[255] *Ira* II. 18. 2; *Ep.* 108. 3.      [256] *Ep.* 90. 6.
[257] *Ira* I. 6. 2-4; cf. *Clem.* I. 2. 2.      [258] *Clem.* I. 22. 1-3.
[259] *Ira* I. 19. 7; I. 16. 2.      [260] *Ep.* 94. 3.

only extensive extant work, the *Lives of the Caesars*, in which he has written the biographies of the Roman emperors from Julius Caesar to Domitian. In this series of biographies we find some points on princely conduct quoted ostensibly from the emperors themselves, and a few observations from the impersonal author himself. The material is naturally meager, owing to the very nature of the biographies. Suetonius's work, in one book, in defense of Cicero's *De republica* has not survived.[261]

The idea of divine right is perhaps suggested in the boast of the Julian house of its descent from the "sacred majesty of kings, the chiefest among men, and the divine majesty of gods, to whom kings themselves are subject."[262] Augustus felt it a privilege to have restored peace and prosperity to the state, and laid the foundations for future development.[263] Tiberius believed the prince should be a servant to the state and the common people.[264] The prince should be a shepherd to his people,[265] should allow freedom of speech,[266] should severely punish informers in order to stop their activities,[267] and should not be prone to consider apparent insult against the person of the prince as a serious charge.[268] He should be merciful against wrongdoers,[269] and assiduous in his duties.[270]

Among characteristics noted as objectionable we may mention that a prince governed by his freedmen or his wives is not a prince, but merely a tool.[271] Nero boasted that no one before him ever knew the extent of his power;[272] and Caligula frequently quoted the line, "Let them hate me, if only they fear me."[273] He also boasted that he was a law unto himself.[274]

---

[261] The best text of Suetonius is that of M. Ihm, *De vita Caesarum libri viii* (Leipzig, 1925); his works are translated by J. C. Rolfe, *Suetonius*, in the "Loeb Classical Library," 2 vols. (New York, 1914).

[262] *Jul.* 6. 1.  [263] *Aug.* 28.  [264] *Tib.* 29.
[265] *Tib.* 32. 2.  [266] *Tib.* 28.  [267] *Dom.* 9. 3; cf. *Calig.* 15. 4.
[268] *Aug.* 51. 55.  [269] *Nero* 10; cf. *Aug.* 65.  [270] *Aug.* 33.
[271] *Claud.* 29. 1.  [272] *Nero* 37. 3.  [273] *Calig.* 30. 1.

[274] *Calig.* 29. 1. It should be remembered that in these biographies material on statecraft, directly or by implication, is very incidental. It seems to me to be beside the point to cite material at length, which by its very nature can only be applicable by implication. This holds true also of the material from the *Scriptores historiae Augustae*, and the body of material known as the *Panegyrici Latini*, both referred to later. Perhaps the main justification for their inclusion here is the fact that Erasmus knew and used them.

## PLUTARCH, ?46-?120

Plutarch, the learned Greek who has left so much of interest for us in connection with western, especially Roman, civilization,[275] wrote among his many works a collection of eighty-three pieces now gathered under the title of *Moralia*.[276] Among these essays, which vary from strictly ethical treatises to discourses on religion, political science, literary interpretation, and physics, there is one which is strictly a mirror of princes, the *Discourse to an Unlearned Prince*. This, together with *A Discourse on the Training of Children, How to Know a Flatterer from a Friend, The Philosopher Is to Discourse with Good Men, On the Three Forms of Government: Monarchy, Democracy, and Oligarchy*, contains most of the material cited here. A few random references to other works have been included when their pertinence demanded it.[277]

Of the three most usual forms of state — monarchy, aristocracy, and democracy — Plutarch believes monarchy to be the

[275] The commonly known stories of Plutarch's intimate knowledge of the Imperial Court at Rome, his friendship with Vespasian, his appointment as consul of Greece, his dedication of a work on the education of a prince to Trajan are all without true foundation, as recent scholarship has proved.

[276] The best complete text of Plutarch's *Moralia* is that by G. M. Bernardakis, *Moralia*, 7 vols. (Leipzig, 1888-96) ; a translation of the *Moralia* in 14 vols. (of which three have appeared) is being prepared by F. C. Babbitt in the "Loeb Classical Library" (New York, 1927-) ; for certain of the essays, including *The Discourse to the Unlearned Prince*, there is a translation by T. G. Tucker and A. O. Prickard, 2 vols. (Oxford, 1913 and 1918) ; for the remaining essays there is only *Plutarch's Miscellanies and Essays . . . by Several Hands* (1694), revised by W. W. Goodwin (6th ed., 5 vols., 1898), which is on the whole poor because of its fundamental unevenness of scholarship. See also R. Hirzel, *Plutarch* (Leipzig, 1912), for the influence of Plutarch; and especially, Scott "Plutarch and the Ruler Cult," *T. A. P. A.*, LX (1929), 117-35.

[277] Cf. also the *Lives, Should an Aged Man Meddle in State Affairs, Political Precepts, Moral Virtue, Virtue and Vice, The Fortune or Virtue of Alexander the Great, On the Control of Anger*. These works all contain moral precepts not only applicable to princes but to others equally well; consequently they have not been abstracted here. It is more difficult in the case of Plutarch than in that of many writers to decide arbitrarily what material should or should not be referred to. The decision is here based largely on the evidence of what Erasmus actually used, directly or indirectly, in his own treatise; but even that criterion presents difficulties, for he almost certainly employed in one place (see p. 186 of our translation, and n. 131 thereto) Plutarch's essay, *Which are the Most Crafty, Water Animals or Land Animals*, and again (p. 186 and n. 130), *Isis and Osiris, or the Ancient Religion and Philosophy of Egypt*.

only safe one, for a good prince is restrained as much by
the state as the state is by the prince. The prince is created by
the people; he can be removed by them.[278] The good prince is the
image of God;[279] as God placed the sun and the moon in the
skies as symbols of His power and glory, so the prince, the vicar
of God, is resplendent on earth.[280] A good man is happy when
he does a good deed; how happy a prince should be who can
do good deeds to so many at once.[281] The prince should be an
example to his people; he should be the strictest in his obser-
vance of the laws.[282] He should first of all learn to control
himself, lead a virtuous life, and set a pattern for his people
to follow.[283] The vices of a prince are especially conspicuous
because of his position;[284] therefore the man who corrupts a
prince is worse than he who corrupts a commoner.[285]

Justice is the measure of royal greatness;[286] the state, as
Anacharsis said, is most felicitous when the only inequality is
the advancement of its virtuous citizens and the subjection of
the wicked.[287] The prince is the administrator of divine power
for the good of his people.[288] This the philosopher-prince is
best able to do.[289] Deliberation is a great quality.[290] The good
prince fears for his subjects, the tyrant fears because of
them;[291] the former is repaid by the fears of his people for his
own safety.[292] It is better to have one's kingdom firmly established than greatly enlarged.[293]

Education is an important matter; a prince without education is like a golden statue filled with sand.[294] Philosophy once
inculcated will never be lost.[295] It is difficult for a prince to get
a good training, for instead of instruction and correction, he
usually gets flattery.[296] Education is a better security for good
order than a complexity of laws.[297] Good training will replace
native ability in many cases.[298] If princes are wise and well

[278] Govern., passim, esp. 4.

[279] Prince 3.     [280] Prince 3.     [281] Philosopher 3.

[282] Banquet 7.     [283] Prince 3.     [284] Prince 7.

[285] Philosopher 3.     [286] Agesilaus 23, 5.     [287] Banquet 11.

[288] Prince 3.     [289] Children 10; cf. Banquet 7.

[290] Prince 6.     [291] Prince 4.     [292] Banquet 7.

[293] Prince 1.     [294] Prince 2.     [295] Philosopher 4.

[296] Flatterer 16.     [297] Lycurgus 13. 1, 2.     [298] Children 4.

trained, just, good, and magnanimous, they greatly increase the happiness and prosperity of their people.[299] Consequently the position of tutor to a prince is honorable and valuable to the state.[300] A flatterer is a grave danger to both prince and state.[301] The suitable tutor is virtuous, well mannered, and experienced.[302] Almost of equal importance are the companions of the young prince,[303] for the young mind is most impressionable.[304] True happiness consists in the possession of true virtue; [305] the pleasures of the wicked are turbulent and restless.[306]

## Dio Chrysostom, 40-?117

Dio Chrysostom, so named for his golden-tongued oratory, was born in the city of Prusa in Bithynia and came to Rome some time in the reign of Vespasian. After suffering banishment under Domitian he returned again, to be held by Nerva and Trajan in even greater esteem than he had been before. It was to the latter emperor that he directed his four dialogues On Kingship (I-IV), of which the first and third were delivered in the presence of the prince. His political ideas, which echo much of Plato and Xenophon, are also found in the essay, Diogenes or On Tyranny (VI), his Agamemnon or On Kingship (LVI), and his On Kingship and Tyranny (LXII).[307]

[299] Philosopher 1.
[300] Philosopher 3.
[301] Flatterer 18, 19; cf. Children 17.
[302] Children 7.
[303] Children 6; cf. 17.    [304] Children 5.    [305] Children 8.
[306] Philosopher 2. Cf. Is Vice Sufficient to Cause Unhappiness, 2, 4; Virtue and Vice, 3.
[307] The latest text of Dio is that by G. de Budé, Dionis Chrysostomi orationes, 2 vols. (Leipzig, 1916-19), who has also translated the complete works (Corbeil, 1927). Dio has been done into German by Karl Kraut, Dio Chrysostomus aus Prusa (Ulm, 1901); a French translation (with the Greek text) of "On Kingship" IV was made by L. François (Dion Chrysostome . . . Paris, 1922), and an English translation of "On Kingship" II, "On Tyranny," et al is available by G. Wakefield, Select Essays . . . (London, 1800). J. W. Cohoon is preparing a translation of the complete works for the "Loeb Classical Library"; Vol. I (1932) alone has appeared. See also Hans von Arnim, Leben und Werke des Dio von Prusa (Berlin, 1898), and V. Valdenberg, "La Theorie monarchique de Dio Chrysostome," Revue des études grecques, XL (1927), 142-62; idem, "Philosophie politique de Dio Chrysostome," Bull. de l'Academie des sciences de l'U.R.S.S., 1926, 943-75, 1281-1307, 1533-54; ibid., 1927, 287-306 (in Russian). The greatest importance attaches to essays On Kingship I-IV which occupy

Dio, like many others, discusses the three forms of government, with their perverted equivalents, and decides that monarchy is best.[308] The good king should be manly, loving, kind, fond of his people, eager to be good, virtuous, ready to help the needy and to reform the wicked.[309] He should be the guardian, the savior, the guiding mind, possessed of courage, wisdom, and power, for "under such a king the people prosper." [310] If the prince acts wisely, loves and protects his people, shares his goods with his subjects, then they are also blessed and the ruler is a true king.[311] "Know well that you will not be a king before you have made your character pleasant, and until you have taken pains, as is proper, to show yourself a real ruler, a free and kingly man, not . . . a slave, a bondsman. . . ." [312] A good prince brings good to all; [313] his position and title are based upon his superiority over the common people.[314] Not everyone possessing a scepter is a king; only those who give thought to the good of their subjects are kings,[315] for otherwise children playing at being kings would really be kings.[316] The outward signs of princely power are not essential.[317]

The real prince should strive first of all to know himself.[318] After reverencing the gods he should respect good men.[319] He should lead a life simple, kind, and magnanimous, after the pattern of the gods,[320] maintaining an interest in philosophy, rhetoric,[321] manly occupations, and dress,[322] as opposed to wanton music, dancing, companionship,[323] avarice, voluptuousness.[324] He should deport himself with truthfulness and frankness.[325] Working diligently, fairly, and justly,[326] acting only according to the law,[327] always moderate and god-fearing,[328]

---

100 pages in Budé's text. They are cited below under the Roman numerals I-IV.

[308] III. 45-50.      [309] II. 77.      [310] III. 9 = Homer *Od.* XIX. 114.

[311] III. 39.      [312] IV. 75.      [313] III. 3-11.

[314] II. 71.      [315] I. 12.      [316] IV. 47.

[317] IV. 61. Here Dio refers to the Persian custom of decking out those condemned on capital charges in royal raiment, setting them on thrones, and then leading them off to death (IV. 67).

[318] IV. 56, 57.      [319] I. 17.      [320] II. 26.      [321] II. 26.

[322] II. 34-38; 49-51; IV. 61-66.      [323] II. 55.      [324] IV. 84-133.

[325] I. 26.      [326] I. 35.      [327] III. 44.      [328] I. 43.

the prince will be beloved of all his people. None is safer than he whom all love and who has no enemy.[329] "He is the best king whom good men are not ashamed to applaud either in the present or for future time." [330] The happy memory of the past and the hope for the future are the best things in life; therefore the life of a good king is indeed a happy one.[331]

The good prince is the shepherd of his people,[332] who watches over them with forethought, protection, guardianship. There is the same difference between a king and a cruel master as between a shepherd and a butcher.[333]

Who is more concerned for the herd than the herdsman? Who is more helpful and good to the flock than the shepherd? Who loves horses more than the man who has charge of many horses, especially if he profits from them? What man is thus more likely to be well-disposed toward his fellowmen than he who has power over them, especially if he is looked upon with respect by men? It is a disgrace if those who rule over strange and wild animals are kinder to their charges than the king ruling over men of our own group and tribe.[334]

If the prince would rule according to the idea and model of Zeus, he would have a good state.[335] Zeus, the king of gods and men, is called the guardian of the city, the friend, the provider of good-fellowship, a member of the same race, the protector of suppliants, the god of refuge, the protector of strangers, and addressed by many other epithets, "all good and the causes of good." [336] Those same titles are also becoming to a prince, as are also protector of property, and guardian of the fruits.[337] The good king is the father of his people.[338] With these pictures we are long familiar from other sources, but Dio also draws a homely comparison, the idea of which he borrowed from Homer,[339] between the bull of the herd and the head of the state: as the bull leads a simple life, fights for his herd, leads them to pasture, refrains from undue hostility with other leaders, so the prince should act for his people.[340]

[329] I. 35.  [330] I. 33.
[331] III. 58-61. The qualities of a good prince are set forth in considerable detail, among other places in I. 12-36.
[332] I. 13; IV. 44.  [333] IV. 44.  [334] I. 17, 18.
[335] I. 45.  [336] I. 39.  [337] I. 36-42.
[338] I. 22.  [339] *Iliad* II. 412-18.  [340] II. 66, 67.

If, failing to yield to the gods as if to good herdsmen,[341] he is cowardly, hurts his own people, is violent, unjust, lawless, weak, lusts for pleasure, is resentful, greedy for wealth, suspicious, crafty, mean, envious, unfriendly, unteachable, unreasonable, then he is replaced by Zeus as unkingly.[342]

A pilot and a general must take countless precautions to be alert to gain a successful end; so in all ways the good king is the one who is happiest because he is busiest.[343] The physician and the pilot both study to qualify in their profession; in just the same way a prince should strive to know his duties.[344]

It is just as impossible to be a real prince and bad, as it is to be inherently good and bad at once. The real prince is the best of all men, the bravest, the most just, the most invincible to the attacks of troublous toil and all passions. Would you select as a charioteer one who knows not how to drive, or as a pilot one who knows nothing of navigation, or as a physician one who is not thoroughly versed in the healing art? Of course not! Well, then, as it is not possible to sail a ship unless by a pilot's knowledge, so it is not possible to rule as a king unless one knows kingship, even if all the Greeks and all the barbarians say so, and attach to the person of the king many diadems, scepters, and tiaras, in the same fashion that one fastens necklaces on children that are exposed, so that they may not be unidentifiable.[345]

"It is not possible to take cities, to depose tyrants, and to command everything everywhere without power." [346] This power may be of several forms, as Dio points out in the long story about Heracles and his accomplishments, without wealth and accompanying forces,[347] in the course of which we are introduced to the goddess Kingship and her attendants Order, Peace, Law, and also to her opposite, Tyranny, who is accompanied by Cruelty, Insolence, Lawlessness, Dissent, Flattery, all in the most gaudy display.[348] Mere accomplishment of great deeds by one with absolute power is nothing [349] unless the one who performs them acts through wisdom, courage, justice, and foresight.[350]

---

[341] II. 72.          [342] II. 72-76.          [343] III. 64-85.

[344] III. 28, 29. Amid all his many duties the prince must have relaxation; Dio recommends riding and hunting (III. 133-36).

[345] IV. 24, 25.          [346] I. 63.          [347] I. 62-84.          [348] I. 74-83.

[349] The interlocutor here has been setting forth the deeds of Xerxes (III. 12-24, 30, 31) to which Socrates replies.          [350] III. 32.

Who has need of greater wisdom than he who plans all great things? ... Who needs a keener sense of justice than he to whom all things are possible? Who needs greater courage than he who keeps all things safe? But, however, to him who rules many others, there must also be this great expense of soldiery, both infantry and cavalry, as well as that of walls, ships, and engines of war, if he intends to keep his subjects in control and to ward off hostile peoples and to subdue any who revolt.[351]

The most valuable asset is friendship;[352] the power of a ruler increases as his friends increase in power.[353] Most worldly possessions are not needed in peace.[354] Friends are the eyes, [?ears], tongues, and hands of the good prince,[355] and they can be of the greatest assistance in the good administration of the state. "That is not really good fortune which has no one sharing its happiness."[356]

With a tyrant (despot), everything is changed. A prince listens to good men as to the gods,[357] and the king, like the king (queen) bee, has no sting.[358] The tyrant is unwise, greedy, unkind,[359] and lacks the good will and friendship of his people.[360] He fears peace, for in it his people have leisure for hatching plots and war, because it ferments trouble among the people;[361] he fears humility as false, and frankness he considers insolence.[362] He is never free from the dread of plots,[363] for he fears the rich because of their power, and the poor because of their longing for power.[364] The tyrant must always be surrounded by an armed guard against his subjects, but he cannot even trust his guard.[365]

## PSEUDO-SALLUST, CIRCA 150

In the manuscripts containing the works of Sallust there are at the end several which are usually considered not to have been written by that author, but which have never been identified with anyone else. These two short *suasoriae*, one in the form of a speech and the second in the form of a letter

[351] LXII. 3, 4. He who is most capable of waging war is likewise best able to maintain peace (I. 27).
[352] III. 86; 103.    [353] III. 86-89.    [354] III. 95-96.    [355] III. 104-106.
[356] III. 102.    [357] I. 16.    [358] IV. 63.
[359] III. 40-42. Cf. the material already cited from II. 72-76; I. 78-83.
[360] VI. 59.    [361] VI. 50, 51.    [362] VI. 56-58.    [363] VI. 35-37; 41-46.
[364] VI. 47, 48.    [365] VI. 38.

addressed to Caesar, are thought to be school exercises by two different persons, probably in the period of Fronto.[366] The problem is still being discussed.

The ruler should be great in adversity;[367] rule with mercy and kindness,[368] and without interest in worldly wealth.[369] He should beware of boasters;[370] and be virtuous, brave, and rule over the best possible subjects.[371] The results of virtue are to be carefully guarded;[372] harmony makes a state endure.[373] Retribution and rewards are slow but sure.[374] If the ruler is feared by his people, it reflects evil upon him.[375] When the public welfare is bound up in one man, then he should be allowed to have full power.[376] The ruler should be fair in his requirements of military service.[377] War should only be waged in order to perpetuate peace.[378] Such a war, once ended, brings problems of peace time, in which good advice is needed.[379] A strong senate is a good thing.[380]

## MARCUS AURELIUS, 121-80

The emperor Marcus Aurelius, the true philosopher-prince, has left for us his *Thoughts* in twelve books. This miscellaneous collection of inner communings with himself, as it were, naturally has more in common with ethics than political philosophy, but there is interwoven a good deal of value for our study. Not without point is the fact that these ideas were written down by a ruling emperor while engaged in the actual task of government.[381]

[366] The text of these short pieces is found in the works of Sallust, e.g., in the edition by Kurfess, *C. Sallustii Crispi epistulae ad Caesarem . . .* (2d. ed. Leipzig, 1930); they are translated by J. C. Rolfe, in the "Loeb Classical Library" (New York, 1921). A recent study by B. Edmar (*Studien zu den Epistulae ad Caesarem senem de re publica*, diss., Lund, 1931) favors the Sallustian authorship. Cf. also H. Dahlmann, "Sallusts politische Briefe," *Hermes*, LXIX (1934), 380-89.

[367] *Ep.* 1. The letter is cited as *Ep.*; the speech as *Or.*

| | | | |
|---|---|---|---|
| [368] *Or.* 3. | [369] *Ep.* 7; *Or.* 7, 8. | [370] *Ep.* 3. | [371] *Or.* 1. |
| [372] *Or.* 1. | [373] *Or.* 5. | [374] *Ep.* 12. | [375] *Or.* 3. |
| [376] *Ep.* 6. | [377] *Or.* 8. | [378] *Or.* 6. | [379] *Or.* 1. |
| [380] *Ep.* 10. | | | |

[381] The most recent text is that by H. Schenkl, *Marci Antonini imperatoris . . . libri XII* (Leipzig, 1913); the latest translation is by C. R. Haines, in the "Loeb Classical Library" (New York, 1916).

Marcus Aurelius believes that the true state should have "one law for all, based upon individual equality and freedom of speech, and of a sovranty which prizes above all things the liberty of the subject. . . ." [382] States are essential, for man is a social animal. [383]

At any rate to begin with among irrational creatures we find swarms and herds and bird-colonies and, as it were, love associations. For already at that stage there are souls, and the bond of affinity shews itself in the higher form to a degree of intensity not found in plants or stones or timber. But among rational creatures are found political communities and friendships and households and gatherings, and in wars treaties and armistice. [384]

Man has been created for his fellow man. [385] Since men are possessed of reason, the prince should treat them as fellow creatures. [386] The prince should be kind, [387] independent, frugal, serious, free from interest in worldly pleasures, [388] self-controlled, [389] an assiduous worker, [390] simple, dignified, uncorrupted, just, god-fearing, gracious, brave, and philosophic. [391] He should never break his word, hate, suspect, or play false to anyone. [392] He should be careful of his speech, [393] truthful, [394] and willing to meet people midway in arguments. [395]

The prince should act only as reason dictates, [396] that is, only as a good man should. [397] His acts should be worth while rather than numerous. [398] He should always be ready to listen to suggestions for the common good, [399] but ready also to examine all ideas carefully, [400] to adhere to good principles, [401] be persistent in his activities, to be clear in thought and speech, [402] and ready to receive help in his labors. [403] He should always be dignified without affectation, [404] slow to anger, [405] happy in high-mindedness, simplicity, kindness of heart, and purity of life, [406]

[382] I. 14.
[383] VIII. 34; cf. IV. 4; V. 30; VII. 55.
[384] IX. 9.
[385] VIII. 59; cf. V. 30; IX. 23.
[386] VI. 23; cf. IV. 4.
[387] I. 8, 15; VII. 31; X. 4; XI. 18.
[388] V. 5.
[389] I. 8, 10, 14, 15; II. 10; V. 31; VI. 6.
[390] VI. 2.
[391] VI. 30; cf. X. 8.
[392] III. 7.
[393] I. 10; VIII. 30.
[394] I. 15.
[395] I. 7.
[396] IX. 12.
[397] IV. 10.
[398] IV. 24.
[399] I. 16; IV. 12; cf. IX. 23; X. 6.
[400] III. 11; IV. 2.
[401] V. 9; cf. VII. 31.
[402] VIII. 51.
[403] VII. 7.
[404] I. 9, 15; II. 5.
[405] I. 9; VII. 24; XI. 18.
[406] V. 9.

and slow to take vengeance.[407] He should beware of flatterers,[408] in fact, should try to suppress flattery.[409] He should walk with the gods,[410] for it is possible to live well in an imperial court.[411] Therefore he should show no interest in games or in slander.[412] Since life is short and ineffectual at best,[413] let the prince scorn great worldly wealth [414] and consider rather the power and grandeur of the gods and the universe.[415]

## DIO CASSIUS, ?150-?235

Dio Cassius, born of a well-known Greek family of Bithynia, came to Rome about 180 and soon entered upon a distinguished state career. The only one of his works which has survived is his *Roman History*, in eighty books, of which only Books 36-60 (covering the material of the years 68 B. C.-A. D. 47) have completely survived. Since Dio spent the ten years, 201-210, in gathering his material, and the next twelve years, 211-223, in writing the first seventy-two books of his work (which began with the arrival of Aeneas in Italy and was to come down to his own day) the passage in which we are interested must have been written at just about the turn of the third century A. D. Book LII opens with two speeches, the first and shorter of which (LII. 1-13) is reported as if spoken by Agrippa, in an attempt to dissuade Augustus from establishing a permanent monarchy; the second (LII. 14-40) is really a miniature mirror of princes, which is addressed, supposedly, by the chancellor Maecenas to Augustus, in support of the establishment of the monarchy.[416]

The prince should be regarded by his people as a father and a savior.[417] This can only be justified if he is upright and self-controlled, and is not insolent nor greedy, if he enjoys a simple private life and does not wrong his subjects.[418] He must always be moderate, wise, prudent,[419] frugal in the arrangement of

---

[407] VI. 6.    [408] XI. 18.    [409] I. 16.    [410] V. 27; cf. VII. 31.
[411] V. 16.    [412] I. 5.    [413] II. 17; cf. IV *passim*; VI. 24.
[414] I. 16.    [415] II. 1-4.

[416] The latest text of Dio Cassius is that by U. P. Boissevain, *Cassii Dionis Cocceiani historiarum Romanarum quae supersunt* (Leipzig, 1895-1926); the work has been translated most recently by E. Cary (based on the translation of H. B. Foster) in the "Loeb Classical Library," 9 vols. (New York, 1914-27).

[417] 39.    [418] 39.    [419] 14.

the royal household,[420] and free from jealousy.[421] He should also be liberal, reward the good,[422] honor God,[423] and remember that virtue makes a prince good.[424] The prince should receive only moderate honors from his people.[425] It is not statues and temples that make the lasting memory of a prince but his image graven in the hearts of his loving subjects.[426] The people readily imitate their prince; he of necessity is ever before their eyes. Therefore whatever he would want his subjects to do, that he should do himself.[427]

It is possible for a good and sensible prince to rule well and with no danger to himself.[428] He should find out, if possible, what the people really think about him [429] and should try to think what acts he can perform in the regular course of duty which will make his subjects love him; [430] and above all, he should realize that it is easier to rule over a wide empire than it is to win it, although even the ruling is often difficult.[431] In this connection Dio gives us the familiar picture of the ship of state, but in a new connection, with a new purpose:

Our city, like a great merchantman manned with a crew of every race and lacking a pilot, has now for many generations been rolling and plunging as it has drifted this way and that in a heavy sea, a ship as it were without ballast. Do not, then, allow her to be longer opposed to the tempest; for you see that she is water-logged. And do not let her be pounded to pieces upon a reef; for her timbers are rotten and she will not be able to hold out much longer. But since the gods have taken pity on her and have set you over her as her arbiter and overseer, prove not false to her, to the end that, even as now she has revived a little by your aid, so she may survive in safety for the ages to come.[432]

The good ruler should do the best he can himself, and try to educate others to be his good assistants.[433] Lazy and abandoned subjects make no end of trouble.[434] He should appoint censors to oversee public morals.[435] Since one prince cannot manage all the affairs of state by himself, however hard he try, it is necessary to have good and honorable men to help

[420] 29.   [421] 33.   [422] 34, 37.   [423] 36.
[424] 35.   [425] 35.   [426] 35.   [427] 34.
[428] 18.   [429] 38.   [430] 38.   [431] 18.
[432] 16.   [433] 26.   [434] 26.   [435] 21.

him.[436] The general crowd of people, however, should not be allowed to partake directly in the rule,

for the boasted freedom of the mob proves in experience to be the bitterest servitude of the best element to the other and brings upon both a common destruction; whereas this freedom of which I speak everywhere prefers for honor the men of prudence, according to their deserts, and thus gives happiness impartially to all who enjoy this liberty.[437]

Yet every citizen should be made to feel that he has a direct part in the state:

I declare that the citizens ought every one actually to be given a share in the government, in order that, being on an equality with us in this respect also, they may be our faithful allies, living as it were in a single city, namely, our own, and considering that this is in very truth a city, whereas their own homes are but the countryside and villages.[438]

The prince should adorn the capital city; [439] keep the open lands cultivated by regular tenants; [440] seek only peace, yet be prepared for war; [441] enact good laws; [442] choose a good senate composed of mature men,[443] which should be empowered to receive embassies, actually enact the laws and perform like acts; [444] he should see that the secret ballot is employed in voting by the senate, so as to maintain the full confidence of the voters.[445] He should demand that only the royal coinage be used everywhere,[446] should levy taxes as lightly as possible and distribute the burden equally upon all citizens,[447] reduce public expenses if possible,[448] and maintain a small professional army so that agriculture and the occupations of peace may not be interrupted through military service.[449] The prince should set up a good system of courts and judges,[450] serve himself as an appellate court,[451] allow freedom of speech,[452] disregarding alleged cases of lèse-majesté,[453] and be mild in the punishment of those whom it is necessary to convict.[454]

[436] 14.          [437] 14.

[438] 19. In chapters 22-23 Maecenas sets forth details of district government, as to appointments, salaries, types of officials, procedure, etc., and in 24-25 adds much the same materials for the second class of appointees, the knights.

| [439] 30. | [440] 28. | [441] 37. | [442] 15. |
| [443] 19, 20. | [444] 31. | [445] 33. | [446] 30. |
| [447] 28. | [448] 30. | [449] 27. | [450] 20. |
| [451] 33. | [452] 33. | [453] 31. | [454] 31. |

Obviously, the worries and responsibilities of a prince are great. He must always be self-controlled [455] in spite of the jealousies aroused by his position,[456] for people always want gifts and honors.[457] When the prince apportions such favors only to the deserving, dissension is started at once.[458] In all this, flattery and deceit [459] are ever present; flattery eventually destroys the prince.[460]

And apart from these considerations, if one is to speak about matters which touch your personal interests, how could you endure to administer affairs so manifold, not only by day but also by night? How could you hold out if your health should fail? What human blessings could you enjoy, and how could you be happy if deprived of them? In what could you take genuine pleasure, and when would you be free from the keenest pain? For it is quite inevitable that a man who holds an office of this kind should have many anxieties, be subject to many fears, and have very little enjoyment of what is most pleasant, but should always and everywhere both see and hear, do and suffer, only that which is disagreeable.[461]

In the speech of Agrippa, from which the above quotation is taken, the distinctions made with regard to the acts of citizens and the interpretations placed upon those acts, under monarchy or democracy, are really the same as those which other writers point out between a good monarchy and a tyranny. In Agrippa's argument monarchy is practically synonymous with tyranny. He says that in a monarchy private citizens take no pride in their individual achievements; [462] that rich men are afraid to employ their riches for fear of being considered rivals of the prince; [463] that the common people contribute taxes and free gifts less readily, for they feel that these go only to the prince's private gain; [464] that people are afraid to display their abilities and good qualities; [465] that army leaders constitute common danger.[466] All is construed unfairly; justice is taken as revenge; leniency as an attempt to gain favor.[467]

## SCRIPTORES HISTORIAE AUGUSTAE

The collection of biographies known as the *Scriptores his-*

[455] 3.        [456] 28.        [457] 12.        [458] 12.        [459] 3.
[460] 10.       [461] 10.        [462] 9.         [463] 6.         [464] 6.
[465] 5.        [466] 8.         [467] 6, 7.

*toriae Augustae* contains the lives of the emperors and usurp-
ers from Hadrian to Carus (A. D. 117-284). This material,
written by six authors, may very well have been intended to
follow directly the work of Suetonius, but as it now stands
with a portion missing at the beginning, there are no biographies of Nerva and Trajan. The material on the perfect
prince is very meager, but like that in Suetonius (and the
*Panegyrici*) cannot be entirely passed over because of its use
by Erasmus.[468]

Fortune creates the prince, therefore it is essential that only
those who are really worthy should be in a position to ascend
the throne.[469] The prince should be wise, kind, well educated,
thinking only of the state, self-restrained, a friend of the people, pure in heart, serious, and "such as we have always prayed
for." [470] A state fares worse under a group of evil advisers to
the prince than under a prince who is himself evil,[471] for many
wicked people cannot be held in check. The nature of the
prince is of great importance.[472] Greed is a serious failing; [473]
no one needs great jewels.[474] Mercy is a big asset to a
prince; [475] cruelty is the mark of a tyrant.[476] The prince should
not take vengeance for personal wrongs.[477]

The prince should be brave, steadfast, tested in experience, unimpeachable.[478] A good prince takes thought for his
wife and children.[479] The prince must have good friends and
advisers, for since he cannot see all things for himself, he
must take the recommendation of others.[480] Flatterers are dangerous.[481]

[468] The latest text is by E. Hohl, *Scriptores historiae Augustae* (Leipzig,
1927); the best translation, with elaborate notes, is by D. Magie, *Scriptores
historiae Augustae*, 3 vols., in the "Loeb Classical Library" (New York, 1922-
32).

[469] *Elagab.* 34. 4, 5.          [470] *Carus, Carinus, and Numerianus* 18. 4.
[471] *Alex. Sev.* 65. 4.          [472] *Carus, Carinus, and Numerianus* 1. 4.
[473] *Avid. Cass.* 8. 5.          [474] *Alex. Sev.* 41. 1.
[475] *Avid. Cass.* 11. 5.         [476] *Maximini duo* 8. 7, 8.
[477] *Avid. Cass.* 12. 5.         [478] *Macrianus* 4, 5.
[479] *Avid. Cass.* 10. 2.         [480] *Gordiani* 25. 4.

[481] *Alex. Sev.* 18. 1. For good acts and similar qualities, which by implication
are of interest, cf. *Ant. Pius* 6-9, 12, 13; *Marc. Aurel.* 4, 11, 22, 24, 27; *Pertinax*
8, 9; *Sept. Sev.* 23; *Alex. Sev.* 22, 24-26, 30, 32, 34, 39.

## PANEGYRICI LATINI

Under this title have been gathered together a group of twelve panegyrics or eulogies written in honor of several of the later Roman emperors. By far the most famous, as well as the longest and earliest, is that by the younger Pliny, which he addressed to Trajan (98-117). Of the remaining eleven, four are dedicated to Constantine. The brief references to them are given at this point, rather than earlier, for most of the treatises fall between 289 and 313.[482] As we might have expected, the direct references to the perfect prince are not many, and casual references, mainly by implication, are really not to the point here. Naturally enough, any panegyricist will emphasize the desirable points of his addressee, and references to a good building program, to successful campaigns, to consideration for the needs of the people, and the like, will be common points in the narrative about any ruler but the worst. They can hardly be regarded as direct references to our *genre*; consequently only the work of Pliny is cited in any detail, and that mainly to illustrate the material. The other essays do not contain the sections of abstract theory that are often found in panegyrics.

Pliny tells us that the prince should be not the lord (*dominus*) but the father (*pater*) of his people,[483] mild and gentle by nature, merciful, self-controlled, free from lusts and greed.[484] He should be liberal and generous,[485] surpassing all in strength, dignity, appearance, virtue, and ability; [486] brave,[487] magnanimous and moderate,[488] truthful, not susceptible to flattery,[489] rejoicing in the general welfare of his people,[490] so that everyone may be happy in his kindness.[491] The best protection for the prince is the love and respect of his subjects.[492] He should reform the youth,[493] correct evil practices,[494] estab-

---

[482] The best text is that by W. Baehrens, *XII Panegyrici Latini* (Leipzig, 1911). The *Panegyrici*, except that of Pliny, were first known in 1433 through the discovery of a single manuscript, now lost, from which it is agreed all the many others have been copied.

[483] 2.  [484] 2, 3, 27.  [485] 28-31, 37, 50.  [486] 4, 67, 82.
[487] 13.  [488] 58.  [489] 41.  [490] 44.
[491] 22.  [492] 49.  [493] 47.  [494] 53.

lish just legal procedure,[495] be himself subject to the law,[496] possess good friends [497] and good advisers.[498] He should travel so as to understand various peoples, places, and conditions.[499]

We are ruled indeed by you and subject to you, but in the same manner as we are subject to the laws. They check our desires and passions, but nevertheless are with us and of us. You surpass us, you excel us, as honor, or power, which are over man, but nevertheless are of man too. Before your accession, princes, through a certain scorn for us and a fear of equality, as it were, lost the use of their feet. They were carried above us on the shoulders and backs of slaves; you are raised above those very princes through glory, devotion of your people, and freedom.[500]

A dominion and a principate are very different.[501] Everyone gladly follows the good prince and imitates him.[502] His example is needed.[503]

You know in what the true and lasting glory of a prince is placed. These are the honors against which no flames, no breakdown of old age, no successor may avail. Arches and statues and even temples are demolished and obscured in oblivion, neglected and attacked by posterity. But the spirit that scorns, conquers, and checks ambition and unlimited power flourishes by its very antiquity. It is praised by none more than by those who are least obliged to praise it. Besides, as each prince is created, straightway his reputation (good or bad as the case may be) is made lasting. The enduring fame which awaits a prince against his will is not to be sought, but only the good fame. That latter is not passed on through images and statues, but through virtue and deeds of merit. Nay, even the less important matters of the prince's form and figure may not be better expressed and preserved in gold or silver than in the favor of mankind.[504]

The others [505] tell us that the greatest good a prince can do is to furnish a new deal to his people; [506] his surest bodyguard is the love of his people.[507] "It is the part of a good ruler to move with deliberation in planning for the correction of difficulties, to fail not when fortune calls in favorable times."[508] He must be noble, wise, brave, dignified, kind, merciful, just,

---

[495] 36.    [496] 65.    [497] 44.    [498] 88.    [499] 15.
[500] 24.    [501] 45.    [502] 45, 46.    [503] 45.    [504] 55.
[505] The remaining writers are cited by the Roman numeral prefixed to their essays in the edition of Baehrens; the Arabic numerals indicate the chapters.
[506] II. 27.    [507] III. 24.    [508] XII. 15.

devoted to his people, chaste in his private life, moderate, generous, truthful, prudent, self-restrained, and modest.[509] The prince should be a good soldier;[510] he should show mercy to the enemy,[511] provide for his people in peace,[512] reward the deserving and help the needy,[513] correct public morals and check the royal expenditures;[514] and he should be a leader in mind and example [515] who is himself hard working and good.[516] "It is the part of a good prince to see that his people are happy, but of a better one, to see them at work." [517] To foster education and help in the establishment of schools is one of the greatest boons that a prince can grant.[518] "Indeed, the essence of efficiency in a prince is to fail not in council even though he fail in strength; but he should be readier to act than to order, since he controls by his warning, helps by his efforts, and fires by his example."[519]

## JULIAN, 331-63

The emperor Julian, usually called "the Apostate" because of his adherence to the pagan religion, has left us several panegyrics in which we find the conventional material, including a section on the "perfect prince." This student-emperor addressed the first panegyric, his best work, in 355 to his cousin Constantius (whom he hated and feared) ; the second, entitled *The Heroic Deeds of the Emperor Constantius, or On Kingship*, is in the nature of a sequel to the first and must have been written before 359. The third is a sincere expression of thanks to the empress Eusebia, the first wife of Constantius, who had been kind to Julian; it was probably written in 355 or shortly thereafter. In spite of his enforced residence at the western court from 355 to 359 Julian apparently developed no abilities in Latin; his works are entirely in his native Greek.[520]

[509] II. 6, 16, 20, 24, 31, 40; III. 24, 36; IV. 16, 33; V. 2; VI. 6, 10, 19, 20; VIII. 3-5; XII. 4.
[510] II. 8-11; III. 24.　　[511] VI. 10.　　[512] III. 12.　　[513] V. 2.
[514] II. 13, 14; cf. III. 5.　[515] IV. 29.　　[516] III. 12-14.　　[517] V. 7.
[518] IX. 19.　　　　　　[519] IV. 29.
[520] The best text of Julian's works is that of Hertlein, *Juliani opera* (Leipzig, 1875-76) ; they have been translated by W. C. Wright, in the "Loeb Classi-

According to Julian the good prince is the shepherd of his people;[521] he is also like the able pilot who can bring his ship safely through a storm.[522] He should be just,[523] merciful,[524] temperate, virtuous,[525] for "all the gold beneath the earth and above ground is too little to give in exchange for virtue."[526] The prince should also be simple in his dress,[527] and in his manner,[528] never insolent,[529] nor greedy for worldly wealth,[530] controlled in his emotions and pleasures,[531] God-fearing,[532] of sound moral character,[533] and willing to follow good counsel.[534] True nobility comes from virtue, not from birth.[535]

It is not wealth, either ancestral or newly acquired and pouring in from some source or other, that makes a king, nor his purple cloak, nor his tiara and sceptre, and diadem and ancestral throne, nay, nor numerous hoplites and ten thousand cavalry; not though all men should gather together and acknowledge him for their king, because virtue they cannot bestow on him, but only power, ill-omened indeed for him that receives it, but still more for those that bestow it.[536]

The prince possesses his power for good or evil;[537] his best defense is the love of his subjects.[538] Born of good parents, the prince should respect them;[539] he should have an education suited to his station,[540] for literature and study are invaluable assets.[541] His wife should be good, wise, and prudent,[542] so that she may partake of his plans and counsel him.[543] The prince himself should submit to nature and the law.[544] He should select good judges[545] and good officials[546] for his magistracies, not fearing to share honors and offices with the good men of his state.[547] Julian mentions the analogy, in connection with the prince, of the queen bee without the sting, but proffers another analogy, that of the prince as the prophet and vice regent

cal Library" (New York, 1913-23). Cf. W. D. Simpson, *Julian the Apostate* (Aberdeen, 1930).

521 II. 86.

522 I. 25.

523 I. 48; II. 89.

524 I. 49; II. 100; III. 115.

525 I. 3-5, 45; II. 79, 80, 100.

526 II. 81 = Plato *Laws* 728 A.

527 I. 7.

528 III. 121.

529 II. 50.

530 II. 85.

531 II. 84.

532 II. 70, 86.

533 I. 47; II. 87.

534 I. 47; cf. III. 119.

535 II. 83.

536 II. 83.

537 III. 121.

538 I. 8.

539 II. 86.

540 I. 10, 11.

541 III. 124-126.

542 III. 109.

543 III. 114.

544 I. 14, 45; II. 87.

545 II. 89, 90.

546 II. 91.

547 II. 90.

of God.[548] He is to honor the good and punish the wicked; [549] to travel about, to know and mix with his people,[550] to help its needy,[551] and to prevent heavy taxation.[552] No war should be entered upon except for the good of the people.[553] When a prince really is good, then he is himself happy and his people are blessed.[554]

## SYNESIUS, ?370-?413

Synesius, the bishop of Ptolemais, was sent in 398 on an embassy to the emperor Arcadius, and while at the latter's court presented him with his treatise *On Kingship*.[555] It is not surprising that parts of this oration of high ethical tone bear close relation to Plato and Dio Chrysostom.

The good king, after the fashion of God, helps all his peoples and cities.[556] The glory of a prince has value in direct proportion to his virtue.[557] The real prince should study philosophy,[558] learn to rule himself,[559] lead a proper private life,[560] beware of flattery,[561] avoid proud displays of raiment,[562] and let his people see him practice his doctrines of virtue.[563] The good will of his subjects is the prince's best protection.[564] He has no better possession than his friends, for through them he is able to see, hear, and think as with a supplementary self.[565]

---

[548] II. 90.  [549] II. 87-89.  [550] I. 13.  [551] I. 16.
[552] I. 21; cf. II. 87.  [553] II. 94.

[554] II. 93. Intimately associated with Julian and the other rulers of the period are two distinguished orators who attained great prominence in public life. Themistius (310/20-95) in his many essays on religion, political problems, humanism, and moral studies offered much important advice to the emperor in a day when flattery was rife. Libanius (314-91), who did not reach the same intellectual heights as Themistius, has left us an even greater bulk of material (including some six hundred letters) in which his views on statecraft are embodied in a variety of places. Neither writer is quoted here because their material is incidental, and not needed to establish the direct tradition of *specula*. Both were greatly influenced by the orators and writers of the classical period. See V. Valdenberg, "Discours politiques de Thémistius dans leurs rapports avec l'antiquité," *Byzantion* I (1924), 557-80. Erasmus knew Libanius and edited three of his *Declamationes* (Allen, Ep. 177).

[555] The text is available in Migne, *Patrologia Graeca, LXVI*, cols. 1054-1107, with Latin translation. An English translation is found in A. Fitz Gerald, *The Essays . . .* (London, 1930) ; and a French one in H. Druon, *Oeuvres de Synésius . . .* (Paris, 1878).

[556] 5.  [557] 3.  [558] 2, 3, 21.  [559] 6, 3.
[560] 10.  [561] 8.  [562] 12.  [563] 6.
[564] 14.  [565] 7.

There can be no safer rule than that based on love and kindness.[566]

The greater one's fortune, the greater the attendant worry.[567] The prince has little time for rest.[568] The prince should be a good soldier; [569] in peace he should help the needy, construct public works, and engage in other similar activities.[570] Taxes should be as light as possible.[571] Good should be inculcated and evil destroyed; [572] good judges should be established over the courts.[573] The good prince is the shepherd of his people; [574] the tyrant is the very opposite.[575]

Equally divided stand the king and the tyrant, I assert, and yet Fortune's gifts are alike to each. Each of the two rules over many men, but he that disposes himself for the manifest good of the governed, and is willing to suffer that there may be no suffering for them, and to encounter danger that they may live without fear, and to keep night vigils, and to sup with cares at his board, that day and night they may have rest from anxieties, this is a shepherd amidst his sheep, a king amongst men. But whoso exploits his leadership for luxury's sake, whoso squanders his resources in revelling, esteeming that he must needs gratify all his desires, considering that what makes the subject class suffer is the guerdon of his rule among many, and that the pleasure of his soul is to be served by many, and in a word, he who does not fatten his flock, but himself desires to be fattened by it, that man I call a butcher amongst his cattle, and I declare him to be a tyrant whenever that which he rules over is a people endowed with reason.[576]

## AUGUSTINE, 354-430

Saint Augustine, the famous bishop of Hippo in his native Africa, has left posterity a prolific collection of writings of which the most famous and influential is his *City of God*. This work in twenty-two books represents the labor of fifteen years (A. D. 413-426) and, as might be expected, embodies a great many ideas on religion, ethics, philosophy of history, and political science. Augustine, who was to have so profound an influence upon the political thinking of the later Church Fathers, did not hesitate to use pagan as well as Christian material in his text. The main sources of political significance

| | | | | |
|---|---|---|---|---|
| [566] 9. | [567] 3. | [568] 3. | [569] 9-15. | [570] 17. |
| [571] 19. | [572] 13. | [573] 21. | [574] 3. | [575] 3. |
| [576] 3. | | | | |

are Plato and Cicero. While Augustine does not quote freely from Plato, he was thoroughly conversant with his doctrines (in fact Books VIII and IX are mainly discussions of Platonic doctrines), and there naturally are many parallels in ideas.[577]

Augustine believes that there are three circles of society: the family, the state, and the world.[578] The state is composed of the people, an assemblage associated by a community of interests;[579] it is a "civic community which is nothing else than a multitude of men bound together by some associating tie."[580] There can be no such tie without justice, for a mutual understanding of "right" is the tie.[581] Man, then, is a social animal.[582] Just as when various musical instruments, properly directed and playing the same theme, unite in harmony, so in a state in which the lower, middle, and upper classes are mutually complementary there is a harmony in matters of state.[583] The position of ruler should not be sought, but such a task should be undertaken if it falls to one's lot.[584] The ruler should be a lover of good,[585] for if there can be good pagan princes, there surely should be good Christian rulers.[586] Augustine has given us one of the most famous pictures of the perfect prince.

[577] The text, with explanatory notes, excellent introduction, and commentary, is available in the edition of J. E. C. Welldon, *S. Aurelii Augustini de civitate Dei*, 2 vols. (London, 1924); the latest text is by B. Dombart (3d ed., Leipzig, 1905); a complete translation with notes is that by M. Dods, *St. Augustine's City of God* (Edinburgh, 1872). Another translation of selections (from which many politically important passages are omitted) is by J. Healy, *The City of God* . . .(new print., London, 1931). On Augustine's political significance see, among others, J. N. Figgis, *The Political Aspects of St. Augustine's City of God* (London, 1921); A. J. Carlyle, "St. Augustine and the City of God," in *The Social and Political Ideas of Great Mediaeval Thinkers*, ed. by F. J. C. Hearnshaw (New York, 1923); G. Combès, *La Doctrine politique de Saint Augustin* (Paris, 1927).

[578] Cf. XIX. 16. "Since, then, the house ought to be the beginning or element of the city, and every beginning bears reference to some end of its own kind, and every element to the integrity of the whole of which it is an element, it follows plainly enough that domestic peace has a relation to civic peace. . . ."

[579] II. 21.        [580] XV. 8.        [581] XIX. 21.

[582] In X. 14, Augustine represents the development of the "social animal": "The education of the human race, represented by the people of God, has advanced, like that of an individual, through certain epochs, or, as it were, ages, so that it might gradually rise from earthly to heavenly things, and from the visible to the invisible."

[583] II. 21.        [584] XIX. 19.        [585] XIV. 7.        [586] V. 18.

For neither do we say that certain Christian emperors were therefore happy because they ruled a long time, or, dying a peaceful death, left their sons to succeed them in the empire, or subdued the enemies of the republic. . . . But we say that they are happy if they rule justly; if they are not lifted up amid the praises of those who pay them sublime honours, and the obsequiousness of those who salute them with an excessive humility, but remember that they are men; if they make their power the handmaid of His majesty by using it for the greatest possible extension of His worship; if they fear, love, worship God; if more than their own they love that kingdom in which they are not afraid to have partners; if they are slow to punish, ready to pardon; if they apply that punishment as necessary to government and defence of the republic, and not that iniquity may go unpunished, but with the hope that the transgressor may amend his ways; if they compensate with the lenity of mercy and the liberality of benevolence for whatever severity they may be compelled to decree; if their luxury is as much restrained as it might have been unrestrained; if they prefer to govern depraved desires rather than any nation whatever; and if they do all these things, not through ardent desire of empty glory, but through love of eternal felicity, not neglecting to offer to the true God, who is their God, for their sins, the sacrifices of humility, contrition, and prayer.[587]

The best guide is one's own conscience;[588] our souls rule, our bodies obey.[589] If justice is removed, kingdoms are mere bands of robbers.[590] There is no peace for the wicked; it would be a happier lot to be a slave to a fellowman than to a dominating lust.[591] In fact, the lust for rule frequently destroys the prince.[592] The love for glory should be surpassed by the love for goodness.[593] Success often changes the good prince.[594]

Augustine is distinctly anti-imperialistic. Kingship itself is first conferred by God;[595] the glory and desire for praise actuate rulers to expand their original realms.[596] A large empire is not good.[597] Men worship a God or gods who will help them in their rule, not from a desire to be good but to rule.[598]

[587] V. 24.        [588] V. 12.        [589] XI. 9 = Sallust *Cat.* 1.
[590] IV. 4. This is one of the most famous expressions in the *Civ. Dei*: "*Iustitia remota, quid regna nisi latrocinia.*"
[591] XIX. 15; IV. 3.
[592] XIX. 15. Cf. XIV. 15; this illustrates the unexpectedness with which one encounters political references in nonpolitical contexts; Book XIV is devoted to "lusts" in general.
[593] V. 14.        [594] XVII. 20.        [595] V. 1.        [596] V. 12-17; cf. XIX. 7.
[597] IV. 15.        [598] XV. 7.

Extensive rule brings a proportionate amount of trouble.[599]
This thought naturally involves a theory of war and peace.
Augustine is essentially opposed to war, especially wars of
conquest.[600] A "just war" is that which is undertaken in self-
defense or for the sake of honor.[601] But even such wars bring
untold miseries:

But, say they, the wise man will wage just wars. As if he would not
all the rather lament the necessity of just wars, if he remembers that he
is a man; for if they were not just he would not wage them, and would
therefore be delivered from all wars. For it is the wrong-doing of the
opposing party which compels the wise man to wage just wars; and this
wrong-doing, even though it gave rise to no war, would still be a matter
of grief to man because it is man's wrong-doing. Let every one, then,
who thinks with pain on all these evils, so horrible, so ruthless, acknowledge that this is misery.[602]

Men cannot be happy under the conditions just described.[603]
War makes neither for the safety nor the dignity of the human
race.[604] "The lust of sovereignty disturbs and consumes the
human race with frightful ills." [605] The desire to conquer is
comparable only to robbery,[606] which is sin. Augustine concludes one of his invectives on this subject epigrammatically:
"By craving to be more, man becomes less." [607] Peace is the
only happy condition. "Every man seeks peace by waging war,
but no man seeks war by making peace." [608] We have already
in Augustine our "war to end war:" "[The state] desires
earthly peace for the sake of enjoying earthly goods, and it
makes war in order to attain this peace." [609] This peace of a
state is defined as "the well-ordered concord" of the citizens
in the matter of command and obedience. "Peace of all things
is the tranquillity of order. Order is the distribution which
allots things equal and unequal, each to its own place." [610]

[599] IV. 3.  [600] Cf. XII. 22; IV. 14.  [601] XXII. 6.
[602] XIX. 7.  [603] IV. 3.  [604] V. 17.
[605] III. 14.  [606] IV. 6.  [607] XIV. 13.
[608] XIX. 12.  [609] XV. 4.  [610] XIX. 13.

# IV

## THE ANCIENT SOURCES OF THE INSTITUTIO

The authors examined in the previous chapter fall in the period between 500 B. C. and A. D. 500. This limit was determined upon for two reasons: its boundaries are essentially those of the classical period of ancient literature, and, more specifically, the writers named by Erasmus himself all come within its scope.[1] The possible relation of Erasmus's work to the various medieval *specula* is discussed in Chapter VI. The several authors analyzed in the preceding chapter have been examined primarily for their own intrinsic value in the development of the particular phase of political theory under discussion. But since Erasmus specifically acknowledges his indebtedness to a number of them in numerous passages of his own treatise and must unquestionably have followed them, consciously or unconsciously, in many places,[2] it is not out of place to discuss at this point his relation to antiquity.

In dealing with the sources employed by a writer, the material falls at once into two groups — that which is specifically acknowledged by the name of the author, or the title of the work, or both, and that which, though nowhere specifically named, must beyond any reasonable doubt have been used. In addition, there frequently appears a third group (as in the case of Erasmus), often closely akin to the second, which may or may not have helped to formulate our author's ideas. This last group is very elastic, and almost anything on the general theme, which is not rejected *a priori* for such reasons as anachronism, proven inaccessibility, an unfamiliar medium, could be included. In its broadest sense this group could

[1] Except for the references to Homer, the Bible, and St. Bernard (1090-1153).
[2] References, both direct and indirect, have been cited in detail in notes to the appropriate passages of the translation of the *Institutio*.

furnish more nearly an illustrative commentary rather than genuine source parallels.

The *Institutio*, as we have said in Chapter II, was written about 1516 for the instruction of Prince Charles. Erasmus was at that time about fifty years of age and recognized everywhere in Europe for his classical learning. The orbit of his star was just approaching its zenith.[3] In 1500 he had brought out an enormous collection of *Adages*, compiled from both Greek and Latin writers. During his life he published, translated, or annotated in whole or in part the following: Aesop, Algenus, Ambrose, *Apophthegmata* of the Greeks, Aristotle (in Greek), Arnobius, Athanasius, Augustine, Ausonius, Basil, *Disticha Catonis*, Cicero (mainly philosophical works), Q. Curtius Rufus, Cyprian, Demosthenes, Eucherius of Lyons, Euripides, Galen, Gaza, William Herman of Gouda, Gregory Nazarinensis, Jerome, Haymo of Halberstadt, Hilary, *Scriptores historiae Augustae*, Horace, Irenaeus, Isocrates, John Chrysostom, Josephus, Lactantius, Libanius, Livy, Lucian, Thomas More, Origen, Ovid, Paul, Periander, Persius, Plautus, Pliny the Elder, Plutarch, Prudentius, Ptolomaeus, Seneca, Suetonius, Syrus, Terence, Laurentius Valla, Xenophon, Zasius.[4] Many of these editions were published later than the *Institutio*, but they are mentioned here to show that Erasmus had free access to the complete texts of these writers. An understanding of this classical learning of Erasmus is highly essential for the proper comprehension of the classical parallels in the *Institutio*, especially those which are unacknowledged. For the first three-quarters or more of his essay (as reference to the notes to the translation will show) Erasmus closely follows the ancient ideas; toward the end he adds in greater degree matter that is his own, perhaps borrowed from medieval sources or taken from contemporary events.[5]

[3] Geldner, *op. cit.*, p. 63, makes this same point.

[4] This information I have taken from the *Bibliotheca Erasmiana, liste sommaire, 2me série, auteurs publiés, traduits ou annotés par Érasme*, Vols. II-III, 3-67.

[5] See chap. i, n. 104; and chap. vi, *passim*.

There is no suggestion at any point that Erasmus used one author consistently for some period of time and then put him aside for another. It would appear that he drew largely from the vast storehouse of classical learning in his mind and made little use of the texts at the actual time of writing. This conclusion is based on the following evidence:

1. There are seldom more than two or three references to a single author in succession, with the exception of a series of biblical passages near the middle of the treatise and again at the end. No conclusion can be drawn from these citations to the Bible. One biblical idea naturally suggests another, whereas one idea from Plato may very well suggest something from Aristotle or Augustine, rather than Plato again. Furthermore, even within this series there are several other references.

2. Erasmus mentions as direct sources the Bible, Aesop, Aristotle, Augustine, St. Denis, Homer, Plato, Julius Pollux, Plutarch, ancient proverbs, Seneca, Vergil, and Xenophon.[6] But with the exception of the passages from the Bible, the ancient proverbs, Julius Pollux, and one or two lines from Homer and Vergil, all the material taken from these sources is paraphrased rather than quoted. The nature of the quotation from Julius Pollux (a long list of adjectives describing the king and the tyrant) makes it very probable that Erasmus had the book before him as he quoted it. The biblical, proverbial, Homeric, and Vergilian references could easily have been quoted from memory.

3. There are many passages that are as direct paraphrases of an ancient writer as those referred to in the preceding paragraph, and yet Erasmus makes no mention of his source.[7]

4. Erasmus refers very often to the character of famous persons in antiquity; for example, Croesus, Carneades, Augustus, and Tiberius, but with no mention of the author from whom he draws his information. This suggests one of two things: that he did not think the exact source was important; or that, from the fullness of his own knowledge, he expected

---

[6] These thirteen sources have been cited approximately 100 times.
[7] Cf. reference to Plutarch, *Discourse to an Unlearned Prince*, p. 159, below.

the reader to be as familiar with the passage and the source as he was. In most cases the source used is a well-known, readily accessible work.

5. In publishing his *Adages* Erasmus had gone over much of this material before and was therefore thoroughly conversant with it, especially as he kept revising his own collection from time to time.

In discussing the sources of anyone so close to the Middle Ages as Erasmus, some consideration must be given to the *florilegia* and the possibility that they (rather than the full text) were used for source purposes. The fact that Erasmus translated or edited so many of the authors quoted makes it highly improbable that he chose his references from *florilegia*. Furthermore the frequency and range of the quotations found in the treatise of Erasmus are not usually found in books of selections. Plato, the chief single source of Erasmus [8] is the only one of the more frequently used authors who is not included in the list of works edited by Erasmus. St. Augustine quotes Plato often. Is it possible that Erasmus may have found his Platonic material in Augustine or some medieval writer or compendium? As Erasmus cites many references to Plato that are not found in St. Augustine, the first possibility is precluded. But Plato was very popular with the humanists,[9] and texts were readily available. Therefore, it seems improbable that Erasmus did not have a copy of Plato's works. Whether or not the authors from whom only a few quotations were taken were used at first hand, it is impossible to decide conclusively without examination of many *florilegia*.[10]

[8] There are over 70 passages from Plato.

[9] Plato was translated into Latin in 1477 by Ficino, president of the Platonic Academy at Florence founded by Cosimo de' Medici in 1450. Sir Thomas More in his *Utopia* leans heavily upon Plato.

[10] Those who are interested in a detailed discussion of the problem of sources should consult the unpublished master's thesis of Agnes Marie Knight, *The Sources of Erasmus' Institutio principis Christiani from the Fourth Century B. C. through the Fourth Century A. D.*, Western Reserve University, 1931. Miss Knight quotes the parallel passages in detail in connection with the passage from Erasmus, and has appended three tables showing the citations in the order of their occurrence (I), the frequency of the citations by pages of the text (II), and the number of citations arranged according to author (III).

Reference to the direct citations found in the text of the *Institutio* is sufficient to establish the fact that Erasmus was indebted most of all to Plato, as we have already said, and, in close position for second place, Cicero, Seneca, and Plutarch. The numerous almost indisputable parallels which are not acknowledged completely confirm the point. The conclusion, to state the obvious, can only be that the Academic and Stoic schools exerted tremendous weight upon the views of Erasmus. He could not, of course, accept all of their tenets; e.g., while he ardently supported Plato's doctrine of the philosopher-king, yet he could not adopt his scheme for the rule of an aristocracy. Undoubtedly two basic principles cause Erasmus to lean most upon the philosophy of the later Stoics. One was the high degree of morality inherent in the doctrines, and the other was the universality of its thought. The composite theory of statecraft which resulted from an eclectic choice of the finest points from the teachings of Christianity, the doctrines of more than one school of philosophy, and a reform-program based on an appreciation of contemporary needs may not present a unified system but it does present a good theory.[11]

[11] Geldner (*op. cit.*, pp. 134-37), is in substantial agreement with this view, although he feels that Erasmus "separated himself, not to his advantage, from the unified systems of the despised scholastics" (p. 137).

# V

## THE PERFECT PRINCE FROM THE SIXTH CENTURY
## TO THE SIXTEENTH CENTURY

In the last chapters we examined in detail the all-important classical background of the *Institutio*. Many of the works considered did not properly belong to the special type represented by the treatise of Erasmus but rather to general political literature. Just how far back into antiquity the roots of this *genre*, the *speculum principis*, reach, is not yet completely proven. That there is a continuous line of succession at least from the time of Isocrates with his treatise *Ad Nicoclem* to the twentieth century is beyond question.[1] Although no account

[1] W. Münch, *op. cit.*; E. R. Goodenough, "The Political Philosophy of Hellenistic Kingship," *Yale Classical Studies*, I, 55-102; L. K. Born, "The *Specula principum* of the Carolingian Renaissance," *Revue belge de philologie et d'histoire*, XII (1933), 583-612; *idem*, "The Perfect Prince: a Study in Thirteenth- and Fourteenth-Century Ideals," *Speculum*, III (1928), 470-504; *idem*, "Erasmus on Political Ethics. . .," *Political Science Quarterly*, XLIII (1928), 520-43 (bibliography, 540-43); R. M. Smith, "The Speculum principum in Early Irish Literature," *Speculum*, II (1927), 411-45; Halil Ganem, *Éducation des princes ottoman* (Bulle, 1895); A. Hillebrandt, "Ueber die altindische Erziehung der Prinzen zu Politik," *Deutsche Revue*, XLI (1916), 196-202; U. Kühne, "Das Herrscherideal des Mittelalters und Kaiser Friederich I," *Leipziger Studien auf dem Gebiet der Geschichte*, V (1898), 4 ff., 57 ff.; F. Schönherr, *Die Lehre von Reichsfürstenstande des Mittelalters* (Leipzig, 1914); F. von Stromer-Reichenbach, *Der deutsche Fürstenspiegel* (Dresden, 1925); E. Booz, *Fürstenspiegel des Mittelalters bis zur Scholastik* (diss., Freiburg i. B., 1913); A. Werminghoff, "Die Fürstenspiegel der Karolingerzeit," *Historische Zeitschrift*, LXXXIX (1902), 193-214; *idem*, "Drei Fürstenspiegel der 14. u. 15. Jahrhunderts," *Studien an A. Hauck zum 70. Geburtstage* (Leipzig, 1916); K. Bartsch, "Das Fürstenideal des Mittelalters im Spiegel deutscher Dichtung," *Gesammelte Vorträge und Aufsätze* (Freiburg, 1883), 185-220; H. Jacobius, "Die Erziehung des Edelfräuleins im alten Frankreich nach Dichtungen des XII., XIII., und XIV. Jahrhunderts," *Zeitschrift f. roman. Philologie*, Beiheft 16 (Halle, 1908); Fietz, "Prinzenunterricht in 16. und 17. Jahrhunderts . . .," *Jahresbericht des neustädter Realgymnasiums zu Dresden*, 1887; W. Rein, *Encyclopädisches Handbuch* (Langensalza, 1895-99), V, 497-504, *s. v.* "Prinzenerziehung," with select bibliography; E. M. Roloff, *Lexicon der Pädagogik* (Freiburg, 1913), II, cols. 139-47, *s. v.* "Fürstenspiegel," with select bibliography; F. Buisson, *Dictionnaire de pédagogie et d'instruction primaire* (Paris, 1882-1887),

will be taken here of the Byzantine writers, the Latin tradition
alone sustains the point. There is clearly a Western tradition
that begins early and continues long.[2]

In this chapter we shall study certain significant treatises falling roughly one in each century between the end of the classical
period and the writing of the *Institutio*. By following this
biographico-chronological scheme, we shall establish the con-
tinuity of the tradition and demonstrate that Erasmus's treatise was but part of a literary *genre* which was to continue for
three centuries after his day with even greater impetus. That
the frequency with which these works were written should
increase in the later centuries is not surprising. In fact, it is
what should be anticipated. There were not only more kingdoms and principalities, each with its sovereign ruler for whom
these works could be written, but there gradually came into
being the spirit of nationalism, which made generalizations
by any scholar less appropriate than particular treatises written
by a citizen of the particular country for whose prince he was
writing. This goes hand in hand with the growing use of the
vernacular languages as a medium of expression for scholarship and literary endeavor. Finally, there is the ever increasing
fomentation of political thought that accompanied nationalism
and the spread of the vernacular. But it should be clearly un-

---

I^re parte, 2435-39, "Éducation de princes," with select bibliography. Other
books and articles could be cited dealing with special authors or periods, but
the above selected list will suffice to indicate the salient points to any who may
be interested in pursuing the matter further.

  [2] That there is an independent body of oriental literature on this *genre* is
clear from such studies as those of Wu, *Ancient Chinese Political Theories*
(Shanghai, 1928), which has a great deal of interesting material arranged
chronologically, and E. D. Thomas, *Chinese Political Thought* . . . (New York,
1927), which covers much of the same material, but under very carefully
planned chapter and topical headings. The second book of *The Constitution of
Chow* contains many provisions for the education of princes, and really is a
genuine *speculum*. The civilizations contemporary with the Chinese, the Baby-
lonian, and the Egyptian, do not seem to have provided us with comparable
material, although the codes, and the passing references to the divinity and
splendor of the kings supply some indication of their ideas. The Old Testament
material needs no introduction. Some helpful suggestions for material in India
are found in B. K. Sarkar, *Political Institutions and Theories of the Hindus*
(Leipzig, 1922), and U. Ghoshal, *A History of Hindu Political Theories*. . .
(London, 1923).

derstood that this by no means precluded the use of certain treatises as "general."

Not the least interesting point is that, when local references, suggestions for current problems, and theories peculiar to an individual or a school are removed, the essentials of form, substance, and method are the same in all times and places. In the later centuries (the sixteenth to the twentieth) the difficulty of isolating the works to be considered, and of limiting the points to be noted, increases greatly. But even when all except clear-cut treatises are eliminated, the field is still a large one.

It is strange that so many works in the great transition period discussed in the early part of the present chapter should have been so completely neglected.[3] Generalizations based on selected passages of the more prominent authors have long appeared in the reliable handbooks. But it seems unsound that those many other works which do not rise to any heights of originality themselves or form part of the *opera* of some distinguished statesman-scholar, should be relegated to a mere note or to utter oblivion before they have been examined in some detail. The several writers here analyzed vary greatly in importance, but they are products of their times and help to establish the general tradition.

## MARTIN OF BRACARA, died 580

St. Martin, the bishop of Bracara, addressed his little treatise, entitled *The Formula of an Honorable Life*, to Miro, king of Galicia, not so much for his own use, as for that of his ministers and officials. One of the shortest of all mirrors of princes, this is very pointed and unique in having no citations to, or quotations from, the Bible, the Church Fathers, or lay writers.[4]

The four cardinal virtues — prudence, magnanimity, continence, justice — are to be exemplified by the prince.[5] If the

---

[3] This is especially true of those written before the twelfth-century Renaissance and the rise of scholasticism.

[4] The text used is Migne, *Patrologia Latina*, LXXII, cols. 22-28. The references are to chapters.

[5] Introd.

prince will live a prudent life, all will be well; [6] yet he should not be too slow and restrained in all these qualities, or their opposites may come into effect. [7] He should be patient with the speech of others, [8] gentle in humor, [9] "kindly to all, flattering to none, intimate with a few, just to all;" [10] self-restrained in dress, manner, pleasures. [11] He should take rest and quiet for sound thought between actions, [12] so as to be careful in judgment, and slow in credulity. He should beware of flattery; [13] careful of ideas and words; [14] look to the future in prudence; [15] change as the time calls for change; [16] and stick to the final purpose. [17] He should be just, "for justice is not of our constitution but is divine law, the bond of human society." [18] Everyone loves, respects, and follows a just man. [19] The prince should punish evil-doers, [20] be slow to anger, merciful, and kind. [21] Whatever he does, he should do nothing secretly, [22] for (by implication) there is a mutual bond between men: "whoever is sufficient unto himself has been born rich." [23]

## Isidore of Seville, 570-636

It may be that Isidore did not write a formal treatise on the training of princes, unless A. E. Anspach [24] is correct in suggesting that a hitherto unpublished tract of Isidore may belong to this *genre*. This seems a likely possibility, when we compare the wide scope of certain other essays, and also note Isidore's own attention to the matter of princes and their training in his *Etymologies*, his *Sentences*, and particularly in the *Honor and Duty of Princes*. This last is Book VII of his *Collected Canons*, and consist merely of references to other treatises, all arranged by subject under eleven titles. [25]

[6] 1.    [7] 5-8.    [8] 3.    [9] 3.    [10] 3.    [11] 3.
[12] 1.    [13] 3.    [14] 2.    [15] 1.    [16] 1.    [17] 2.
[18] 4.    [19] 4.    [20] 4.    [21] 3.    [22] 2.    [23] 3.

[24] "Isidori Hispalensis 'Institutionum disciplinae'," *Rhein. Mus.*, LXVII (1912), 556-68. The text occupies only pp. 557-59.

[25] 1. On reverence to be showed by princes to the priests of God; 2. The election of princes; 3. On the praise of royal works; 5. On the protection of princes; 6. On courts of princes; 7. No commoner to fail the prince; 8. On inviolate faith given to princes; 9. On not usurping the royal power; 10. On the faithful followers of kings; 11. On those who flee to the enemy. All references in this collection are to the specific canon. The texts used are Migne, *PL,* LXXXII-

Isidore gives us the traditional definition of "king." [26] The good prince should be mindful of God and of the church; [27] for princes when good are the helpers of God; when wicked, the undoing of the people.[28] That man is no real ruler who does not correct evils in his state; [29] he should not only do no harm but be helpful,[30] for the prince can build up or completely ruin the lives of his people.[31]

The prince should be chaste in his personal life,[32] humble in heart,[33] moderate and just,[34] kind and merciful,[35] for unkindness makes the prince suspect the people, and causes him to be suspected by them in turn.[36] He should remember to return good for evil.[37] He should obey his own laws [38] and be charitable to those who oppose him.[39]

Isidore has much to say of the responsibility of the people to their prince, which it may not be out of place to summarize here, since several avowed mirrors of princes include such sections.[40] The people should always keep faith with their prince,[41] speak no evil of him,[42] guard his safety and his life,[43] and not desert him or seek a new prince while he is still living.[44] By no means should plots or seditious remarks be tolerated,[45] and no one should dare to presume to the throne while there is a reigning prince,[46] or try to usurp it by tyranny after his death.[47] The new prince should be chosen by a general vote of the people.[48]

---

LXXXIV. In citations to the works of Isidore, and subsequently to those of other writers which likewise are available only in the original, the titles are given in their Latin forms for the sake of brevity.

[26] *Sent.* III. 48. 7 ; *Etym.* IX. 3. 4.

[27] *Sent.* III. 51. 6 ; cf. *De hon.* I.

[28] *Sent.* III. 48. 11.  [29] *Etym.* IX. 3. 4.  [30] *Sent.* III. 49. 3.

[31] *Sent.* III. 50. 6.  [32] *Ep. Ricc.* 100. 4.  [33] *Sent.* III. 49. 1, 2.

[34] *Etym.* IX. 3. 5.  [35] *Can. Tol.* IV. 75.  [36] *Can. Tol.* V. 2.

[37] *Sent.* III. 50. 3. The prince (?) should have good nurses, so that he may be trained properly from the very start, then begin studies that will continue such a training: oratory, medicine, law, philosophy, music, etc., so that he may excel in all virtues, help his people and land, obey laws, avoid evil ways and cling to good friends always hoping for the result anticipated in Plato's philosopher-king (*Instit. Discip., passim*).

[38] *Sent.* III. 51.1.  [39] *Sent.* III. 50. 1, 2.

[40] E. g., Jacques de Cessoles, II. 4, and III. 1-8.

[41] *Can. Tol.* IV. 75.  [42] *Can. Tol.* V. 5.  [43] *Can. Tol.* V. 2 ; VI. 17-18.

[44] *Can. Tol.* V. 4.  [45] *Can. Tol.* IV. 75.  [46] *Can. Tol.* IV. 75.

[47] *Can. Tol.* VI. 17.  [48] *Can. Tol.* IV. 75.

## ALCUIN, 735-804

Alcuin seems not to have written any set treatise on the subject of princes and their training, but eleven of his extant letters, addressed to the young kings about him, deal entirely with that subject and really belong to the same *genre* as the much longer epistles of Hincmar and others. In addition to these eleven, Alcuin tells us that he wrote a similar letter to Clodovic, third son of Charlemagne by Hildegarde.[49]

The prince should give thanks to God for his elevation to the throne,[50] and respect the church and its representatives,[51] so that by the help of God he may improve his realm and leave it better for his successors.[52] He should have good advisers: men who are god-fearing, just, desirous of peace, faith, and virtue,[53] for the friendship of good men is very valuable,[54] and it is difficult to avoid flatters.[55] He should be wise in counsel [56] and cautious in speech.[57] If the prince lives a good, moral life, his realm will reap the benefits,[58] for he will be an example to everyone.[59]

The pleasures and rewards of this life are empty.[60] It is essential for the prince to keep faith and hope in God,[61] doing nothing to reflect on his own good name,[62] but following the example of his good predecessors,[63] by being kind, merciful, just, truthful, patient, generous, devoted to all, moderate in taste and dress, and upright in manners and morals.[64] He should be humble and affable,[65] give freely of alms,[66] listen

---

[49] Ep. 120, col. 355. The letters are addressed to Aedilred, king of Northumbria (Ep. 11, dated *c.* 793), to Aedilred, king (Ep. 12, no date), to Charles, the king (Ep. 17, dated *c.* 793), to Pippin (Ep. 38, dated 796), to Offa, king of the Mercii (Ep. 49, no date), to Ecgfrid, king of the Mercii (Ep. 50, no date), to Aerdwulf, the king (Ep. 60, dated 796), to Coenulf, king of the Mercii (Ep. 63, dated 796), to the king (Ep. 100, dated 800), to Charles, the young king (Ep. 119, 120, no date). The text used is Migne, *PL,* C, *passim.* All references are given by the number of the letter.

[50] 60.        [51] 63.        [52] 60, 17.        [53] 119, 63, 11, 38.
[54] 11.        [55] 120.        [56] 11, 120.        [57] 120.
[58] 120, 11.        [59] 119.        [60] 11.        [61] 120, 49.
[62] 119.        [63] 120, 63.
[64] 11. On this general subject of personal characteristics compare in detail *Ep.* 11, 12, 38, 50, 63, 100, 120, where most of the requisites are repeated. Many ideas are repeated in several letters, although duplicated references have rarely been given.        [65] 38.        [66] 11, 38, 50.

to the wretched and try their cases justly,[67] select as judges men who are honest and honorable, who will treat everyone fairly, who will act towards widows and orphans as fathers,[68] and who will not take rewards in return for their decisions.[69] Above all, it is necessary to avoid avarice, greed, licentiousness, moral turpitude, arrogance, perjury, so as to keep peace with one's fellowmen.[70]

## SMARAGDUS OF ST. MIHIEL, DIED ?830

Smaragdus, who became abbot of St. Mihiel in 819, dedicated his treatise, entitled the *Royal Way*, almost certainly to Louis the Pious. The work, which is prefaced by a letter to the king, abounds in the usual biblical references but is unique in the exclusion of examples of both good and bad princes from profane sources.[71]

There seems to be no question of the right of the ruler: "God has elevated you to the worldly throne . . . he has now invested you with the royal purple."[72] The kingly virtue is that which "to all in the palace breaks the bread of joy, to all pours out the wine of happiness, to all assigns sweet kisses, and eagerly enfolds all in outstretched arms."[73] The prince should fear God,[74] pray to Him,[75] follow and honor Him in all his deeds,[76] seek His aid at all times.[77] In this way his "peace will be fruitfully multiplied and his joys will overflow as a river forever."[78] It is divine wisdom which justifies good princes; guards their acts and persons; makes them wise, just, brave, merciful, virtuous, and sober,[79] so that they adhere to virtue and righteousness[80] and try through their personal efforts to keep others in the path of truth and right.[81]

The prince should be patient,[82] should guard against arrogance[83] and flatterers;[84] should be prudent and act only after sound counsel,[85] which will bring discretion and enable him to

---

[67] 120.         [68] 11.         [69] 120.         [70] 11.

[71] The text used is Migne, *PL*, CII, cols. 935-70. The references are to chapters.

[72] 11.         [73] 1.         [74] 1.         [75] 32.

[76] 11.         [77] 31.         [78] 2.         [79] 4.

[80] 4.         [81] 18.         [82] 7.         [83] 21.

[84] 25.         [85] 20, *passim*.

gain and hold other peoples;[86] should restrain his wrath (not return evil for evil) [87] since he can so readily give way to it.[88] He should also be just,[89] but he should temper justice with mercy,[90] for clemency and compassion [91] make for universal happiness.[92] Judges should be carefully instructed not to take rewards on this earth and to decide cases without regard to the social status of the plaintiff or the defendant.[93]

The prince should be pure in heart and adhere to the cause of peace; [94] be simple in his life,[95] without avarice [96] or faith in worldly riches,[97] remembering not to glory in wealth,[98] which causes bitterness, discord, arrogance and wrath,[99] but in humbleness.[100] God has granted enough for all; the prince should not strive to collect from the poor,[101] but rather to help them, the weak and oppressed, the stranger and the forsaken.[102] The prince should not hesitate to give freely of alms to them from his own goods,[103] for his reward will come in heaven.[104]

### HINCMAR OF RHEIMS, ?806-82

Hincmar's earliest treatise on the subject at hand was his essay entitled *The Person of the King and the Royal Minister* (*Reg. pers.*) written at the request of Charles the Bald. The next work, which is no longer extant, was addressed to Louis in 877 and entitled *The Disposition of the Advantages of the Kingdom and the Pursuit of the Plan and Advice of the Emperor, Your Father.* In the same year he wrote another work for Louis, the *Instruction of a New King in the Correct Administration of a Kingdom* (*Reg. inst.*). That is followed by a very short essay to the emperor, entitled *The Establishment of Suitable Tutors and Advisors for the Royal Sons of Louis the Bald* (*Ad Carol. imp.*). In 879 there appeared a very important treatise, *To the Nobles of the State, for the Instruction of Carlomman the King, and on the Administration of the Palace* (*Pro inst.*), of which chapters xiii-xxxvii

| | | | | |
|---|---|---|---|---|
| [86] 5. | [87] 23. | [88] 24. | [89] 8, 9. | [90] 8. |
| [91] 10. | [92] 19. | [93] 28. | [94] 17. | [95] 6. |
| [96] 26. | [97] 15. | [98] 16. | [99] 22. | [100] 16. |
| [101] 27. | [102] 9, 30. | [103] 10. | [104] 10. | |

are based directly on a similar work, now lost, by Adelhard of Corbie. The last work from which we have extracted references here is entitled *A Second Address to the Bishops of the Kingdom* (*Ad episc.*).[105]

The king has his power by the grace of God.[106] The happiest conditions are found when the ruler has specific training for his task.[107] A good king with his good advisers makes for success,[108] for it is to the mutual good of kings and the people if a good king has a long rule.[109] The two outstanding royal virtues are justice and devotion;[110] the prince "should preserve in himself the dignity of his name."[111] He should hold to the word of God[112] and Christ.[113] If he fails in his task, he will suffer eternal punishment.[114]

Cupidity is the root of all evils in a state.[115] The prince should be more pleased with evidence of justice, truth, and hope than with gold.[116] He should beware of flattery and bribery,[117] be a model character for his subjects,[118] and keep good company.[119] In this connection come the officers of the court,[120] who should be good men,[121] discreet and thoughtful,[122]

[105] These works are found in Migne, *PL*, CXXV, cols. 833-56, 983-1018. Manitius, *op. cit.*, I, 339-54, does not mention the fourth and sixth items.

[106] *Reg. pers.* 1. God divided the temporal and ecclesiastical powers so that there would not be too much power in the hands of any one man. Each, pope or king, is to obey the rules of the other under appropriate circumstances (*Ad episc.* 1) ; but the pope is the higher of the two (*Ad episc.* 2, 3).

[107] *Reg. pers.* 5.

[108] *Reg. inst.* 1, 2. E.g., the prince should ascertain from his ministers, after their travels, the condition of his own and neighboring kingdoms (*Pro. inst.* 36).

[109] *Reg. pers.* 6.

[110] *Ad episc.* 17.

[111] *Pro. inst.* 6. Cf. *Ad. Carol. imp.* 3-5, where the prince is told to love justice, to honor the church and God, to preserve law and order, to live piously and purely, and to read Pseudo-Cyprian, *On the Twelve Abuses*, 9 (which is quoted in full in *Ad episc.* 7-8; cf. *Pro. inst.* 6).

[112] *Pro. inst.* 2. Cf. *ibid.*, 3-5, 7, on the duties of churchmen toward the temporal kingdom.

[113] *Reg. pers.* 16.

[114] *Pro. inst.* 10.        [115] *Reg. inst.* 8.        [116] *Reg. inst.* 9.

[117] *Reg. pers.* 21.        [118] *Pro. inst.* 6.

[119] *Ad Carol imp.* 2; *Pro. inst.* 10, 11; *Reg. pers.* 22.

[120] On the various officers, their origin and duties, cf. *Pro. inst.* 15-17, 19-26, 32, 33, 35; on the rules for their assemblies, etc., cf. *ibid.*, 27-30.

[121] *Reg. inst.* 8; *Ad episc.* 9, 10, 14; *Reg. pers.* 4.

[122] *Pro. inst.* 18, 31.

free from avaricious desires and from scandal.[123] If they do
wrong they should be shown no more leniency than others.[124]
A good administration is a sign of extensive power.[125]

The prince should keep his palace in order and rule the state
in the same fashion,[126] taking special care not to transgress the
laws himself.[127] According to divine law no one should be
ignorant of the laws [128] or disobey them; [129] hence they should
be upheld by the good prince.[130] Judgment should be rendered
in accordance with the established law,[131] through love of justice,[132] not for personal vengeance,[133] since all persons have
the right to equal justice.[134] The prince should be the corrector
of wicked men,[135] even using compulsion if necessary.[136] The
death penalty is justifiable as a warning to others.[137] Occasion-
ally justice should be tempered with mercy [138] and love,[139] but
always with discretion and moderation.[140] In certain cases pardon should be granted; [141] e.g., when a sin is universal among
a people, it must obviously be overlooked, since a whole state
could not be punished.[142] This same condition should extend to

[123] *Reg. inst.* 6; *Pro. inst.* 10.

| [124] *Reg. pers.* 29. | [125] *Reg. pers.* 3. | [126] *Pro. inst.* 12. |
| [127] *Pro. inst.* 9. | [128] *Pro. inst.* 8. | [129] *Pro. inst.* 8; *Ad episc.* 13. |

[130] *Reg. pers.* 27. At this point it may not be out of place to summarize briefly
the pertinent ideas in the essays *On the Twelve Abuses* (*De XII abusivis*) just
referred to, although it belongs to some period earlier than this, and does not
strictly come under the category of treatises being discussed.

Christ is the *end* of law: those without law are without Christ, and *vice versa*
(12); an undisciplined common people makes no end of trouble for everyone
(11). There is no power except from God (6), and consequently the prince
loses all his power unless he follows God (6). He should be just (this is discussed at length, occupying cols. 956-57 of the Migne text), for this justice and
truth are the firmest foundations for princely power (9). The prince should not
only be free from unjust and improper acts himself but should keep all others from
the ways of transgression (9). Any injustice on his part will effect the future
of his kingdom as well as its present status (9). Therefore his first duty is to
correct and perfect his own character (9), so that the three essential characteristics of fear, order, and love may be properly balanced (6). The text used
was Migne, *PL*, IV, cols. 947-60. Cf. S. Hellmann, *Pseudo-Cyprian: De XII
abusivis* (Munich, 1909), who dates the work between A. D. 630 and 700, and
Carlyle, *op. cit.*, III, 108, n. 1, for his discussion of this same point, and I, 222-24,
for the general discussion of the work.

| [131] *Pro. inst.* 8. | [132] *Reg. pers.* 18. | [133] *Reg. instr.* 9. |
| [134] *Ad episc.* 13. | [135] *Reg. pers.* 25, 26. | [136] *Reg. pers.* 17. |
| [137] *Reg. pers.* 23, 24. | [138] *Reg. pers.* 28. | [139] *Reg. pers.* 32. |
| [140] *Reg. pers.* 19. | [141] *Reg. pers.* 20. | [142] *Reg. pers.* 33. |

public sinners if they show contrition;[143] but the prince should be careful not to exercise this privilege in favor of his own family unless they have truly repented.[144] War in the name of God is not sin;[145] but only necessity should make a prince wage war to expand his territory.[146] Those who drag out a war do not please God,[147] for He grants victory to whom He pleases,[148] and mere numbers are of no avail.[149]

### Peter Damiani, 1007-72

Peter Damiani, the cardinal bishop of Ostia, wrote his treatise, entitled *The Duties of a Prince in Coercing the Wicked, to which is added a second discussion on the same point,* for Godfrey, duke of Tuscany. In this work are found the usual biblical citations and occasional references to historical sources in support of examples of princes, good and bad.[150]

"Toward your people, who have been entrusted to your care, act always with justice."[151] While it is necessary for the prince to place some of his authority and responsibilities on others,[152] yet it is also necessary to watch those others carefully.[153] The prince's advisers should be pious and prudent.[154] The prince should sit in court himself.[155] He should remember the proverb, "Spare the rod and spoil the child,"[156] for too lenient a rule may lead to excessive liberties.[157] Duties should be thoroughly carried out,[158] for the people are too often in turmoil and upset when the prince is guided by too much consideration.[159] But there is nothing more glorious in the eyes of God than helping the weak, widows and orphans, the oppressed and despoiled, to regain their own.[160] The punishment of evildoers is a sacrifice on the altars of God.[161] The judge

---

[143] *Reg. pers.* 31.    [144] *Reg. pers.* 30.    [145] *Reg. pers.* 9.
[146] *Reg. pers.* 7, 8.    [147] *Reg. pers.* 10.    [148] *Reg. pers.* 12, 13.
[149] *Reg. pers.* 14.
[150] The text is Migne, *PL,* CXLV, cols. 819-30. The references are to parts I and II and the chapters.
[151] I. 5.    [152] I. 1.    [153] II. 1.    [154] I. 4.
[155] II. 1.    [156] *Prov.* 13.    [157] II. 1.    [158] I. 1.
[159] I. 3.    [160] II. 1.
[161] I. 3. Many quotations from the Bible are advanced to support this view.

who does not punish the wicked is the minister of the devil;[162] sparing the criminal increases crime.[163] Even the death penalty is justifiable in the eyes of God and the church, if it is imposed justly.[164]

## John of Salisbury, circa 1110-80

The Policraticus of John of Salisbury is the earliest elaborate medieval treatise on politics. . . .[165] It [is] a landmark in the history of political speculation for two reasons. It is the only important political treatise written before western thought had once more become familiar with the Politics of Aristotle. . . . In the second place it comes just before the important turning-point in the institutional development at the end of of the twelfth, and the beginning of the thirteenth century, when legal precision began to be stamped on a great number of previously indefinite relationships. . . . It contributed a heritage of ideas whose momentum made them, in spite of the newer influences, the dominant force in political thought down to at least the middle of the sixteenth century.[166]

Salisbury is really interested only in monarchy,[167] and so he begins at once with the place of the prince (i.e., a single leader) in the state, which is likened to the human body. The prince is the head, and is "subject only to God and to those who exercise His office and represent Him on earth;" the senate fills the place of the heart, and the judges and governors of the princes represent the eyes, ears, and tongue; officials and soldiers are the hands; the constant attendants of the prince correspond to the sides; officers of the treasury are like the stomach; and the farmers are like the feet, "which always cleave to the soil . . . and deserve aid and protection . . . since it is they who raise, sustain, and move forward the entire weight of the body." [168]

From this it is clear that Salisbury foreshadows the theory of divine right, and in Chapter VI of the same book, he says that the prince is established in his seat by God. However, he

[162] I. 2.          [163] I. 1.          [164] II. 2.

[165] Salisbury wrote the *Policraticus* in 1159. For the latest treatment of this work, see the partial translation by John Dickinson, *The Statesman's Book of John of Salisbury* (Knopf: New York, 1927), particularly the introduction, pp. xvii-lxxxii. The best text is that of C. C. I. Webb (Oxford, 1909), 2 vols.

[166] Dickinson, *op. cit.*, pp. xvii, xviii.

[167] IV. 1 ff.

[168] V. 2. This is the first formulation of the "organic analogy."

does not believe in absolute hereditary succession. The prince may only hope to have his son succeed him if that son is worthy of his father. Succession in the family, then, is both a reward to a good ruler for the proper training of his son and an incentive for the son to be deserving.[169] The evils that spring from the strife over rights of succession are many.[170]

The duties of a good prince are manifold.

[He] should be chaste and avoid avarice;[171] he should be learned in letters;[172] he should be humble;[173] he should banish from his realm actors and mimes, buffoons and harlots;[174] he should seek the welfare of others and not his own;[175] he should wholly forget the affections of flesh and blood and do only that which is demanded by the welfare and safety of his subjects; he should be both father and husband to them;[176] he should correct their errors with the proper remedies;[177] he should be affable of speech and generous in conferring benefits; he should temper justice with mercy;[178] he should punish the wrongs and injuries of all, and all crimes, with even-handed equity;[179] he has duties to the very wise and the very foolish, to little children and to the aged;[180] his shield is a shield for the protection of the weak, and should ward off the darts of the wicked from the innocent;[181] he must act on the counsel of wise men;[182] he must protect the widow and the orphan;[183] he must curb the malice of officials and provide for them out of public funds to the end that all occasion for extortion may be removed;[184] he must restrain the soldiery from outrage;[185] he should be learned in law and military science;[186] he must in all things provide for the welfare of the lower classes;[187] he must avoid levity;[188] he is charged with the disposal of the means of the public welfare;[189] and is the dispenser of honour;[190] he must not close his ear to the cries of the poor;[191] he must raise aloft the roof-tree of the Church and extend abroad the worship of religion;[192] he must protect the Church against sacrilege and rapine;[193] and finally, he must ever strive so to rule that in the whole community over which he presides none shall be sorrowful.[194]

The prince who is to perform all these many obligations

[169] IV. 11; cf. also V. 6.       [170] V. 6-7; cf. IV. 11.
[171] IV. 5.      [172] IV. 6.      [173] IV. 7.      [174] IV. 4.
[175] IV. 8.      [176] IV. 3.      [177] IV. 8.      [178] IV. 8.
[179] IV. 2.      [180] IV. 3.      [181] IV. 2.      [182] V. 6.
[183] V. 6.      [184] V. 10.      [185] VI. 1.
[186] The discussion on military service is based largely on Vegetius, *De re militari*, and occupies chap. ii-xix of book VI.
[187] VI. 20.      [188] VI. 23.      [189] VI. 24.      [190] VI. 26.
[191] VI. 27.      [192] VI. 2.      [193] VI. 13.
[194] VI. 6. Quoted from Dickinson, *op. cit.*, pp. l-li.

must have good advisers. They are to be chosen from among the old men (following the successful practice of both the Greeks and Romans) and such as fear God.[195] "Unjust men are therefore to be excluded and men who are overbearing and avaricious and all such manner of human plagues. Nought, indeed, is more deadly than the unrighteous counsellor of a rich man."[196] The prince must also bear in mind that there is no greater glory than the favor and praise which comes from good men,[197] and that he shall place his friendship only in such honorable men.[198] Obviously flattery and association with toadies is to be shunned at all times.[199] Luxury and the dissipations of lust lead only to undoing.[200] The prince should never forget that he and his money both belong to his people,[201] for the love of wealth for its own sake can lead only to great evil.[202] An evil prince is the nucleus of countless evils to the state.[203] "Then, and then only, will the health of the commonwealth be sound and flourishing when the higher members shield the lower, and the lower respond faithfully and fully in like measure to the just demands of their superiors, so that each and all are as it were members one of another by a sort of reciprocity, and each regards his own interest as best served by that which he knows to be most advantageous for the others."[204]

The original state of society was good, and in it we may infer there was no need of checks and laws,[205] but now that state no longer exists and there is a prince and there are laws.[206] The prince is the "envoy of God on earth" and holds his power from Him.[207] If the prince controverts the law of God, his subjects are justified in refusing obedience.[208] But this is not to be a violent disobedience.[209] The prince is to serve his fellow-servants of God[210] and is responsible for his state, not to it,[211] and will be judged in heaven for the discharge of

---

195 V. 9.          196 V. 9.          197 VIII. 14.          198 III. 12.
199 III. 4-7.          200 VIII. 6.          201 IV. 5.          202 VII. 17.
203 VI. 20.          204 VI. 20.          205 VIII. 17.
206 Salisbury refers to the well-ordered social state of the bees (VI. 21), which is so much used by later writers. It is taken from Vergil's *Georgics* IV. 153-218.
207 IV. 1, 10, 12; V. 2, 6, 25, 26; VI. 1.
208 VI. 9, 12, 25.          209 V. 6; cf. VII. 20.          210 IV. 7.          211 V. 7.

his trust.[212] Therefore, according to divine law the prince is subject to the law,[213] albeit the will of the prince has the force of law.[214] This is explained by the fact that as soon as the prince acts contrary to the established law, he ceases to be a prince and becomes a tyrant. In enforcing these laws to which he himself is subject, the prince should be regular and consistent,[215] although officials are to be punished more severely for their misdeeds than are the commoners.[216] Laws, which only catch the lowly and allow the great to go unpunished, are like spider webs which catch the flies but do not hold the larger creatures.[217] But the prince should not fail to temper his justice with mercy.[218]

Salisbury believes that liberty and virtue are inseparable,[219] and that real liberty can only be obtained if there is freedom of speech.[220] Hence the good prince in a good state should "accept with patience the words of free speaking, whatever they may be. Nor [should] he oppose himself to its words so long as these do not involve the casting away of virtue."[221] Consequently, in hearing a charge of lèse-majesté,[222] it is important to investigate the character of the accused, to see if he could have committed the offence, and, if so, if he was of sane mind at the time. "Nor ought a mere slip of the tongue to be drawn into punishment." [223]

From a discussion of lèse-majesté it is but a step to that of tyrannicide.[224] Salisbury says, "it is just for public tyrants to be killed and the people set free for the service of God." [225] The origin of tyranny he gives as springing from pride and "ambition, to wit, the lust of power and glory." [226] Cupidity is the companion of folly. If a man possessing these qualities succeeds in gaining the highest position, from which he may

[212] V. 11; VI. 1.  [213] IV. 4.  [214] IV. 1.  [215] IV. 6, 7.
[216] VI. 1.  [217] VII. 20.  [218] IV. 8.  [219] VII. 25.
[220] VII. 25.  [221] VII. 25.
[222] This was one of the most serious offenses possible and was severely punished upon conviction.
[223] VI. 25.
[224] Dickinson points out that Salisbury was the first to formulate a real doctrine on this subject.
[225] VIII. 20, passim.  [226] VII. 17.

"oppress a whole people by rulership based on force," he is a tyrant.[227] With an accumulation of arguments and examples to show that all tyrants come to a bad end, Salisbury brings his *Policraticus* to a close.

## THOMAS AQUINAS, 1226-74

It is in the essay *On the Training of Princes* that Aquinas develops most fully his concept of the duty of the prince, and it is to this treatise, therefore, that our attention will be chiefly devoted. It was written for the king of Cyprus (probably Hugh III, who died in 1267) about 1265-66. The work, which is in four books, is commonly considered to be by the hand of Aquinas only as far as II. 4. This short treatise does not cover all the political ideas of the author, but nothing of vital importance is omitted. Although overshadowed by the greater works of Aquinas, it has enjoyed a wide popularity, having been translated into French, German and Italian.[228]

Man is a social and political animal,[229] and therefore it is necessary to have the organization of society, with someone at its head.[230] This Aquinas illustrates by the organic analogy and the commonplace of the social life of the bees.[231] All other creatures have their necessities of life created for them, but man has to provide his own. Since it is not possible for each individual to do everything himself, the community developed.[232] According to Aquinas, the rule of one has been proved best in practice,[233] and consequently that form of government

---

[227] VII. 17. For a comparison of a tyrant and a king see VIII. 17.

[228] I have used the text of the *Opera omnia* (Parma, 1852-71), XVI, 224-90. The work is also conveniently found in Mandonnet, *Opuscula omnia*, I (Paris, 1927), 312-487. J. J. Baumann, *Die Staatslehre des H. Thomas von Aquino* (Leipzig, 1873), has a translation of books I and II, 1-4, with a discussion of selections from the *De regimine Iudaeorum*, the *Commentary on Aristotle's Politics*, the *Summa theologica*, and the *Summa contra gentiles*. C. A. Bosone, *Der Aufsatz "De regimine principum" von Thomas von Aquino* (diss., Bonn, 1894), is a chapter by chapter summary of the four books with notes and discussion.

[229] I. 1.

[230] I. 1; cf. *Sum. theol.* 1ª, 2ᵃᵉ, Quaes. 96, Art. 4.

[231] I. 2; cf. I. 3 and 12; *Com. polit.* III. 12.

[232] I. 1; cf. IV. 3, 4; *Com. polit.* III. 5.

[233] I. 2.; cf. I. 5, 6; I. 1-11 are devoted to the general subject of the necessity, preference, and advantage of a monarchy for both the prince and the people. All dominion is based on the example of God, the single ruler of the

which has the least evil in it should be chosen.[234] Those states
not governed by a single prince have to endure many misfortunes and internal dissentions.[235] However, Aquinas does not
advocate an absolute and unqualified monarchy.[236] Constitutional power in the original state of innocence was best.[237]
Under present conditions,[238] however, the most advantageous
is absolute monarchy.[239]

Peace is an indispensable requisite for the attainment of
good through social organization,[240] and this peace can only
be attained through the efforts of a good prince,[241] following,
to the best of his ability, the ways of God.[242] "A true and per-

---

universe (III. 1-6). Aquinas thus defines the term "prince." "Him we call
a prince, to whom the supreme authority in human affairs has been committed"
(I. 14; cf. I. 1). Some of the duties of a prince are summed up in I. 12, and the
best ways of ruling the state in I.14, 15. The idea of peace, unity, and harmony
as requisites of the good state is elaborated by the later writers.

[234] I. 5.        [235] I. 2.

[236] I. 6; cf. Sum. theol., 1ᵃ, 2ᵃᵉ, Quaes. 90, Arts. 3, 4, and also ibid., Quaes.
105, Art. 2, where Aquinas declares that a monarchy is best, but that a limited
monarchy is necessary since it is difficult to secure a good prince, and ibid.,
Quaes. 105, Art. 1: "In the good direction of princes in any state or people, two
things must be present; all should have a share in the principate, for this preserves the peace of the people. . . . Whence the best form of principate is in a
state in which one man is the head. . . . Under him are some others of authority,
but nevertheless such a principate belongs to everyone, not only because these
men can be chosen by all, but because they are so chosen. Such is the organization of every polity that it is a combination of monarchy, in so far as one man
rules, an aristocracy, in so far as many have ruling authority, and a democracy,
that is, power of the people, in so far as the prince can be chosen by the common people and the election of princes is a function of the people."

[237] II. 8, 9.

[238] Cf. IV. 8. "There are certain provinces of a servile nature. Such ought to
be governed by a despotic government, including in 'despotic,' 'regale.' Those
men, however, who are of strong character, bold in heart, and reliant upon their
own intelligence, cannot be ruled except by a dominium politicum." On the importance of this whole distinction and its later development, see Dickinson,
op. cit., pp. xli, xlii. John Fortescue, in his The Difference between an Absolute
and a Limited Monarchy (written after 1471), goes one step further and says
that there are two forms of government especially to be considered — dominium
regale, i.e., absolute monarchy, and dominium politicum et regale, i.e., constitutional monarchy (I-IV). In the first, the people are ruled by laws which
are made by the prince alone without their consent (II). In the second (and
better) form, the people's assent is essential (I). But if the prince is a good
prince, this form is really advantageous for him, for he "mey therby the more
surely do justice, than bi is owne arbitrment" (II.) But if the prince rules
per ius regale, i.e., by royal decree, and his people are subjected to dire oppression, it is really a state of tyranny (IV).

[239] II. 9; cf. III. 11.        [240] I. 2.        [241] I. 15.        [242] I. 13.

fect polity is like a physical body functioning properly, in
which the organs are in perfect condition. If supreme virtue,
which is reason (*ratio*), controls the lower powers . . . then
there results a calmness and perfect affinity of the forces one
to the other. This is called 'harmony.' " [243] It is clear then,
that the members of a community are unlike as individuals,
but are one in the common association.[244] The prince looks out
for the common good.[245]

There are three main obstacles to the permanent existence
and good order of the state. By nature, man cannot endure
long in this life. This the prince should offset by care in training the younger generation to replace the previous one.[246] A
second difficulty is caused by "radicals" or chronic objectors.
The corrective for them is found in laws, precepts, and punishments to check the existing trouble and to forestall similar
conditions in the future.[247] The third is for external causes such
as war. The only protection in that case is to guard against all
possible enemies. In addition, the prince should do his best to
keep firm the bonds of peace and mutual good will within the
state and to provide for the essentials of a normal life.[248]

It is the work of a prince to rule his subjects well,[249] for he
is in the state what the soul is in the body, and what God is in
the universe.[250] Nothing is more fitting for a prince than magnanimity,[251] and he should consider the friendship of his people
the best thing to be achieved.[252] The prince should realize that
glory is not the only reward he will achieve as a result of his
good administration; in fact it is a thing scorned by Christian
philosophers. The true reward will come from God.[253]

If the prince has the task, or privilege, of instituting a new
state, he should carefully select a region that is fertile, suited
for cities, towns, universities, camps, military maneuvers, and

[243] IV. 23.
[244] I. 1; cf. *Sum. theol.* 1ᵃ, 2ᵃᵉ, Quaes. 96, Art. 4.
[245] I. 1; cf. *Com. Polit.,* III. 6.
[246] I. 15.     [247] I. 15.     [248] I. 15.     [249] I. 8.
[250] I. 12. The government of the universe (and therefore of the state) is likened to the good navigation of a ship, by means of which the pilot brings it
safely to the right port (I. 14).
[251] I. 7.     [252] I. 10.     [253] I. 7-9.

business, with places for religious worship and law courts.[254] The climate should be temperate,[255] healthful,[256] and favorable to the abundant production of food stuffs.[257] The region should also be attractive in natural beauty,[258] with a natural wealth of vines, groves, forests,[259] with large herds of cattle and draft animals.[260] Dependence upon commerce for the staples of life is a great evil.[261] In his administration the prince should have sufficient wealth to carry on properly the various departments of the government.[262]

In this he should be aided by ministers carefully selected with regard to the kind of state they will serve.[263] The prince should have his own system of coinage, which should be kept stable. From this much good will come, and not the least will be sound commercial standards.[264] A standard system of weights and measures should also be established.[265] Roads and highways should be kept open and safe. That will do much to promote internal peace and also to stimulate commerce.[266]

Aquinas devotes some time to a discussion of tyranny,[267] which he believes is more liable to come from democracy than from monarchy.[268] The opportunity for tyranny is to be carefully avoided by tempering the prince's original power.[269] A prince voids the mutual agreement of defense and support with his people by his acts of tyranny,[270] and therefore tyrannicide is justifiable.[271] But no move should be made against the tyrant except by public authority, for all order would be overthrown if private citizens could commit homicide on the grounds of tyranny.[272] At all events tyrants seriously err in forsaking the care of justice for mundane powers,[273] for they only store up more charges against themselves.[274] The reward of a good prince will not only be of this world, but will be in heaven.[275]

[254] I. 13.  [255] II. 1.  [256] II. 2.  [257] II. 3.
[258] II. 4.  [259] II. 5.  [260] II. 6.  [261] II. 5.
[262] II. 7; cf. I. 14; II. 5. The poor should be provided for from the public treasury (II. 15).
[263] II. 8, 10.  [264] II. 13.  [265] II. 14.  [266] II. 12.
[267] I. 3, 6, 9-11; cf. II. 9; III. 9.
[268] I. 5. This is in accord with the general ideas of both Plato and Aristotle.
[269] I. 6.  [270] I. 6.  [271] I. 6; cf. I. 7-11.
[272] I. 6.  [273] I. 10.  [274] I. 11.  [275] I. 9.

## AEGIDIUS ROMANUS, 1247-1316

Aegidius, a pupil of Thomas Aquinas at Paris, wrote his treatise, *On the Governance of Princes*, in three books, at the request of Philip the Fair, about 1287. Upon his accession to the throne, Philip ordered the work translated from the original Latin into French. The treatise is a clear and more complete expression of the ideas of Aquinas who died before he had completed his own work. Aegidius's ideas on the state and "the perfect prince" are very definite.[276] Hereditary monarchy, he believes, is the best form of government,[277] just as tyranny is the worst;[278] aristocracy is placed second,[279] and democracy last.[280] Very interesting is his belief in the benefits that come from the establishment of cities and towns;[281] namely, convenience in procuring the necessities of life, the enjoyment of a full life, and the use of laws. He also understood the value of a strong middle class [282] which prevents the evils that arise from the great contrast between the very rich and the very poor and makes possible for all a life according to reason and law.

The perfect prince for this state must have many virtues. In fact, he should be endowed with all virtues.[283] The prince must be prudent.[284] As a means of attaining this virtue, the prince should ponder deeply the affairs of his realm. He should be dignified, sympathetic, kindly,[285] and truthful; and, if he has this last quality, he will not be boastful.[286] He should also be energetic, vigorous, and ready to encourage pleasures among his people.[287] He should also be just,[288] for without justice the state could not exist.[289] Yet justice should be tempered with mercy.[290] The prince should be courageous,[291] but

---

[276] There have been numerous editions of Aegidius's treatise. Of these, the edition of the French text by S. P. Molenaer in 1899, under the title, *Les Livres du gouvernement de rois; a XIII Century Version of Egidio Colonna's Treatise, De regimine principum, now first published from the Kerr MSS*, is the most easily accessible and is here cited.

[277] III. 1. 2; III. 2. 5.          [278] III. 2. 7.          [279] III. 2. 4.

[280] He also disapproves of "communism" (III. 1. 4).

[281] III. 1. 1; III. 2. 31.

[282] III. 2. 31.          [283] I. 2. 27.          [284] I. 2. 6-8.          [285] I. 2. 28, 29.

[286] I. 2. 30.          [287] I. 2. 31.          [288] I. 2. 10.          [289] I. 2. 11, 12.

[290] III. 2. 13.          [291] I. 2. 13, 14.

should not become rash.[292] Moderation in all things, especially physical activities, is very important.[293] Yet generosity is not to be excluded, although it must be carefully guarded so as not to become a vice,[294] because it wins the love of the people. The prince should be magnanimous and munificent in his undertakings. These virtues inspire the possessor to great things and prevent discouragement and misfortune.[295] He should love honor,[296] but at the same time he should not forget to be humble,[297] and he should be on friendly terms with his subjects.[298] However, he should at all times be so dignified and worthy of respect that his authority be not diminished.[299] As a result of this attitude, the people should obey their prince and his laws. From this will come a condition of peace.[300]

In his home, which should be such as becomes his station, but not too elaborate,[301] the prince should be master just as he is in the state,[302] but his wife should be his equal and well endowed with "temporal, physical, and spiritual goods." She should be such an one that she may share the prince's secrets and help him with advice.[303] Toward his children the prince should be affectionate, but he should devote his especial attention to their welfare.[304]

All men, princes in particular, should love the common good, not merely their own advancement.[305] They should desire only the welfare of the state.[306] Princes should work diligently to see that their states are so ordered that their subjects may enjoy the highest benefits — virtue, knowledge, and temporal goods.[307] Wise men and enlightened priests should be encouraged to settle in the state, so that education may be widely diffused.[308]

Princes should be powerful enough to keep off enemies from their realms,[309] but should not enlarge their territory by injur-

[292] I. 3. 6.        [293] I. 2. 15, 16.        [294] I. 2. 17-21.        [295] I. 2. 22, 23.
[296] I. 2. 24.        [297] I. 2. 25, 26.        [298] III. 2. 34.        [299] III. 2. 9.
[300] III. 2. 32, 33.        [301] II. 3. 1-8.        [302] II. 3. 11-18.        [303] II. 1. 9-21.
[304] II. 2. 1-18. The training of his daughters receives especial attention (II. 2. 19-21).
[305] I. 3. 3.        [306] I. 3. 4, 5.        [307] II. 2. 8, 9.        [308] III. 2. 8.
[309] Aegidius gives a rather elaborate summary of Vegetius, De re militari, in III. 3. 1-22. From this it is obvious that he expects his prince to be a good general, as well as a good peace-time ruler.

ing others.[310] As a means of preventing internal disorder, in addition to these things already named, the prince should not allow small fortresses to be built within his realm; should respect, however, the position of all his people; should choose the best men for his officials, and move them about frequently; should keep the country well policed; and, above all, should learn from experience and never repeat a mistake once made.[311]

Aegidius devotes some space to the subject of law.[312] The laws of a state are to be established in accordance with the customs of the peoples.[313] Natural law differs from the law of men in that the former recognizes the offense, the latter defines the degree of guilt and punishment.[314] To be effective, the laws must be promulgated,[315] and once so published must be observed.[316] Nor should they be rashly amended.[317] In rendering judgment, the judges should not be swayed by private inclinations [318] or emotions,[319] but should realize that the law is the basis of judgment, for it would not have been created unless there was need for it.[320] But withal, justice should be tempered with leniency and compassion.[321]

We may conclude with one of the most important of Aegidius's suggestions. The prince should surround himself with wise men and counselors. Their advice should be given in private and after due deliberation. Above all, they should speak the truth even though it may not please the prince. It is not enough for these counselors to be wise — they must be practical and should spend their time only on the larger problems of the state, such as the collection of the income and the preservation of wealth, commerce, especially in providing food for cities and towns, trade laws, maintenance of internal order, declaration of war, and the formulating of laws.[322] Under such a plan, with a good prince, we hope for the best.

## THOMAS OCCLEVE, ?1370-?1450

Occleve's poem, which is composed entirely in English, but

310 III. 2. 9.    311 III. 2. 13.    312 III. 2. 18, 19.    313 III. 2. 24.
314 III. 2. 23.    315 III. 2. 25.    316 III. 2. 29.    317 III. 2. 29.
318 III. 2. 19.    319 III. 2. 18.    320 III. 2. 18.    321 III. 2. 20.
322 III. 2. 14-17.

was entitled in Latin the *De regimine principum* (*The Governance of Princes*), contains 5,460 lines.[323] It was written in the years 1411-12 and dedicated to Henry V (then Prince of Wales). Occleve himself tells us that his work is based on three main sources (exclusive of the Bible) : the *Secretum secretorum* (*The Secret of Secrets*), which purports to be a letter from Aristotle to his pupil, Alexander the great; the *De regimine principum* of Aegidius Romanus; and *The Game of Chess Moralized* by Jacques de Cessoles.

In order to be successful the king must know his duties and his responsibilities — no archer can hit his target unless he sees it. So it is with a prince; he cannot accomplish his end unless he understands it.[324] Let us see then, what Occleve enjoins upon the prince:

> First and forwarde the dignitee of a Kyng
> Impressed be in the botme of your mynde;
> Consideryng how a changeable a thyng
> That office is, for so shalle ye it fynde.[325]

The exalted position of a ruler shows the real character of the prince, and the good in him is extolled.[326] The king should be chary of his speech, with the result that his people will be eager and heedful when he does address them.[327] The prince should remember that his burdens are not light, for he is one of the chosen few. He should always be true to his oath, and his word alone should be worth more than the sworn oath of the common man.[328] Above all he is to obey the laws:

> Prince excellent, have your lawes in chere,
> Observe hem and offende hem by no wey;
> By othe to kepe it bounden is the powere
> Of Kyng, and by it is Kynges nobley

[323] The first edition is by Thomas Wright and was published in 1860. If we may judge by the number of extant manuscripts the poem seems to have enjoyed great contemporary popularity. Cf. H. F. Aster, *Verhältniss des altenglischen Gedichtes "De regimine principum" . . . zu seinen Quellen . . .* (diss. Leipzig, 1888) ; and A. H. Gilbert, "Notes on the Influence of the *Secretum secretorum," Speculum,* III (1928), 84-98.

[324] 174. The lines are not numbered and the references are therefore given to the pages of Wright's edition; each page contains four stanzas of seven lines each, except the first page which contains only three stanzas.

[325] 78.          [326] 103.          [327] 87-88.          [328] 85.

> Sustened; lawe is bothe lokke and key
> Of seurté; while lawe is kept in londe,
> A prynce in his estate may syker stonde.[329]

In dealing with his people the prince should be patient,[330] remembering that

> Prudence and temperance, strengthe and ryght,
> The foure ben vertues principalle.[331]

He should be of unquestioned morals and should surpass his people in virtue; [332] he should be continent, temperate, self-restrained, and magnanimous;[333] he should be honorable in his administration, for

> Love without a goode governaile
> A Kyng hathe none . . .; [334]

he should realize that the avoidance of flatterers and dissuaders is essential to that end; [335] he should be merciful in dealing with the less powerful,[336] for power without mercy is tyranny.[337] He should not be avaricious,[338] for if he sets his aim at worldly wealth, his people will suffer in proportion.[339] He should not forget, however, that although avarice is worse than prodigality,[340] prodigality is likewise a great evil.[341] Largesses should be tempered with common sense: [342]

> Largesse mesurable unto you tye,
> And foole largesse voidethe from you clene;
> For free largesse is a vertuous mene.[343]

If the prince can accomplish all this, his people will have rest, peace, wealth, joy, and happiness.[344]

Occleve also has something to say on justice and the laws. In the first place everyone should make it a point to try to keep his fellow man from going astray.[345] Justice, he says, is of the nature of God and is something which restrains bloodshed, punishes guilt, defends possessions, and keeps the people safe

---

[329] 100.    [330] 129.    [331] 171.

[332] 130. Pages 130-40 are occupied with examples of the ancients, both biblical and pagan, who have been model characters in this respect.

[333] 138, 140.    [334] 173.    [335] 79; cf. 109-111, 174.

[336] 119-124.    [337] 123.    [338] 161.

[339] 144.    [340] 165.    [341] 158, 167.

[342] 147-157.    [343] 170.    [344] 174.    [345] 90.

from oppression.[346] We have already shown that the prince should obey the laws.[347] As the soul is the motivating power behind the body, so with justice in the state — when it flourishes, all is peace and quiet.[348] Those who pass judgment should be careful not to be swayed by anger or hatred or love, above all, by bribery; [349] for it is a grievous situation that permits the great to break the laws while the weak are apprehended.[350] From this unequal regulation of the law, the common folk are stirred to uprisings.[351] In the execution of justice the death penalty should be used only as a means of saving the innocent lives of others.[352]

In all his official capacities a prince should not act without counsel, and that from great and low alike,[353] bearing always in mind that a man's advice may be sound even though it opposes his preconceived opinions.[354] Especially should a prince be on guard, because evils done by his ministers, although unknown to him, are laid to his door and there is no excuse which he can make: [355]

> Counceil may wele be likenede to a bridelle,
> Which that an hors kepethe up from fallyng.[356]

If that be its purpose, then old men with years of experience should be selected as advisers.[357] The young men may be just as sincere, but they are too bold; they are the ones to execute the actions.[358]

The poem closes with a plea for peace. War, Occleve tells us, springs from ambition and covetousness, as the example of the Roman empire shows.[359] The only justification for war is to bring unbelievers into the faith of Christ; [360] and terms of

[346] 90.        [347] 100.        [348] 98.        [349] 97-98.

[350]
    Smalle tendernesse is hade nowe of our lawes;
      For yf so be that one of the grete wattes
    A dede do, which that ageyn the lawe is,
      Not at alle he pynysshede for that is.
    Right as lop-webbes flyes smale and gnattes
      Taken, and suffren grete flyes go,
    For alle this world lawe is reulede so.

[351] 102.        [352] 114.        [353] 174.        [354] 176.
[355] 91-92.      [356] 177.       [357] 177.        [358] 178.
[359] 187.        [360] 195.

victory should not be severe.[361] The prince "is sette in his reame for his peples ese and releef;" [362] accordingly peace is his goal. This is attained in three ways: conforming to the will of God; humility of being; tranquility of thought. This last is especially important, because there can be no peace if one is filled with grievous and angry thoughts.[363]

> By concorde, smale thynges multiplien;
>     And by discorde, hate, ire, and rancour,
> Perisshen thynges grete, and waste, and dyen.
>     Pees hathe the fruyte, ese in his favour;
> To gete pees holsom is the labour.
>     And kepe it wele, whan that a man hath it caught,
> That ire ne discorde banysshe it nought.[364]

The very last lines of the poem are addressed to the kings of France and England, the mirrors of the world, from whose peaceful unity so much good could and should come.[365]

[361] 116-17.    [362] 166.    [363] 180; cf. 180-end.
[364] 186.    [365] 191.

# VI

## SUMMARY OF THE MEDIEVAL PERIOD

Some of the conclusions to be drawn from the material of the previous chapter are very obvious and applicable to the entire period. There is little originality displayed; the main argument is nearly always supported by wholesale quotations; the methods and topics are nearly all the same. Most of the works were written for a specific prince, and many were written in response to a special request.

All the treatises analyzed fall into two main groups — the pre-Aristotelian, and the Aristotelian.

The earlier scholastics, from the ninth to the twelfth centuries, were obliged, in the absence of fuller sources, to follow in their systems the scanty outlines of Stoic and Platonic doctrine that had been transmitted through the Dark Ages in more or less accurate compends. Of Aristotle but few works were known, and these, as Symonds says, "through Latin translations made by Jews from Arabic commentaries on Greek texts." [1]

By the middle of the thirteenth century the great work of Aristotle was available to all Europe.

Before the twelfth century little space is given to economic matters or to education in its strictest sense. This is not so in the succeeding centuries. But, on the other hand, certain important topics of the thirteenth and later centuries are suggested by those who lived before the revived study of Aristotle, namely, the theory of divine right, the relation of church and state, and the organic analogy. This early period forecasts the future as well as it echoes the past. The exact extent of the debt, usually unacknowledged, to Plato, Cicero, and other classical writers of the same type could only be determined by careful examination of countless passages, a labor which probably would not repay the effort. There can

[1] Dunning, *op. cit.*, I, 189-90.

be little doubt that these writers of the earlier Middle Ages were thoroughly acquainted with many of the greater pagan writers, and that they used them constantly,[2] even though not so liberally as did their scholastic and humanistic successors.

In the political thought of the thirteenth and fourteenth centuries (as in the earlier centuries), the central figure about which the whole revolves is the prince. This emphasizes the personal view toward rulership, which is characteristic of the period. Furthermore, in accordance with the medieval attitude the writers of these centuries considered the real in terms of the ideal and were interested in nothing less than the pattern of the perfect prince.

Just how far these later writers in the thirteenth and succeeding centuries directly followed their predecessors (except when they acknowledge their indebtedness), or how much they depended upon the Greek philosopher at first hand, it is not possible to say here; but certainly both forms of indebtedness were present. In addition to Aristotle, most of the great Roman writers were drawn upon for moral precept, philosophy, example, and also for corroborating evidence of evils to be avoided. This combination of Greek thought and Roman vigor, joined with medieval theology, resulted in a mixture of idealism and practicability.

Certain strong and consistent lines of thought may be traced throughout a large part of this period of ten centuries. Perhaps the most striking and prominent thought that we find is the personal attitude toward rulership and rulers. Every one of the writers lays great stress upon the personal moral virtues of the prince. It is from him alone that good or evil, as he wills it, is visited upon the land. Christian goodness is the one great remedy suggested for the surcease of human woes. Con-

[2] Cf. R. Schevill, *Ovid and the Renascence in Spain* (Univ. of California Press, 1913), pp. 6-27; and M. Manitius, *op. cit.*, indices; *idem*, "Beiträge zur Geschichte des Ovidius and anderer römischen Schriftsteller im Mittelalter," *Philologus*, Suppl. VII (1899), 723-67; *idem*, "Zu römischen Schriftsteller im Mittelalter," *ibid.*, LXI (1902), 455-72. The manuscripts of classical writers, with contemporary glosses, written during this period, give further evidence. Whether the debt is direct or through commentaries, such as that of Boethius on Aristotle, is beside the point here.

sistent with this, and consequent upon it, is the emphasis upon counsel which is so regularly enjoined upon the ruling prince. With the exception of some attention devoted to education, and some suggestions of economic development, in the later writers, the prince's functions are mainly divided between the military and the judicial. This last is particularly stressed, especially by the writers of the later centuries, which again emphasizes the personal element of the whole theory. As a whole, the various authors insist that the prince is "under the law," [3] and is responsible for his acts. Just what this "law" is, they do not state. But this, at least, is clear: the prince must assuredly answer for his conduct before the law of God.

In summary we may say that the perfect prince of these ten centuries must be wise, self-restrained, just; devoted to the welfare of his people; a pattern in virtues for his subjects; immune from flattery; interested in economic developments, an educational program, and the true religion of God; surrounded by efficient ministers and able advisers; opposed to aggressive warfare; and, in the realization that even he is subject to law and that the need of the prince and his subjects is mutual, zealous for the attainment of peace and unity.

Now that we have examined the development of the *speculum principis* over a period of one thousand years, from the start of the Middle Ages to the end of the Renaissance, what shall we say about Erasmus's place in the tradition? From the summary just given in the preceding paragraph, it is obvious that the same ethical points are common to Erasmus and his medieval predecessors, but that he develops them at greater length. It is also clear that his ideas are much more closely associated with those of the writers after the twelfth century than with the earlier ones, except in the points which all borrowed from classical antiquity.

It does not seem possible to deduce a more direct relationship with any one of the writers, except perhaps with John of Salisbury (many of whose frequent classical references are also found in Erasmus), and with Thomas Aquinas, whose

[3] Divine right is consistently stated up to the tenth century.

organic analogy (first formulated by him as a regular doctrine and used in several places in the *Institutio*) could have been borrowed directly from its source as readily as from one of the later disciples.[4] The emphasis on economic factors in state-craft is common to several late medieval writers; Erasmus could have taken his ideas from any one of them. But we must not forget, in this pursuit of possible dependences or inter-relations, that quasi-independence (if not originality) is not to be excluded. The points which Erasmus's work has in common with the works of his predecessors are, in the main, not of such a nature as to indicate clear reliance upon any one writer or any group of writers. Except for occasional refer-ences Erasmus seems independent of direct borrowing from the material between the sixth and the sixteenth centuries.[5]

There remains one matter which deserves a separate dis-cussion. What was the relationship of Thomas More's *Utopia*, also published in 1516, to the *Institutio* of Erasmus? The close personal friendship of the two authors needs no further proof; their frequent and continuous interchange of ideas is readily shown from the correspondence of Erasmus. That

[4] Erasmus edited neither Salisbury nor Aquinas; there is no subject index in Allen, *op. cit.*, by which references could be checked; the indices in Nichols, *op. cit.*, show no reference to either writer. In this connection it may not be uninteresting to point out that Erasmus was asked (probably by Mercurino Gattinari, chancellor of Charles V) to edit the *De monarchia* of Dante. While the letter (Allen, Ep. 1790a) is undated, Allen places it about March, 1527. Erasmus's reply so far has not been found; however, he must have refused, for the *editio princeps* of the *De monarchia* did not appear until 1559. My information on this matter is taken from P. Toynbee, "Dante Notes," *Mod. Lang. Rev.*, XX (1925), 43-47; for Erasmus, p. 43. See also the introductory remarks in Allen for the political significance of the refusal by Erasmus.

[5] We have already observed in chap. iv, n. 1, that the only medieval author specifically referred to is St. Bernard. Even granting the validity of Geldner's statement (which I have not checked except in the *Institutio*), that Erasmus never cites a medieval writer except when he differs from him, "and yet the instances of similar thought are very numerous" (*op. cit.*, p. 140), I do not find it possible to agree with his generalization that "Erasmus knew of a certainty a large percentage of the medieval mirrors of princes" (p. 138). Certainly there is nothing in Erasmus's essay to prove that he was *not* acquainted with the im-portant writers of the medieval period, but to insist that he borrowed his "modern" ideas from them seems to me to overlook Erasmus's power for inde-pendent thought and to beg the question of the inter-relationship of many of the medieval mirrors themselves. With Geldner's statement (p. 138) that Eras-mus was well acquainted with Thomas Aquinas I concur.

More knew of Erasmus's *Institutio* before its publication, we have already pointed out in a previous chapter. It is not illogical to infer that Erasmus had advance knowledge of the *Utopia*, which embodied, in a very different guise, most of the essential points which he developed in his own work.[6]

Erasmus could not have used the *Utopia* in its finished form, for More sent a manuscript copy to him for his criticism on September 3, 1516,[7] which was acknowledged on October 2, 1516.[8] The *editio princeps* appeared from Martens at Louvain in November, 1516, while Erasmus's own work had already been published in April of that same year. While it is possible that those ideas of Erasmus which partake of the medieval theories may have been engendered or stimulated

[6] The *Utopia* is not subdivided into chapters; the following references, enough to show the similarity in content to Erasmus, are cited by page, from the edition of W. D. Armes, *The Utopia of Sir Thomas More* (New York, 1912): "to find citizens ruled by good and wholesome laws, that is an exceeding rare and hard thing" (p. 25); the prince is the prime source of good or evil for his people (pp. 28-29); most princes are more interested in war than in peace (p. 29); it is better to provide a means of livelihood for everyone than to punish those who steal (p. 33); mercenary soldiers make for immorality, theft, bad social conditions (pp. 36-37); war drives people from their homes, with non-production and higher prices as the result (pp. 39-40); economic conditions must be considered (pp. 42-43); *summum jus* is often *summa injuria* (p. 45; cf. Nichols, *op. cit.*, II, 123); disapproval of capital punishment (pp. 45-52); provision for poor and needy (p. 55); philosophers should be teachers of kings (p. 60); opposition to aggressive warfare (pp. 63-65); corrupt advisers of princes (pp. 65-68); a good prince is the shepherd of his people, and his duties are manifold (pp. 68-72); the best state exists where all men are good (p. 74); economic reform is needed (p. 78); general principles of the "community" life in Utopia (pp. 87-94); public works (pp. 91-96); magistrates (pp. 96-98); farming, weaving and other crafts; opposition to idlers, including priests, etc., (pp. 99-108); a war is just when made to occupy vacant lands (p. 110); travel (pp. 111-18); no value in worldly goods (pp. 123-30); "they [the Utopians] define virtue to be a life ordered according to nature" (p. 134); no real pleasure in vain or worldly honors (pp. 138-39); Greek authors, especially Plato, Aristotle, Plutarch, Lucian, Aristophanes, Homer, Euripides, Sophocles, Thucydides, Herodian are to be read (pp. 150-52); on slavery (p. 155); simple dress for the ruler (p. 164); few laws (pp. 167-70); opposition to war (pp. 170-73); religious freedom for all (p. 187); the clergy should be virtuous (p. 198). See also P. F. Sherwin, "Some Sources of More's Utopia," *Bulletin Univ. of New Mexico*, I (1917), 167-91, in which some importance is given to Erasmus as a background, although he has not read the *Institutio* and apparently has not used such obvious material as Janet, *op. cit.*, and others but followed only Seebohm, *The Oxford Reformers.*

[7] Allen, Ep. 461.

[8] *Ibid.*, Ep. 474.

by discussion with the author of the *Utopia* at a time when both friends were outlining a similar plan of social reform, of course the exact opposite of this situation is also possible. A definite statement cannot, in my opinion, be safely made, but one is tempted to feel that Erasmus is the stronger personality. The fact that Erasmus, in contrast to More in company with many other contemporary theorists, makes no direct or indirect reference to the New World or its problems and possibilities must not be overlooked.[9]

[9] By an interesting coincidence, Geldner (*op. cit.*, pp. 175-79) closes his study with an "Anhang" on the interrelation of the *Utopia* and Erasmus. He distinctly feels the influence of Erasmus on More. "Der Morus der *Utopia* bekennt sich zu denselben Grundsätzen, die der wirkliche Morus im Leben geübt; durch die Maske des Raphael spricht hier Erasmus von Rotterdam (p. 179)."

# THE EDUCATION OF A CHRISTIAN PRINCE

Three virtues should be taught the royal heir. The first is the virtue of moderation, so that he may learn the fundamental principle of how to live. The second is the virtue of adaptability, so that he may learn the fundamental principle of how to conduct himself. The third is the virtue of filial duty, so that he may learn what is in accordance with nature and what is in contradiction to it. — *Constitution of Chow.*

## [DEDICATORY EPISTLE]

### TO THE MOST ILLUSTRIOUS PRINCE CHARLES, GRANDSON OF THE INVINCIBLE CAESAR MAXIMILIAN, DESIDERIUS ERASMUS OF ROTTERDAM SENDS GREETINGS

Wisdom is not only an extraordinary attribute in itself, Charles, most bountiful of princes, but according to Aristotle [1] no form of wisdom is greater than that which teaches a prince how to rule beneficently. Accordingly, Xenophon was quite correct in saying in his *Oeconomicus* [2] that he thought it something beyond the human sphere and clearly divine, to rule over free and willing subjects. That kind of wisdom is indeed to be sought by princes, which Solomon as a youth of good parts, spurning all else, alone desired, and which he wished to be his constant companion on the throne. This is that purest and most beautiful wisdom of Sunamite, by whose embraces alone was David pleased, he that wisest son of an all-wise father. This is the wisdom which is referred to in *Proverbs*: [3] "Through me princes rule, and the powerful pass judgment." Whenever kings call this wisdom into council and exclude those basest of advisers — ambition, wrath, cupidity, and flattery — the state flourishes in every way and, realizing that its prosperity comes from the wisdom of the prince, rejoices rightly in itself with these words: [4] "All good things together come to me with her [i.e., wisdom]." Plato [5] is nowhere more painstaking than in the training of his guardians of the state. He does not wish them to excel all others in wealth, in gems, in dress, in statues and attendants, but in wisdom alone. He says that no state will ever be blessed unless the philosophers are at the helm, or those to whom the task of government falls embrace philosophy. By "philosophy" I do not mean that

[1] E.g., *Pol.* 9.  [2] *Econ.* XXI. 12.  [3] *Prov.* 8: 16.
[4] *Wisdom* 7:11.
[5] E.g., *Laws* IV. 715; *States.* 311; *Rep.* VI. 503.

which disputes concerning the first beginnings, of primordial matter, of motion and infinity, but that which frees the mind from the false opinions and the vicious predilections of the masses and points out a theory of government according to the example of the Eternal Power. It was something such as this that Homer [6] had in mind when [he had][7] Mercury protect Ulysses against the potions of Circe with the molu flower. And not without reason did Plutarch [8] say that no one serves the state better than he who imbues the mind of the prince, who provides and cares for everyone and everything, with the best of ideas and those most becoming a prince. On the other hand, no one brings so serious a blight upon the affairs of men as he who has corrupted the heart of the prince with depraved ideas and desires. He is no different from one who has poisoned the public fountain whence all men drink. Likewise Plutarch [9] judges not inapposite that celebrated remark of Alexander the Great: Departing from the talk he had had with Diogenes the Cynic, and still marveling at his philosophic spirit, so proud, unbroken, unconquered, and superior to all things human, he said, "If I were not Alexander, I should like to be Diogenes." Nay, as great authority is exposed to so many storms, the more was that spirit of Diogenes to be sought after, since he could rise to the measure of such towering tumults.

But as much as you surpass Alexander in good fortune, mighty prince Charles, so much do we hope you will surpass him in wisdom. For he had gained a mighty empire, albeit one not destined to endure, solely through bloodshed. You have been born to a splendid kingdom and are destined to a still greater one. As Alexander had to toil to carry out his invasions, so will you have to labor to yield, rather than to gain, part of your power. You owe it to the powers of heaven that you came into a kingdom untainted with blood, bought through no evil connection. It will be the lot of your wisdom to keep

[6] *Od.* X. 305.
[7] Throughout the translation, words in square brackets are not found in the original text.
[8] *Mor.* 778D.        [9] *Alex.* 14; *Mor.* 782A.

it bloodless and peaceful. You have the inborn nature, the soundness of mind, the force of character, and you have received a training under the most reliable preceptors. So many examples from your ancestors surround you on every side, that we all have the highest hopes that Charles will some day do what the world long hoped his father Philip would do. And he [Philip] would not have disappointed the popular expectation if death had not cut him off before his time. And so, although I am not unaware that your highness does not need the advice of anyone, and least of all my advice, yet it has seemed best to set forth the likeness of the perfect prince for general information, but addressed to you. In this way those who are being brought up to rule great kingdoms will receive their theory of government through you and take their example from you. At the same time the good from this treatise will spread out to all under your auspices, and we of your entourage may manifest somewhat by these first fruits, as it were, the zeal of our spirit toward you.

We have done into Latin Isocrates's precepts on ruling a kingdom. We have fashioned ours, set off with subject headings so as to be less inconvenient to the reader, after the fashion of his, but differing not a little from his suggestions. That sophist was instructing a young king, or rather a tyrant: one pagan instructing another. I, a theologian, am acting the part of teacher to a distinguished and pure-hearted prince — one Christian to another. If I were writing these things for a prince of more advanced age, I should perhaps come under the suspicions of some for flattery or impertinence. But since this little book is dedicated to one who, although he evidences the highest hopes for himself, is still so youthful and so recently installed in his power that he could not as yet do many things which people are wont to praise or censure in princes, I am free from suspicion on both charges and cannot appear to have sought any object beyond the public welfare. That to the friends of kings (as to kings themselves) ought to be the only aim. Among the countless distinctions and praises which virtue, by the will of God, will prepare for you, this will be no small part: Charles was such an one that anyone could without the mark of flattery present [to him] the likeness of a pure and true Christian prince, which the excellent prince would happily recognize, or wisely imitate as a young man always eager to better himself.

With best wishes.[10]

[10] This letter is found in Allen (Ep. 393) as well as in both editions of the *Opera omnia* where it immediately precedes the text of the *Institutio*. In the title to the work itself, which immediately follows, Erasmus does not use *capitula*, the obvious word for "chapters." His Latin reads *aphorismis digesta*, which could also be translated as "marked off with side-headings."

# THE EDUCATION OF A CHRISTIAN PRINCE

separated into pertinent chapters so that
it may be less burdensome to read

by

Desiderius Erasmus of Rotterdam

# I

## [THE QUALITIES, EDUCATION, AND SIGNIFICANCE OF
## A CHRISTIAN PRINCE]

[B 433, L 562] [1] When a prince is to be chosen by election it is not at all appropriate to look to the images of his forefathers, to consider his physical appearance, his height of stature (which we read that some barbarians once most stupidly did) and to seek a quiet and placid trend of spirit.[2] Seek rather a nature staid, in no way rash, and not so excitable that there is danger of his developing into a tyrant under the license of good fortune and casting aside all regard for advisers and counselors. Yet have a care that he be not so weak as to be turned now this way and now that by whomsoever he meets.[3] Consider also his experience and his age — not so severe as to be entirely out of sympathy with frivolity, nor so impetuous as to be carried away by flights of fancy. Perhaps some consideration should also be paid to the state of health of the prince so that there will be no danger of a sudden succession to be filled, which would be a hardship on the state.[4]

BIRTH AND REARING OF A PRINCE

HEALTH OF THE PRINCE

---

[1] These references give the pages in the *Opera omnia* (Basle, 1540), IV (designated as B), and in the *Opera omnia* (Leyden, 1703-6), IV (designated as L), in which the Latin text of the *Institutio* is most easily accessible.

[2] Cf. Plato *Laws* IV. 715; see also Seneca *Ep. Mor.* XLIV. 3-4. Throughout the translation references specifically cited or quoted by Erasmus have been cited in the notes; references to passages which may well have suggested the thought to Erasmus because of his familiarity with the writer from whom they are taken or because they are such striking parallels that mere coincidence would be hard to explain, have also been cited, but always prefixed by "cf." No attempt has been made to load the text with miscellaneous learning; any critic could suggest many more passages to add as general parallels or illustrative material. Such information is contained in detail in Chapters III and V of the Introduction and is not repeated here.

[3] Cf. Plato *States.* 311; *Rep.* VI. 503.

[4] The Latin word is *respublica*, "commonwealth." Since Erasmus is not concerned with the discussions of the "state" in connection with sovereignty, etc., and regularly employs the word *civitas* to mean city, I have consistently rendered *respublica* as "state." Any other word so rendered has been noted in the text where it occurs.

In navigation the wheel is not given to him who surpasses his fellows in birth, wealth, or appearance, but rather to him who excels in his skill as a navigator, in his alertness, and in his MEANS dependability. Just so with the rule of a state: most naturally OF JUDGING the power should be entrusted to him who excels all in the A PRINCE requisite kingly qualities of wisdom, justice, moderation, foresight, and zeal for the public welfare.[5]

Statues, gold, and gems contribute no more to state government than they do to a master in steering his ship. That one idea which should concern a prince in ruling, should likewise REGARDING concern the people in selecting their prince: the public weal, THE PUBLIC free from all private interests.[6] GOOD

The more difficult it is to change your choice, the more circumspectly should your candidate be chosen, or else the rashness of a single hour may spread its retributions over a lifetime. There is no choice, however, in the case of hereditary succession of princes. This was the usual practice with various barbarian nations of old, as Aristotle [7] tells us, and it is also almost universally accepted in our own times. Under that con-EDUCATION dition, the chief hope for a good prince is from his education, OF A PRINCE which should be especially looked to. In this way the interest in his education will compensate for the loss of the right of election. Hence, from the very cradle, as it were, the mind of WITH WHAT the future prince, while still open and unmolded, must be filled THE PRINCE with salutary thoughts.[8] Then the seeds of morality must be MUST IMME-DIATELY BE sown in the virgin soil of his spirit so that little by little they IMBUED may grow and mature through age and experience, to remain firmly implanted throughout the course of life. Nothing remains so deeply and tenaciously rooted as those things learned in the first years. What is absorbed in those years is of prime importance to all, especially in the case of a prince.

When there is no opportunity to choose the prince, care CHOOSING should be exercised in the same manner in choosing the tutor THE PRINCE'S to the future prince. That a prince be born of worthy character TUTOR

[5] Cf. Plato *Rep.* VI. 487-89; see also Aristotle *Pol.* III. 13; II. 9; I. 13.
[6] Cf. Cicero *De off.* I. 25. 85.
[7] *Pol.* III. 14.
[8] Cf. Plato *Rep.* II. 377; Plutarch *Training of Children* 5.

we must beseech the gods above; that a prince born of good parts may not go amiss, or that one of mediocre accomplishments may be bettered through education is mainly within our province. It was formerly the custom to decree statues, arches, and honorary titles to those deserving honor from the state. None is more worthy of this honor than he who labors faithfully and zealously in the proper training of the prince [B 434], and looks not to personal emolument but rather to the welfare of his country. A country owes everything to a good prince; him it owes to the man who made him such by his moral principles.[9] There is no better time to shape and improve a prince than when he does not yet realize himself a prince. This time must be diligently employed, not only to the end that for a while he may be kept away from base associations, but also that he may be imbued with certain definite moral principles. If diligent parents raise with great care a boy who is destined to inherit only an acre or two, think how much interest and concern should be given to the education of one who will succeed not to a single dwelling, but to so many peoples, to so many cities, yea, to the world, either as a good man for the common gain of all, or an evil one, to the great ruination of all! It is a great and glorious thing to rule an empire well, but none-the-less glorious to pass it on to no worse a ruler: nay, rather it is the main task of a good prince to see that he does not become a bad one. So conduct your rule as if this were your aim: "My equal shall never succeed me!" In the meantime, raise your children for future rule as if it were your desire to be succeeded by a better prince. There can be no more splendid commendation of a worthy prince than to say that he left such a successor to the state, that he himself seemed average by comparison. His own glory cannot be more truly shown than to be so obscured. The worst possible praise is that a ruler who was intolerable during his life is longingly missed as a good and beneficial prince each time a worse man ascends the throne. Let the good and wise prince always so educate his children that he seems ever to have remembered

THE PRINCE TO BE SHAPED AT ONCE

TO WHAT END THE SONS OF PRINCES ARE TO BE EDUCATED

[9] Cf. Plutarch *A Philosopher Is to Converse with Great Men* 1-3.

THOSE BORN
FOR THE
STATE ARE
TO BE EDU-
CATED FOR
THE STATE that they were born for the state and are being educated for the state, not for his own fancy. Concern for the state must always be superior to the personal feelings of the parent. However many statues he may set up, however many massive works he may erect, a prince can have no more excellent monument to his worth than a son, splendid in every way, who is like his excellent father in his outstanding deeds. *He does not die, who leaves a living likeness of himself!* The prince should choose for this duty teachers from among all the number of his subjects — or even summon from every direction men of good character, unquestioned principles, serious, of long experience and not merely learned in theories — to whom advancing years provide deep respect; purity of life, prestige; sociability and an affable manner, love and friendship. Thus a

tender young spirit may not be cut by the severity of its training and learn to hate worthiness before it knows it; nor on the other hand, debased by the unseasoned indulgence of its tutor, slip back where it should not.[10] In the education of anyone, but especially in the case of a prince, the teacher must adopt a mid-course; he should be stern enough to suppress the wild pranks of youth, yet have a friendly understanding to lessen and temper the severity of his restraint.[11] Such a man should the future prince's tutor be (as Seneca elaborately sets forth),[12] that he can scold without railing, praise without flattering, be revered for his stainless life, and loved for his pleasing manner.

Some princes exercise themselves greatly over the proper care of a beautiful horse, or a bird, or a dog, yet consider it a matter of no importance to whom they entrust the training of their son. Him they often put in the hands of such teachers as no common citizen with any sense at all would want in charge of his sons [L 564]. Of what consequence is it to have begot a son for the throne, unless you educate him for his rule?

Neither is the young prince to be given to any sort of nurse, but only to those of stainless character, who have been pre-

---

[10] Cf. Seneca *Ep. Mor.* LII; Plutarch *Training of Children* 7.
[11] Cf. Seneca *De ira* II. 21. 3; Plato *Rep.* VII. 536.
[12] *Ep. Mor.* LII. 8, 9.

viously instructed in their duties and are well trained. He should not be allowed to associate with whatever playmates appear, but only with those boys of good and modest character; he should be reared and trained most carefully and as becomes a gentleman.[13] That whole crowd of wantons, hard drinkers, filthy-tongued fellows, especially flatterers, must be kept far from his sight and hearing while his mind is not yet fortified with precepts to the contrary.[14] Since the natures of so many men are inclined towards the ways of evil, there is no nature so happily born that it cannot be corrupted by wrong training.[15] What do you expect except a great fund of evil in a prince, who, regardless of his native character (and a long line of ancestors does not necessarily furnish a mind, as it does a kingdom), is beset from his very cradle by the most inane opinions; is raised in the circle of senseless women; grows to boyhood among naughty girls, abandoned playfellows, and the most abject flatterers, among buffoons and mimes, drinkers and gamesters, and worse than stupid and worthless creators of wanton pleasures. In the company of all of these he hears nothing, learns nothing, absorbs nothing except pleasures, amusements, arrogance, haughtiness, greed, petulance, and tyranny — and from this school he will soon progress to the government of his kingdom! Although each one of all the great arts is very difficult, there is none finer nor more difficult than that of ruling well. Why in the case of this one thing alone do we feel the need of no training, but deem it sufficient to have been born for it? To what end except tyranny do they devote themselves as men, who as boys played at nothing except as tyrants?[16]

CORRUPT EDUCATION OF A PRINCE

THE ART OF RULING ESPECIALLY TO BE LEARNED

[B 435] It is too much even to hope that all men will be good, yet it is not difficult to select from so many thousands one or two, who are conspicuous for their honesty and wisdom, through whom many good men may be gained in simple fashion. The real young prince should hold his youth in dis-

13 Cf. Plutarch *Training of Children* 6.
14 Cf. *ibid.*, 17; Seneca *De ira* II. 21. 7-8.
15 Cf. Plato *Rep.* VI. 491; see also *ibid.*, 494; *Laws* III. 691.
16 Cf. Plato *Laws* I. 643; Isocrates *To Nicocles* 4.

trust for a long time, partly because of his inexperience and partly because of his unrestrained impulsiveness. He should avoid attempting any considerable enterprise without the advice of tried men, preferably old men, in whose company he should steadily be, so that the rashness of youth may be tempered by deference to his elders.

Whoever will undertake the task of educating the prince, let him ponder again and again the fact that he is undertaking a duty by no means slight. Just as it is the greatest of all [duties], so is it beset with the most trials. In the first place, he should have an attitude of mind befitting his undertaking; he should not contemplate the number of priestly benefices he can gain as a result, but rather in what way he can repay the hopes of his country entrusted to him by giving it a prince heedful of his country's needs. Think, you who would teach, how much you owe your country, which has entrusted the source of its fortunes to you! It rests with you whether you are going to turn out a power for good in your country or visit it with a scourge and plague.[17]

The teacher, into whose care the state has given its prince, shall give much careful thought to discover his leanings. Sometimes, too, at this early age it can be discovered by certain signs whether the prince is more prone to petulance or arrogance, to a desire for popularity or a thirst for fame, to licentiousness or dicing or greed, to defense or war, to rashness or tyranny.[18] When he has found the prince's weak spot, there he should strengthen him with goodly doctrines and suitable teachings and try to lead into better ways a spirit still prone to follow. On the other hand, if he finds a nature prone to the good things of life, or at any rate to only those vices which are readily turned to virtue, e.g., ambition and prodigality, he should work the harder and assist advantages of nature with refinement. It is not enough just to hand out precepts to restrain the prince from vices or to incite him to a better course — they must be impressed, crammed in, inculcated, and in one

[17] Cf. Plutarch *A Philosopher Is to Converse with Great Men* 2.
[18] Cf. Plato *Rep.* VI. 486.

way and another be kept before him, now by a suggestive
thought, now by a fable, now by analogy, now by example, now
by maxims, now by a proverb. They should be engraved on
rings, painted in pictures, appended to the wreaths of honor,
and, by using any other means by which that age can be interested, kept always before him. The deeds of famous men fire
the minds of noble youths, but the opinions with which they
become imbued is a matter of far greater importance, for
from these sources the whole scheme of life is developed. In
the case of a mere boy, we must immediately be on guard, to
see that he gets only the virtuous and helpful ideas and that he
be fortified as by certain efficacious drugs against the poisoned
opinions of the common people. But if the prince happens to
be somewhat tinged with the thoughts of the common people,
then the first effort must be to rid him of them little by little,
to weed out the seeds of trouble and replace them by wholesome ones. As Aristo says in Seneca,[19] "It is no use to teach
a crazy man how to speak, how to act, how to conduct himself
in public, how alone, until you have driven out the root of the
malady." Just so is it fruitless to attempt advice on the theory
of governing, until you have freed the prince's mind from
those most common yet most truly false opinions of the common people. There is no chance for the tutor to avoid or shrink
his responsibility if he unfortunately encounters a headstrong
and untractable nature. There is no beast so wild, so terrible,
that the skill and endurance of his trainer will not tame him.
Why should the tutor judge any man to be so coarse and so
forsaken that he will not be corrected by painstaking instruction? [20]

FIRST OF ALL,
BASE IDEAS
MUST BE
TORN OUT

On the other hand, if the tutor encounters a better character that is no excuse for ceasing his efforts. The better the
nature of the soil, the more it is wasted and filled with worthless weeds and shrubs if the farmer does not take care. So it
is with a man's character: the richer, the more noble, the more

[19] *Ep. Mor.* XCIV. 3.
[20] Cf. Plutarch *Training of Children* 4.

righteous it is, the more it is beset with shameful vices, unless improved by wholesome teachings.[21]

Those shores which receive the severest pounding of the waves we are wont to bulwark most carefully. Now there are countless things which can turn the minds of princes from the true course — great fortune, worldly wealth in abundance, the pleasures of luxurious extravagance, freedom to do anything they please, the precedents of great but foolish princes, the storms and turmoils of human affairs themselves, and above all else, flattery, spoken in the guise of faith and frankness.[22] On this account must the prince be the more sincerely strengthened with the best of principles and the precedents of praiseworthy princes.

Just as one who poisons the public fountain from which all drink deserves more than one punishment, so he is the most harmful who infects the mind of the prince with base ideas, which later produce the destruction of so many men.[23] If anyone counterfeits the prince's coinage, he is beaten about the head [B 436]; surely he who corrupts the character of the prince is even more deserving of that punishment. The teacher should enter at once upon his duties, so as to implant the seeds

GOOD IDEAS ARE TO BE INTRODUCED AT ONCE of good moral conduct while the senses of the prince are still in the tenderness of youth, while his mind is furthest removed from all vices and tractably yields to the hand of guidance in whatever it directs. He is immature both in body and mind, as in his sense of duty. The teacher's task is always the same, but he must employ one method in one case, and another in another. While his pupil is still a little child, he can bring in his teachings through pretty stories, pleasing fables, clever parables. When he is bigger, he can teach the same things directly.[24]

When the little fellow has listened with pleasure to Aesop's fable [25] of the lion and the mouse or of the dove and the ant,

[21] Cf. Plato *Rep.* VI. 491.
[22] Cf. Augustine *Civ. Dei* XVII. 20.
[23] Cf. Plutarch *A Philosopher Is to Converse with Great Men* 3.
[24] Cf. Plato *Rep.* VI. 498.
[25] *Fabulae* 256, 296, 7 (ed. C. Halm).

and when he has finished his laugh, then the teacher should point out the *new* moral: the first fable teaches the prince to despise no one, but to seek zealously to win to himself by kindnesses the heart of even the lowest peasant (*plebs*), for no one is so weak but that on occasion he may be a friend to help you, or an enemy to harm you, even though you be the most powerful. When he has had his fun out of the eagle, queen of the birds, that was almost completely done for by the beetle, the teacher should again point out the meaning: not even the most powerful prince can afford to provoke or over-look even the humblest enemy. Often those who can inflict no harm by physical strength can do much by the machinations of their minds. When he has learned with pleasure the story of Phaeton, the teacher should show that he represents a prince, who while still headstrong with the ardor of youth, but with no supporting wisdom, seized the reins of government and turned everything into ruin for himself and the whole world. When he has finished the story of the Cyclops who was blinded by Ulysses, the teacher should say in conclusion that the prince who has great strength of body, but not of mind, is like Polyphemus.

USE OF FABLES

THE USE OF MYTHS

[L 566] Who has not heard with interest of the govern-ment of the bees and ants?[26] When temptations begin to descend into the youthful heart of the prince, then his tutor should point out such of these stories as belong in his educa-tion. He should tell him that the king[27] never flies far away, has wings smaller in proportion to the size of its body than the others, and that he alone has no sting.[28] From this the tutor should point out that it is the part of a good prince always to remain within the limits of his realm; his reputation for clem-ency should be his special form of praise. The same idea should be carried on throughout. It is not the province of this treatise to supply a long list of examples, but merely to point out the

THE USE OF ANALOGIES

[26] Cf., on bees, Vergil *Georgics* IV. 67-87, 153-218; Pliny *Natural History* XI. 5 (4); and on ants, *ibid.*, 30 (36).

[27] Erasmus follows the majority of the ancients in referring to the queen bee as the "king."

[28] See the references in note 26, above.

theory and the way. If there are any stories that seem too coarse, the teacher should polish and smooth them over with a winning manner of speech. The teacher should give his praise in the presence of others, but only within the limits of truth and proportion. His scoldings should be administered in private and given in such a way that a pleasing manner somewhat breaks the severity of his admonition. This is especially to be done when the prince is a little older.

CHRISTIAN DOGMAS TO BE INSTILLED AT ONCE

Before all else the story of Christ must be firmly rooted in the mind of the prince. He should drink deeply of His teachings, gathered in handy texts, and then later from those very fountains themselves, whence he may drink more purely and more effectively. He should be taught that the teachings of Christ apply to no one more than to the prince.

No "GOOD" EXCEPT ONE

The great mass of people are swayed by false opinions and are no different from those in Plato's cave,[29] who took the empty shadows as the real things. It is the part of a good prince to admire none of the things that the common people consider of great consequence, but to judge all things on their own merits as "good" or "bad." [30] But nothing is truly "bad" unless joined with base infamy. Nothing is really "good" unless associated with moral integrity.

WHAT IS TRUE "GOOD?"

Therefore, the tutor should first see that his pupil loves and honors virtue as the finest quality of all, the most felicitous, the most fitting a prince; and that he loathes and shuns moral turpitude as the foulest and most terrible of things. Lest the young prince be accustomed to regard riches as an indispensable necessity, to be gained by right or wrong, he should learn that those are not true honors which are commonly acclaimed as such. True honor is that which follows on virtue and right action of its own will. The less affected it is, the more it redounds to fame. The low pleasures of the people are so far beneath a prince, especially a Christian prince, that they hardly become any man. There is another kind of pleasure which will endure, genuine and true, all through life. Teach the young

[29] *Rep.* VII. 514-15.
[30] Cf. Isocrates *To Nicocles* 50.

prince that nobility, statues, wax masks, family-trees, all the pomp of heralds, over which the great mass of people stupidly swell with pride, are only empty terms unless supported by deeds worth while. The prestige of a prince, his greatness, his majesty, must not be developed and preserved by fortune's wild display, but by wisdom, solidarity, and good deeds.

Death is not to be feared, nor should we wail when it comes to others, unless it was a foul death.[31] The happiest man is not the one who has lived the longest, but the one who has made the most of his life. The span of life should be measured not by years but by our deeds well performed. Length of life has no bearing on a man's happiness. It is how well he lived that counts.[32] Surely virtue is its own reward [B 437]. It is the duty of a good prince to consider the welfare of his people, even at the cost of his own life if need be. But that prince does not really die who loses his life in such a cause. All those things which the common people cherish as delightful, or revere as excellent, or adopt as useful, are to be measured by just one standard — worth. On the other hand, whatever things the common people object to as disagreeable, or despise as lowly, or shun as pernicious, should not be avoided unless they are bound up with dishonor.[33]

These principles should be fixed in the mind of the future prince. They should be impressed in his tender young heart as the most hallowed laws, *les lois les plus sacrées*.[34] Let him hear many being praised for these ideas and others reprimanded for diverse ones. Then he will be accustomed from the start to expect praise as a result of good things and to abhor

---

[31] In addition to the various passages in the *Testament*, cf. also Seneca *Ep. Mor.* IV.

[32] Cf. Seneca *Ep. Mor.* XCIII. 2-5.

[33] Cf. Augustine *Civ. Dei* V. 14.

[34] The reading of the Basle edition here is *leges sanctissimae, θεσμοί ἀκίνητοι*; that of the Leyden edition, *leges sanctissimae καὶ ἀκίνητοι*. I have followed the reading of the Basle edition since nowhere else in the *Institutio* does Erasmus mix a Greek construction with his Latin as an integral part of the syntax. The words are always parenthetical, as here, or quoted. I have not been able to examine the reading of the *editio princeps*. In accordance with custom, I have here and throughout the translation rendered the Greek by French to give the effect of the original.

the ignominy that comes from the opposite. But here some one of those frumps at the court, more stupid and worthless than any woman you could name, will interrupt with this: "You are making us a philosopher, not a prince." "I am making a prince," I answer, "although you prefer a worthless sot like yourself instead of a real prince!" You cannot be a prince, if you are not a philosopher; you will be a tyrant. There is nothing better than a good prince. A tyrant is such a monstrous beast that his like does not exist. Nothing is equally baneful, nothing more hateful to all. Do not think that Plato [35] rashly advanced the idea, which was lauded by the most praiseworthy men, that the blessed state will be that in which the princes are philosophers, or in which the philosophers seize the principate. I do not mean by philosopher, one who is learned in the ways of dialectic or physics, but one who casts aside the false pseudo-realities and with open mind seeks and follows the truth.[36] To be a philosopher and to be a Christian is synonymous in fact. The only difference is in the nomenclature.

What is more stupid than to judge a prince on the following accomplishments: his ability to dance gracefully, dice expertly, drink with a gusto, swell with pride, plunder the people with kingly grandeur, and do all the other things which I am ashamed even to mention, although there are plenty who are not ashamed to do them? The common run of princes zealously avoid the dress and manner of living of the lower classes. Just so should the true prince be removed from the sullied opinions and desires of the common folk. The one thing which he should consider base, vile, and unbecoming to him is to share the opinions of the common people who never are interested in anything worth while. How ridiculous it is for one adorned with gems, gold, the royal purple, attended by courtiers, possessing all the other marks of honor, wax images and statues, wealth that clearly is not his, to be so far superior to all because of them, and yet in the light of real goodness of spirit to be found inferior to many born from the very dregs of society.[37]

On What a Prince's Excellence Is Based

---

[35] *Rep.* V. 473; *ibid.*, VI. 487, 499.    [36] Cf. Plato *Rep.* VI. 485.
[37] Cf. Isocrates *To Nicocles* 32; see also Xenophon *Cyropaedia* I. 6. 8.

What else does the prince, who flaunts gems, gold, the royal purple, and all the other trappings of fortune's pomp in the eyes of his subjects, do but teach them to crave and admire the very sources from which spring the foulest essence of nearly all crimes that are punishable by the law of the prince? In others, frugality and simple neatness may be ascribed to want, or parsimony, if you are less kind in your judgment. These same qualities in a prince are clearly an evidence of temperance, since he uses sparingly the unlimited means which he possesses.

What man is there whom it becomes to stir up crimes and then inflict punishment for them? What could be more disgusting than for him to permit himself things he will not let others do? If you want to show yourself an excellent prince, see that no one outshines you in the qualities befitting your position — I mean wisdom, magnanimity, temperance, integrity.[38] If you want to make trial of yourself with other princes, do not consider yourself superior to them if you take away part of their power or scatter their forces; but only if you have been less corrupt than they, less greedy, less arrogant, less wrathful, less headstrong.[39]

No one will gainsay that nobility in its purest form becomes a prince. There are three kinds of nobility: the first is derived from virtue and good actions; the second comes from acquaintance with the best of training; and the third from an array of family portraits and the genealogy or wealth.[40] It by no means becomes a prince to swell with pride over this lowest degree of nobility, for it is so low that it is nothing at all, unless it has itself sprung from virtue. Neither must he neglect the first, which is so far the first that it alone can be considered in the strictest judgment. If you want to be famous do not make a display of statues or paintings; if there is anything praiseworthy in them, it is due to the artist whose genius and work they represent. Far better to make your character the monument to your good parts. If all else is lacking, the very

THREE KINDS
OF NOBILITY

[38] Cf. Xenophon *Agesilaus* X. 1; *Cyropaedia* VIII. 1. 37; Aristotle *Pol.* I. 13.
[39] Cf. Plutarch *Agesilaus* 23. 5; 7. 3.
[40] Cf. Seneca *Ep. Mor.* XLIV. 3-5.

appurtenances of your majesty can remind you of your duty. What does the anointing mean if not greatness, leniency, and clemency on the part of the prince, since cruelty is almost always the companion of great power? What does the gold

THE MEANINGS OF A PRINCE'S VARIOUS INSIGNIA

mean, except outstanding wisdom? What significance has the sparkle of the gems, except extraordinary virtues as different as possible from the common run? What does the warm rich purple mean, if not the essence of love for the state? And why the scepter, unless as a mark of a spirit clinging strongly to justice, turned aside by none of life's diversions? But if the prince has none of these qualities [B 438], these symbols are not ornaments to him, but stand as accusations against him. If a necklace, a scepter, royal purple robes [L 568], a train of attendants are all that make a king, what is to prevent the actors who come on the stage decked with all the pomp of

THE SPIRIT MAKES THE PRINCE

state from being called king? What is it that distinguishes a real king from the actor? It is the spirit befitting a prince. I mean he must be like a father to the state.[41] It is on this basis that the people swore allegiance to him. The crown, the scepter, the royal robes, the collar, the sword belt are all marks or symbols of good qualities in the good prince; in a bad one, they are accusations of vice.

Watchfulness must increase in proportion to his meanness, or else we will have a prince like many we read about of old. (May we never see the like again!) If you strip them of their royal ornaments and inherited goods, and reduce them to themselves alone, you will find nothing left except the essence of an expert at dice, the victor of many a drinking bout, the fierce conqueror of modesty, the craftiest of deceivers, an insatiable pillager; a creature steeped in perjury, sacrilege, perfidy, and every other kind of crime. Whenever you think of yourself as a prince, remember you are a *Christian* prince! You should be as different from even the noble pagan princes as a Christian is from a pagan.[42]

[41] Cf. Cicero *Rep.* II. 26. 47, among many others, for this idea. This could not have been directly used as a source, for the *Republic*, as Erasmus himself tells us, was lost until after his day.
[42] Cf. Augustine *Civ. Dei* V. 18.

Do not think that the profession of a Christian is a matter to be lightly passed over, entailing no responsibilities unless, of course, you think the sacrament which you accepted along with everything else at baptism is nothing. And do not think you renounce just for the once the delights of Satan which bring pain to the Christ. He is displeased with all that is foreign to the teachings of the Gospel. You share the Christian sacraments alike with all others — why not its teachings too? You have allied yourself with Christ — and yet will you slide back into the ways of Julius and Alexander the Great? You seek the same reward as the others, yet you will have no concern with His mandates.

THE PRO-
FESSION OF
CHRISTIANITY

But on the other hand, do not think that Christ is found in ceremonies, in doctrines kept after a fashion, and in constitutions of the church. Who is truly Christian? Not he who is baptized or anointed, or who attends church. It is rather the man who has embraced Christ in the innermost feelings of his heart, and who emulates Him by his pious deeds.[43] Guard against such inner thoughts as these: "Why is all this addressed to me? I am not a mere subject. I am not a priest. I am not a monk." Think rather in this fashion: "I am a Christian and a prince." It is the part of a true Christian to shun carefully all vulgarity. It is the province of a prince to surpass all in stainless character and wisdom. You compel your subjects to know and obey your laws. With far more energy you should exact of yourself knowledge and obedience to the laws of Christ, your king! [44] You judge it an infamous crime, for which there can be no punishment terrible enough, for one who has sworn allegiance to his king to revolt from him. On what grounds, then, do you grant yourself pardon and consider as a matter of sport and jest the countless times you have broken the laws of Christ, to whom you swore allegiance in your bapism, to whose cause you pledged yourself, by whose sacraments you are bound and pledged?

THE TRUE
CHRISTIAN

PRINCE —
THEOLOGIAN

THE
DESERTER

If these acts are done in earnest, why do we make a farce of

[43] Cf. Plato *Laws* IV. 716.
[44] Cf. Plutarch *The Banquet* 7.

them? If they are only sham, why do we vaunt ourselves under the glory of Christ as pretext? There is but one death for all — beggars and kings alike. But the judgment after death is not the same for all. None are dealt with more severely than the powerful.

Do not think you have acquitted yourself well in the eyes of Christ, merely because you send a fleet against the Turks, or build a shrine or erect a little monastery somewhere. There is no better way to gain the favor of God, than by showing yourself a beneficial prince for your people. Guard against the deceit of flatterers who claim that precepts of this kind have no concern for princes but pertain only to that class which they call ecclesiastics. The prince is not a priest, I confess, and therefore does not consecrate the body of Christ. He is not a bishop, and so does not rouse the people on the mysteries of Christianity, nor does he administer the sacrament. He has not professed the rule of St. Benedict, and therefore does not wear the cowl. But what is more than all this, he is a Christian. He has followed the rule of Christ himself. It is from Him that he has received his white robe, not from St. Francis. The prince should vie with the other Christians, if he would have the same reward.

You, too, must take up your cross, or else Christ will have none of you. "What," you ask, "is my cross?" I will tell you: Follow the right, do violence to no one, plunder no one, sell no public office, be corrupted by no bribes. To be sure, your treasury will have far less in it than otherwise, but take no thought for that loss, if only you have acquired the interest from justice. While you are using every means and interest to benefit the state, your life is fraught with care; you rob your youth and genius of their pleasures; you wear yourself down with long hours of toil. Forget that and enjoy yourself in the consciousness of right. As you would rather stand for an injury than avenge it at great loss to the state, perchance you will lose a little something of your empire. Bear that; consider that you have gained a great deal because you have brought hurt to fewer than you would otherwise have done. Do your private emotions as a man — reproachful anger, love for your wife, hatred of an enemy, shame — urge you to do what is not right and what is not to the welfare of the state? Let the thought of honor win [B 439]. Let the concern for the state completely cover your personal ambitions. If you cannot defend your realm without violating justice, without wanton loss of human life, without great loss to religion, give up and yield to the importunities of the age! If you cannot look out for the possessions of your subjects without danger to your own life, set the safety of the people before your very life! But while you are conducting yourself in this fashion, which befits a true Christian prince, there will be plenty to call you a dolt, and no prince at all! Hold fast to your cause. It is far better to be a just man than an unjust prince. It is clear now, I think, that even the greatest kings are not without their crosses, if they want to follow the course of right at all times, as they should.

In the case of private individuals, some concession is granted to youth and to old age: the former may make a mistake now and then; the latter is allowed leisure and a cessation of toils. But the man who undertakes the duties of the prince, while managing the affairs of everyone, is not free to be either a young man or an old one; he cannot make a mistake without a great loss to many people; he cannot slacken in his duties without the gravest disasters ensuing. The ancients used to say that was a costly prudence which came from experience, because each one found it at his own expense.[45] The prince should be sheltered from this by all means. When such experiences occur later, they bring great harm to all the people. If Africanus[46] spoke the truth when he said, " 'I did not think,' is not a fit expression for any wise man," how much more unsuited is it to a prince! For it applies not only to the great man himself, but, alas, to the state as well! For example, a war begun in a moment of rashness by a young prince with no knowledge of war, lasts throughout twenty years.

No Leniency
to a Prince
at Fault

45 Cf. Plato *Symposium* 222.
46 Valerius Maximus VII. 2. 2.

What a vast sea of misfortunes this floods over us! At length when it is too late, he recovers his senses and says, "I did not think." On another occasion he followed his own bent, or listened to the entreaties of others, and appointed corrupt public officials who overthrew the orderly functioning of the whole state. After a while he saw his mistake and said, "I did not think." That sort of wisdom is too expensive for the state, if all else has to be bought at the same high price. Hence the instruction of the prince in accordance with established principles and ideas must take precedence over all else so that he may gain his knowledge from theory and not experience. Long experience which youth precludes will be supplied by the advice of older men.[47]

Do not think you may do anything you please, as foolish women and flatterers are in the habit of telling princes. School yourself so that nothing pleases you which is not suitable. Remember that what is proper for private citizens, is not necessarily becoming in you. What is just a little mistake on the part of anyone else, is a disgrace in connection with a prince. The more others allow you, the less you should permit yourself. As others indulge you, so you should check yourself.[48] Even when everyone marks you with approval, be your own severest critic. Your life is open to all — you cannot hide

THE PRINCE MUST NOT INDULGE HIMSELF

yourself. You have either to be a good man for the common good, or a bad one, bringing general destruction.[49] As more honors are heaped upon you by everyone, you must make a special effort to see that you deserve them. No fitting honors or gratitude can ever be shown a good prince; no punishment can be bad enough for an evil prince. There is nothing in life better than a wise and good monarch; there is no greater scourge than a foolish or a wicked one. The corruption of an evil prince spreads more swiftly and widely than the scourge of any pestilence. In the same proportion a wholesome life on the part of the prince is, without question, the quickest and shortest way to improve public morals. The common people

[47] Cf. Cicero De off. I. 34. 122.
[48] Cf. Plutarch Discourse to an Unlearned Prince 2.
[49] Cf. ibid., 7; Xenophon Cyropaedia VIII. 7. 23.

imitate nothing with more pleasure than what they see their prince do.[50] Under a gambler, gambling is rife; under a warrior, everyone is embroiled [L 570]; under an epicure, all disport in wasteful luxury; under a debauché, license is rampant; under a cruel tyrant, everyone brings accusations and false witness. Go through your ancient history and you will find the life of the prince mirrored in the morals of his people. No comet, no dreadful power affects the progress of human affairs as the life of the prince grips and transforms the morals and character of his subjects.[51]

The studies and character of priests and bishops are a potent factor in this matter, I admit, but not nearly so much so as are those of princes. Men are more ready to decry the clergy if they sin than they are to emulate them in their good points. So it is that monks who are really pious do not excite people to follow their example because they seem only to be practicing what they preach. But on the other hand, if they are sinful everyone is shocked beyond measure. But there is no one who is not stimulated to follow in the footsteps of his prince! For this very reason the prince should take special care not to sin, because he makes so many followers in his wrongdoings, but rather to devote himself to being virtuous so that so many more good men may result.

*THE EXAMPLE OF THE PRINCE IS MOST EFFECTIVE*

*THE GOOD PRINCE*

A beneficent prince, as Plutarch [52] in his great learning said, is a living likeness of God, who is at once good and powerful. His goodness makes him want to help all; his power makes him able to do so. On the other hand, an evil prince, who is like a plague to his country, is the incarnation of the devil, who has great power joined with his wickedness. All his resources to the very last, he uses for the undoing of the human race. Was not each of these, Nero, Caligula, Heliogabalus, a sort of evil genius in the world? [B 440] They were plagues to the world during their lives, and their very memory is open to the curse of all mankind. When you who are a prince, a Christian

*THE BAD PRINCE*

---

50 Cf. Xenophon *Agesilaus* 7. 2; *Cyropaedia* VIII. 1. 21; Isocrates *To Nicocles* 31; Cicero *Rep.* II. 42. 69.
51 Cf. Cicero *Laws* III. 14. 31.
52 *Discourse to an Unlearned Prince* 3.

prince, hear and read that you are the likeness of God and his vicar, do not swell with pride on this account, but rather take pains that you correspond to your wonderful archetype, whom it is hard, but not unseemly, to follow.[53]

Christian theology attributes three prime qualities to God — the highest power, the greatest wisdom, the greatest goodness. In so far as you can you should make this trinity yours. Power without goodness is unmitigated tyranny; without wisdom it brings chaos, not domain. In the first place, then, in so much as fortune gave you power, make it your duty to gain for yourself the best store of wisdom possible, so you may clearly see the objectives to be striven for and the courses to avoid. In the next place, try to fill as many needs as possible for everyone, for that is the province of goodness. Make your power serve you to this end, that you can be of as much assistance as you want to be. But no, your desire in this respect should always exceed your means! On the other hand, always cause less hurt than you could have caused.

THREE
COMPONENTS
IN THE
PRINCE AS
IN GOD

God is loved by all good men. Only the wicked fear Him, and even they have only that fear which all men have of harm befalling them. In like manner, a good prince should strike awe into the heart of none but the evildoers and criminals; and yet even to them he should hold out a hope of leniency, if only they reform. On the other hand, his Satanic majesty is beloved of no one, and is feared by all, especially the virtuous, for the wicked are his appropriate attendants. Likewise a tyrant is hated by every good man, and none are closer to him than the worst element in society. This was clearly seen by St. Denis,[54] who divided the world into three hierarchies: what God is in the heavenly concourse, that should the bishop be in the church, and the prince in the state. He is supreme, and from him flows the fountain of all his goodness. No condition can be more absurd than that in which the greatest portion of all the state's misfortunes arise from him who should be the fountainhead of goodness. The common people are

---

[53] Cf., *inter alios*, Ambrosiaster (Pseudo-Augustine) *Quaest. Vet. et Novi Test.* XCI. 8; XXXV.

[54] *De ecclesiastica hierarchia* V. 2.

unruly by nature, and magistrates are easily corrupted through avarice or ambition. There is just one blessed stay in this tide of evils — the unsullied character of the prince. If he, too, is overcome by foolish ideas and base desires, what last ray of hope is there for the state?

As God is good in all his beneficence and does not need the attendant services of anyone nor ask any recompense, so it should be with the prince who is really great — who is the likeness of the Eternal Prince. He should freely do works of kindness for everyone without thought of compensation or glory. God placed a beautiful likeness of Himself in the heavens — the sun. Among mortal men he set up a tangible and living image of himself — the king.[55] The sun is freely shared by all and imparts its light to the rest of the heavenly bodies. The prince should be readily accessible for all the needs of his people. He should be a virgin source of wisdom in himself, so that he may never become benighted, however blind everyone else may be.

GOD AND THE GOOD PRINCE COMPARED

God is swayed by no emotions, yet he rules the universe with supreme judgment. The prince should follow His example in all his actions, cast aside all personal motives, and use only reason and judgment. God is sublime. The prince should be removed as far as possible from the low concerns of the common people and their sordid desires.

No one sees God in his government of the universe, but only feels Him and His kindness. The prince's native land should not feel his powers, except when its troubles are mitigated through his wisdom and goodness. On the other hand, tyrants are nowhere experienced, except to the sorrow of all. When the sun is highest in the zodiac, then its motion is slowest: so it is with you, the prince. The higher you are carried by fortune, the more lenient and less stern you should be.[56] Loftiness of spirit is not shown by the fact that you will tolerate no

---

[55] Cf. Plutarch *Discourse to an Unlearned Prince* 3. The unusually close similarity of this passage to that of Erasmus is striking, but Erasmus does not mention Plutarch here. Since Erasmus edited some of Plutarch's works, including this essay, the indebtedness can hardly be doubted.

[56] Cf. Plutarch, *loc. cit.*, 6.

affronts, that you allow no one greater empire than your own, but rather that you consider it improper to admit of anything unbecoming a prince.

All slavery is pitiable and dishonorable, but the lowest and most wretched form is slavery to vice and degrading passions. REAL What more abject and disgraceful condition can there be than SERVITUDE that in which the prince, who holds imperial authority over free men, is himself a slave to lust, irascibility, avarice, ambition, and all the rest of that malicious category?[57]

It is an established fact that among the pagans there were some who preferred death for themselves to defending the empire with great waste of human life — men who set the CODRUS welfare of the state above their own lives.[58] What an outrag-AND OTHO eous condition it is, then, for a Christian prince to be concerned with his pleasures and vicious passions in a period of great calamity to the state? When you assume the principate, do not think how much honor is bestowed upon you, but consider rather the great burden of care you have assumed. Do not expend only your wealth and income but also a good deal of thought. Do not think that you have plundered a ship but rather that you have taken the wheel.

[B 441] According to Plato,[59] no one is fit to rule who has not assumed the rule unwillingly and only after persuasion. For whoever strives after the princely place must of necessity either be a fool or else not realize how fraught with care and trial the kingly office really is, or he may be so wicked a man that he plans to use the royal power for his own benefit, not for that of the state, or so negligent that he does not carry out the task he assumed. To be a fit ruler, the prince should at the same time be diligent, good, and wise.

The greater your dominion, the greater care you must exercise to keep down your conceit. Remember that you are thereby shouldering greater cares and responsibilities and that you are bound to give less and less to your leisure and pleasures. Only

---

[57] Cf. Augustine *Civ. Dei.* XIX. 15; see also *ibid.,* IV. 3.

[58] Cf. Augustine *Civ. Dei.* XVIII. 19; Cicero *De off.* III. 27. 100.

[59] *Rep.* I. 347, see also *ibid.,* VII. 520; Cicero *Rep.* I. 17. 27; Augustine *Civ. Dei* XIX. 19.

those who govern the state not for themselves but for the good of the state itself, deserve the title "prince." His titles mean nothing in the case of one who rules to suit himself and measures everything to his own convenience: he is no prince, but a tyrant. There is no more honorable title than "prince," and there is no term more detested and accursed than "tyrant." There is the same difference between a prince and a tyrant as there is between a conscientious father and a cruel master.[60] The former is ready and willing to give even his life for his children; the latter thinks of nothing else than his own gain, or indulges his caprices to his own taste, with no thought to the welfare of his subjects. Do not be satisfied just because you are called "king" or "prince." Those scourges of the earth, Phalaris and Dionysius, had those titles. Pass your own judgment on yourself [L 572]. If Seneca [61] was right, the distinction between tyrant and king is one of fact, not of terminology.

To summarize: In his *Politics* Aristotle [62] differentiates between a prince and a tyrant on the basis that the one is interested in his own pursuits and the other is concerned for the state. No matter what the prince is deliberating about, he always keeps this one thing in mind: "Is this to the advantage of all my subjects?" A tyrant only considers whether a thing will contribute to his cause. A prince is vitally concerned with the needs of his subjects, even while engaged in personal matters. On the other hand, if a tyrant ever chances to do something good for his subjects, he turns that to his own personal gain. Those who look out for their people only in so far as it redounds to their personal advantage, hold their subjects in the same status as the average man considers his horse or ass. For these men take care of their animals, but all the care they give them is judged from the advantage to themselves, not to the animals. But anyone who despoils the people with his rapacity, or wracks them with his cruelty, or subjects them to all sorts of perils to satisfy his ambition, considers free

How the Tyrant Differs from a King

---

[60] Cf. Xenophon *Cyropaedia* VIII. 1. 1; Seneca *De clementia* I. 14. 2.
[61] *De clementia* I. 13. 1.          [62] *Pol.* IV. 10.

citizens even cheaper than the common folk value their draft animals or the fencing master his slaves.

The prince's tutor shall see that a hatred of the very words "tyranny" and "dominion" are implanted in the prince. He shall often utter diatribes against those names, accursed to the whole human race — Phalaris, Mezentius, Dionysius of Syracuse, Nero, Caligula, and Domitian who wanted to be called "God and Lord." [63] On the other hand, if he finds any examples of good princes who are as different as possible from the tyrant he should zealously bring them forth with frequent praise and commendation. Then let him create the picture of each, and impress upon mind and eye, to the extent of his capabilities, the king and the tyrant, so that the prince may burn to emulate the one and detest the latter even more [than before].

Let the teacher paint a sort of celestial creature, more like to a divine being than a mortal: complete in all the virtues; THE PICTURE born for the common good; yea, sent by the God above to OF THE GOOD help the affairs of mortals by looking out and caring for every- PRINCE one and everything; to whom no concern is of longer standing or more dear than the state; who has more than a paternal spirit toward everyone; who holds the life of each individual dearer than his own; who works and strives night and day for just one end — to be the best he can for everyone; with whom rewards are ready for all good men and pardon for the wicked, if only they will reform — for so much does he want to be of real help to his people, without thought of recom- pense, that if necessary he would not hesitate to look out for their welfare at great risk to himself; who considers his wealth to lie in the advantages of his country; who is ever on the watch so that everyone else may sleep deeply; who grants no leisure to himself so that he may spend his life in the peace of his country; who worries himself with continual cares so that

[63] Cf. on Phalaris, e.g., Plutarch *A Philosopher Is to Converse with Great Men* 3; Aristotle *Pol.* V. 10; Seneca *De ira* II. 5; on Dionysius, e.g., Plutarch *loc. cit.,* and *Dion* 7; Aristotle *loc. cit.*; on Nero, Caligula, and Domitian, e.g., see Suetonius *Lives of the Caesars*; on Domitian in particular, Suetonius *Dom.* 13.

his subjects may have peace and quiet.[64] Upon the moral qualities of this one man alone depends the felicity of the state.
Let the tutor point this out as the picture of a true prince!

Now let him bring out the opposite side by showing a frightful, loathsome beast, formed of a dragon, wolf, lion, viper,
bear, and like creatures; [65] with six hundred eyes all over it,
teeth everywhere, fearful from all angles, and with hooked   PICTURE
claws; with never satiated hunger, fattened on human vitals,   OF THE EVIL
and reeking with human blood; never sleeping, but always   PRINCE
threatening the fortunes and lives of all men; dangerous to
everyone, especially to the good; a sort of fatal scourge to the
whole world, on which everyone who has the interests of state
at heart pours forth execration and hatred; which cannot be
borne because of its monstrousness and yet cannot be overthrown without great disaster to the city because its malicious-
ness is hedged about with armed forces and wealth [B 442].
This is the picture of a tyrant — unless there is something
more odious which can be depicted. Monsters of this sort were
Claudius and Caligula. The myths in the poets also showed
Busyris, Pentheus, and Midas, whose names are now objects
of hate to all the human race, to be of the same type.

The main object of a tyrant is to follow his own caprices,
but a king follows the path of right and honor. Reward to a
tyrant is wealth; to a king, honor, which follows upon virtue.[66]
The tyrants' rule is marked by fear, deceit, and machinations
of evil. The king governs through wisdom, integrity, and
beneficence.[67] The tyrant uses his imperial power for himself;   THE
the king, for the state. The tyrant guarantees safety for him-   DIFFERENCE
self by means of foreign attendants and hired brigands. The   BETWEEN A
king deems himself safe through his kindness to his subjects   A TYRANT
and their love for him in return.[68] Those citizens who are distinguished for their moral character, judgment, and prestige
are held under suspicion and distrust by the tyrant.[69] The king,

[64] Cf. Augustine *Civ. Dei.* V. 24; see also Seneca *De clementia* I. 13. 4, 5.
[65] The Latin is *monstra*, "monsters."
[66] Cf. Aristotle *Pol.* V. 10.
[67] Cf. Plutarch *Discourse to an Unlearned Prince* 4.
[68] Cf. Seneca *De clementia* I. 13. 1.
[69] Cf. Plato *Rep.* VIII. 567; Aristotle *Pol.* V. 10.

however, cleaves to these same men as his helpers and friends. The tyrant is pleased either with stupid dolts, on whom he imposes; or with wicked men, whom he puts to evil use in defending his position as tyrant; or with flatterers, from whom he hears only praise which he enjoys. It is just the opposite with a king; every wise man by whose counsel he can be helped is very dear to him. The better each man is, the higher he rates him, because he can rely on his allegiance. He loves honest friends, by whose companionship he is bettered. Kings and tyrants have many hands and many eyes, but they are very different.[70] A tyrant's aim is to get the wealth of his subjects in the hands of a few, and those the wickedest, and fortify his power by the weakened strength of his subjects. The king considers that his purse is represented by the wealth of his subjects; the tyrant strives to have everyone answerable to him either by law or informers. The king rejoices in the freedom of his people; the tyrant strives to be feared, the king to be loved. The tyrant looks upon nothing with greater suspicion than the harmonious agreement of good men and of cities; good princes especially rejoice in this. A tyrant is happy to stir up factions and strife between his subjects and feeds and aids chance animosities. This means he basely uses for the safeguarding of his tyranny. A king has this one interest: to foster peaceful relations between his subjects and straightway to adjust such dissensions among them as chance to arise, for he believes that they are the worst menace to the state that can happen. When a tyrant sees that affairs of state are flourishing, he trumps up some pretext, or even invites in some enemy, so as to start a war and thereby weaken the powers of his own people.[71] The opposite is true of a king. He does everything and allows everything that will bring everlasting peace to his country, for he realizes that war is the source of all misfortunes to the state. The tyrant either sets up laws, constitutions, edicts, treaties, and all things sacred and profane to his own personal preservation or else perverts them to that

[70] Xenophon *Cyropaedia* VIII. 2. 10.
[71] Cf. Plato *Rep.* VIII. 567.

end. The king judges everything by the standard of its value to the state.

Most of the marks or schemes of a tyrant have been set forth at great length by Aristotle [72] in his *Politics*; but he sums them up under three points. The tyrant is first concerned to see that his subjects neither wish to nor dare to rise against his tyrannical rule; next, that they do not trust one another; and thirdly, that they cannot attempt a revolution. He accomplishes his first end by allowing his subjects to develop no spirit at all and no wisdom, by keeping them like slaves and devoted to mean stations in life, or held accountable by a system of spies, or rendered effeminate through pleasure. He knows full well that noble and acute spirits do not tolerate a tyranny with good grace. He accomplishes his second point by stirring up dissension and mutual hatred among his subjects so that one accuses the other and he himself is more powerful as a result of their misfortunes. The third he attains by using every means to reduce the wealth and prestige of any of his subjects, and especially the good men, to a limit which no sane man would want to approach and would dispair of attaining. *THE THREE WICKEDEST SCHEMES OF A TYRANT*

A prince should keep as far as possible from all such ideas, yes, *tout au contraire*,[73] i.e., be clearly separated from them and this is especially true of a Christian prince. If Aristotle, who was a pagan and a philosopher too, painted such a picture among men who were not holy and learned in the Scriptures, how much more is it fit for one who moves in the place of Christ to fulfill the task?

Even in the dumb animals we may find comparisons to both king and tyrant. The king bee [74] has the biggest quarters, but in the middle of the hive, which is the safest place. He is relieved of all physical work, but is the overseer of the work of the others. If he is lost, the whole swarm will break up. Besides, the king is distinguished in form from the others, both as to size and shiny appearance. But according to Seneca [75] *IMAGE OF THE PRINCE*

---

[72] *Pol.* V. 11.          [73] The text reads ἐκ διαμέτρου.

[74] Erasmus again follows the erroneous practice of the ancients in referring to the queen bee as the "king bee."

[75] *De clementia* I. 19. 2, 3.

this is the most outstanding difference, that although bees rise
to such a pitch of anger that they leave their stings in the
wound, yet the king alone has no sting. Nature did not want
him to be cruel and seek vengeance appropriate to a great
personage, and so she withheld his weapon and left his wrath
ineffectual. This should be a great pattern for mighty kings.

[L 574] If you want a comparison for the tyrant, take the
lion, bear, wolf, or eagle, all of which live on their mangled
prey. Since they know they are open to the hatred of everyone
and are beset with ambuscades all around them, they dwell
on rugged cliffs, or hide away in caverns and desolate regions
— unless perchance the tyrant exceeds the savageness even of
TYRANTS these beasts. [B 443] Huge snakes, panthers, lions, and all the
ARE MORE other beasts that are condemned on the charge of savageness
SAVAGE THAN
WILD BEASTS do not rage one against the other, but beasts of like characteristics are safe together. But the tyrant, who is a man, turns
his bestial cruelty against his fellow men and fellow citizens.
In the Holy Scriptures [76] God described the tyrant in these
words:

This will be the manner of the king that shall reign over you: He will
take your sons, and appoint them for himself, for his chariots, and to be
his horsemen; and some shall run before his chariots. And he will appoint him captains over thousands, and captains over fifties; and will set
them to ear his ground, and to reap his harvest, and to make his instruments of war, and instruments of his chariots. And he will take your
daughters to be confectionaries, and to be cooks, and to be bakers. And
he will take your fields, and your vineyards, and your oliveyards, even the
best of them, and give them to his servants. And he will take the tenth
of your seed, and of your vineyards, and give to his officers, and to his
servants. And he will take your menservants, and your maidservants, and
your goodliest young men, and your asses, and put them to his work. He
will take the tenth of your sheep: and ye shall be his servants. And ye
shall cry out in that day because of your king which ye shall have chosen
you; and the Lord will not hear you in that day.

And do not be exercised because he calls him "king" instead
of "tyrant," for of old the title of "king" was as hateful as
that of "tyrant." And since there is no greater benefit than a
good king, why did God in his anger order this image to be set

[76] I *Sam.* 8:11-18.

up before the people, by which he might deter them from seeking a king? He said the power of kings (*ius regium*) was the
power of tyrants (*ius tyrannicum*). Yet Samuel had been a good
king and governed his people's affairs justly and honestly for
many years; but they did not realize their happiness, and, as
is the way of people, begged their king to rule with arrogance
and violence. And yet in this image what a large part consists
of the evils which within our memory we have discovered even
in some Christian princes, to the great misfortune of the whole
world!

Now we come to the description of a good prince, which
God himself gives in the book of *Deuteronomy*.[77] When a king
is established over you,

he shall not multiply horses to himself, nor cause the people to return to
Egypt, to the end that he should multiply horses: ... Neither shall he multiply wives to himself, that his heart turn not away: neither shall he greatly multiply to himself silver and gold. And it shall be when he sitteth upon
the throne of his kingdom, that he shall write him a copy of this law in a
book out of that which is before the priests the Levites: And it shall be
with him, and he shall read therein all the days of his life: that he may
learn to fear the Lord his God, to keep all the words of this law and these
statutes, to do them: That his heart be not lifted up above his brethren,
and that he turn not aside from the commandment, to the right hand,
or to the left: to the end that he may prolong his days in his kingdom,
he, and his children, in the midst of Israel.

DESCRIPTION
OF A GOOD
PRINCE

If a Hebrew king is bidden to learn the law, which gave but
the merest shadowy outlines of justice, how much more is it
fitting for a Christian prince to follow steadfastly the teachings of the Gospels? If He does not wish the king of Judea to
be exalted over his people, but wishes to call them brothers
instead of slaves, how much less does it become a Christian
[prince] to call them slaves whom Christ himself, the Prince
of princes, called brothers?

Now this is what Ezekiel [78] says of a tyrant: "[Her]
princes in the midst thereof are like wolves ravening the prey,
to shed blood." Plato [79] calls princes the guardians of the state,
in that they may be for their country what dogs are for the

[77] 17:16-20.        [78] 22:27.        [79] *Rep.* III. 416.

flocks; but if the dogs should be turned into wolves what hope
would there be for the flocks. Again, in another place [80] he
calls a cruel and rapacious prince a "lion," and in still another [81] he inveighs against shepherds who are taking good care
of themselves, instead of giving attention to their flocks, and
believes that they are like princes who use their power for
themselves alone. And in reference to Nero, Paul [82] said,
"I was delivered out of the mouth of the lion." Now see how
Solomon,[83] in his wisdom, pictured a tyrant with almost the
same idea in mind: "As a roaring lion, and a ranging bear,
so is a wicked ruler over the poor people." And in another
passage he says, "When the wicked beareth rule, the people
mourn" as if surrendered to slavery. In still another, "When
the wicked rise, men hide themselves." There is another in
"Isaiah," [84] according to which the Lord is angry at the misdeeds of the people and threatens them, saying, "And I will
give children to be their princes, and babes shall rule over
them." Can this mean anything else than that no more dire calamity can befall a country than a stupid and impious prince?

But why go on with all this? Christ himself, who is the *one*
Prince and Lord of all, has most clearly set off the Christian
prince from the pagan, saying,[85] "The princes of the Gentiles
exercise dominion over them, and they that are great exercise
authority upon them. But it shall not be so among you." If it is
THE PRINCE  the part of pagan princes to exercise dominion, it does not
ACCORDING  then become Christian princes. But what is the meaning of this
TO THE
GOSPEL  phrase "but it shall not be so among you," unless that the
same thing is not proper for Christians, with whom the principate is [only a matter of] administration, not imperial power, and kingly authority is [a matter of] service, not tyranny.[86]
And no prince should ease his conscience by saying, "These
things are for the bishops, not for me!" They surely are for
you — if you are really a Christian. If you are not, nothing
pertains to you! And do not get excited if perchance you find

---

[80] *Ibid.*, IX. 588.  [81] *Ibid.*, I. 345.  [82] II *Tim.* 4:17.
[83] *Prov.* 28:15; 29:2; 28:28.  [84] 3:4.  [85] *Matt.* 20:25-26.
[86] Augustine *Civ. Dei.* V. 12.

some bishops that have fallen far from this standard. Let them see to what they are doing. Give your attention to what is becoming in yourself.

[B 444] Do not consider yourself a good prince, just because you appear less wicked by comparison with others. And do not think it is correct to do a thing, just because the great run of princes do it. Hold yourself of your own accord to a rule of honor and judge yourself according to it.[87] Even if there be no one for you to surpass, strive against yourself, for surely there is no emulation more honorable or truly worthy of an unconquered prince than a daily effort to be better. If the name, or better, the principles, of a tyrant are repulsive, they will not become more honorable if they are made common to many. If virtue depends on worldly condition, then it does not depend on [the qualities of individual] men. Seneca has expounded impressively that kings who have the inclination of brigands and pirates should be put in the same class with them. For it is the character, not the title, that marks the king.

In his *Politics* Aristotle [88] tells us that in some oligarchies it was customary for the magistrates-elect to take the following oath, "I will persecute the common people with hatred and will strive with all my power to bring trouble upon them." A prince about to assume his functions takes quite a different oath before his subjects. And yet we hear of some who have acted toward the people as if sworn by the old oath of the barbarians to be the open enemy of the affairs of the people in every way.

A BARBARIAN CUSTOM

Surely this savors of tyranny: the best thing for the prince, is the worst thing for the people; the good fortune of the one springs from the misfortunes of the other — just as if a *paterfamilias* ran his affairs so that he would become richer and more powerful through the ill fortunes of his family. Whoever wants to claim the title "prince" for himself and to shun the hated name "tyrant," ought to claim it for himself, not through deeds of horror and threats, but by acts of kindness. For it is of no significance if he is called "prince" and

[87] *Ibid.*    [88] *Pol.* V. 9.

"father of his country" by flatterers and the oppressed, when he is a tyrant in fact. And even if his own age fawns upon him, posterity will not. You can see with what colossal disgust succeeding generations treated the wicked deeds of those once awe-inspiring kings, whom no one dared offend by even a word during their lifetime, and how openly their very names were abominated. The good prince ought to have the same attitude toward his subjects, as a good *paterfamilias* toward his household — for what else is a kingdom but a great family? What is the king if not the father to a great multitude?

THE PRINCE IS THE FATHER OF ONE GREAT FAMILY
He is superior, but yet of the same stock — a man ruling man, a freeman over free men, not untamed beasts, as Aristotle justly comments,[89] and this is what those poets [90] of remotest antiquity meant when they applied to Jupiter — to whom they assign supreme authority of the whole world and the gods, as they say — these words, *père des hommes et des dieux*,[91] that is, "father of gods and men." We have been taught by Christ our teacher that God is the unquestioned prince of all the world, and we call Him "Father." But what is more revolting or accursed than that appellation in Homer,[92] *monstre dévorant ses sujets* [i.e., the devourer of his people],[93] which Achilles, [L 576] I think it is, applied to the prince who ruled for his own benefit, not for that of his subjects, for in his wrath he could find no more fitting epithet for him whom he considered unfit for rule than "man-eater." But Homer, in giving a man the honorary title of "king," calls him the *pasteur de peuple*,[94] "shepherd of the people." [95] There is a very great difference between a shepherd and a robber. On what apparent ground, then, do they take the title "prince" to themselves, who choose just a few of their subjects (and those only the most wicked) through whom by trickery, trumped-up pretexts, and suddenly-created titles, they sap the strength of the people and drain their wealth away at the same time?

---

[89] *Pol.* I. 5.    [90] Homer *Iliad* XV. 47.
[91] The original reads πατὴρ ἀνδρῶντε θεῶντε.
[92] *Ibid.*, I. 231.
[93] The original reads δημοβόρος βασιλεύς.
[94] The original reads ποιμήν λαῶν.    [95] *Ibid.*, I. 263.

What they have unmercifully extorted they transfer to their privy purse, or squander shamefully on pleasures, or spend in cruel wars. Each one that can appear as the cleverest knave in these matters, considers it of prime importance, just as if the prince were the enemy of the people, not the father, with the result that he especially seems to have the prince's concern at heart who bends every effort to thwart the prosperity of the people. As a *paterfamilias* thinks whatever increase of wealth has fallen to any of his house is [the same as if it had been] added to his own private goods, so he who has the true attitude of a prince considers the possessions of his subjects to represent his own wealth. Them he holds bound over to him through love, so that they have nothing to fear at all from the prince for either their lives or their possessions.

It will be worth our while to see how Julius Pollux,[96] who had been the boyhood tutor of Commodus, described to him the king and the tyrant. He at once ranked the king next to the gods, as being nearest and most like them. [B 445] Then he said:

Praise the king with these terms: [call him] "Father," mild, peaceful, lenient, foresighted, just, humane, magnanimous, frank. Say that he is no money-grabber nor a slave to his passions; that he controls himself and his pleasures; that he is rational, has keen judgment, is clear thinking and circumspect; that he is sound in his advice, just, sensible, mindful of religious matters, with a thought to the affairs of men; that he is reliable, steadfast, infallible, planning great things, endowed with influential judgment; that he works hard, accomplishes much, is deeply concerned for those over whom he rules and is their protector; that he is given to acts of kindness and slowly moved to vengeance; that he is true, constant, unbending, prone to the side of justice, ever attentive to remarks about the prince; that he is a check-and-balance on conduct; that he is readily accessible, affable in a gathering, agreeable to any who want to speak with him, charming, and open-countenanced; that he concerns himself for those subject to his rule and is fond of his soldiers; that he wages war with force and vigor, but does not seek opportunities for it; that he loves peace, tries to arrange peace, and holds steadily to it; that he is opposed to changing forcibly the ways of his people; that he knows how to be a leader and a prince and to establish beneficial laws; that he is born to attain honors and has the appearance of a god. There

EPITHETS OF A GOOD PRINCE

[96] *Onomasticon* I. 40-42.

are in addition many things which could be set forth in an address, but cannot be expressed in just a word or two.[97]

This has all been the thought of Pollux. If a pagan teacher developed such a pagan prince, [think] how much more venerable should be the likeness set up of a Christian prince!

Now see in what colors he painted the tyrant.

A wicked price you will censure with the following epithets: tyrant, cruel, savage, violent, property-snatcher, miserly (as Plato says),[98] one greedy for plunder, man-eater (as Homer says),[99] arrogant, proud, exclusive, unsocial, difficult of approach, unpleasant to speak to, hot tempered, irritable, frightful, raging, slave-to-passion, intemperate, immoderate, inconsiderate, inhuman, unjust, regardless of counsel, unfair, wicked, brainless, carefree, fickle, easily taken in, disagreeable, fierce, moody, incorrigible, abusive, instigator of wars, severe, a scourge, untractable, intolerable.[100]

NOTHING MORE HATEFUL TO GOD THAN A WICKED PRINCE

Since God is the very opposite of a tyrant, so it must follow unfailingly that there is nothing more loathsome to Him than a baneful king. Since no wild beast is more deadly than a tyrant, it consistently follows that there is nothing more odious to all mankind than a wicked prince. But who would want to live hated and accursed by gods and men alike? When the Emperor Augustus realized that there were many conspiracies against his life and that as soon as one was put down another straightway sprang up, he said it was not worth while to live if you were a bane to everyone and your personal safety was preserved only at the great cost of life among your subjects.[101] Furthermore, the kingdom is not only more peaceful and pleasant but will steadfastly endure for a longer time.

[97] Erasmus gives this passage, a direct quotation, in the original Greek. At the end of it he says, "Although the Latin language cannot render these phrases handsomely because of the peculiar quality of Greek, yet we will at least turn them into something which can be understood," and then he repeats the thought verbatim in Latin. It seemed to me far better to risk the charge of inconsistency by not turning this and the following quotation into French, as has been done with all other Greek passages, than to incur that of pedantry by doing so.

[98] Xenophon *Memorabilia* I. 2. 5.

[99] *Iliad* I. 231.

[100] Erasmus likewise gives this direct quotation in the Greek and repeats it verbatim in Latin with the introductory comment, "Of which words the following is approximately the thought."

[101] Cf. Seneca *De clementia* I. 9. 5.

For this we find ample proof in the annals of the ancients. No
tyranny is so firmly protected that it will endure for long. No Tyranny
Every state that has degenerated into a tyranny has rushed Long-lived
on into utter dissolution. It is meet for him who is feared by
all, to fear many; [102] and he cannot be safe, whom the majority
of men want removed.

In ancient times, those who ruled their empires well were
decreed divine honors. Toward tyrants the ancients had the Divine Honor
same law which we now apply to wolves and bears — the Given to<br>Good Kings
"reward" comes from the people who have had the enemy in
their very midst. In very early times, the kings were selected
through the choice of the people because of their outstanding
qualities, which were called "heroic" as being all but divine and Manly
superhuman. Princes should remember their beginnings, and Qualities<br>first Made
realize that they are not really princes if they lack that quality Kings
which first made princes.[103]

Although there are many types of state, it is the consensus
of nearly all wise-thinking men that the best form is monarchy.
This is according to the example of God that the sum of all Monarchy
things be placed in one individual but in such a way that, following God's example, he surpasses all others in his wisdom
and goodness and, wanting nothing, may desire only to help
his state. [B 446] But if conditions were otherwise, that would
be the worst form of state. Whosoever would fight it then
would be the best man. If a prince be found who is
complete in all good qualities, then pure and absolute
monarchy is the thing. (If that could only be! I fear it is too
great a thing even to hope for.) If an average prince (as the
affairs of men go now) is found, it will be better to have a
limited monarchy checked and lessened by aristocracy and
democracy. Then there is no chance for tyranny to creep in,
but just as the elements balance each other, so will the state
hold together under similar control. If a prince has the interests of the state at heart, his power is not checked on this
account, so it will be adjudged, but rather helped. If his atti-

102 Cf. Seneca *De ira* II. 11. 3.
103 Cf. Cicero *De off.* II. 12. 42; see also Aristotle *Pol.* III. 17; VII. 3.

tude is otherwise, however, it is expedient that the state break and turn aside the violence of a single man.[104]

Although there are many types of authority (man over beasts, master over slaves, father over children, husband over wife), yet Aristotle [105] believes that the rule of the king is finest of all and calls it especially favored of the gods because it seems to possess a certain something which is greater than mortal. But if it is divine to play the part of king, then nothing more suits the tyrant than to follow the ways of him who is most unlike God. A slave should be judged for his worth in comparison with a fellow slave, as the proverb [106] says, a master with a master, one art with another art, one performance of duty with another. [L 578] But a prince should excel in every kind of wisdom. That is the theory behind good government. It is the part of the master to order, of the servant to obey. The tyrant directs whatever suits his pleasure; the prince only what he thinks is best for the state. But how can anyone who does not know what is best direct it [to be done]? Or even worse, if he considers the wickedest things the most desirable, being utterly misled by his ignorance or personal feelings? As it is the function of the eye to see, of the ears to hear, of the nose to smell, so it is the part of the prince to look out for the affairs of his people. But there is only one means of deliberating on a question, and that is wisdom. If the prince lacks that, he can no more be of material assistance to the state than an eye can see when sight is destroyed.[107]

FROM
ARISTOTLE

Xenophon,[108] in his book called *Oeconomicus*, said that it is a divine rather than a human position to rule over free men at their own consent, but it is dishonorable to rule over dumb creatures, or slaves that are under compulsion. But man is a divinely-inspired animal, and free twice over: once by nature and again by his laws. It is the mark of the highest capacity and clearly of God's inspiration for a king to control his authority in such a way that his people feel only the benefits, not

104 Cf. Plato *Laws* IV. 709; see also Aristotle *Pol.* IV. 1; Plato *Rep.* IX. 580; Isocrates *To Nicocles* 26; Cicero *Rep.* I. 35. 54, 55; II. 23. 43.
105 *Pol.* IV. 2.        106 Aristotle *Pol.* I. 7.
107 Cf. Plato *Rep.* VI. 484, 506-7.        108 xxi. 12.

their subservient condition. Be careful not to consider as yours only those men whose services you employ in your cookshops, in your hunting, and in your domestic services, for very often no men are less yours, but consider all your subjects yours without distinction. If you single out any one at all, take a man of sterling qualities, patriotic and devoted to the state, as your nearest and closest associate. When you travel through the cities of your people, do not harbor such thoughts as these in your mind: "I am the master of these great possessions. All these places are subject to my will. I may do as I please here." But if you want to give some thought [to the occasion], as a good prince should, do so along these lines: "Everything has been placed in my trust; therefore, I must unceasingly strive to hand it over better than I received it." When you look upon the countless throng of your subjects, be careful not to think of them as so many slaves. Hold rather this thought: "These thousands of souls depend on my sincerity alone; they have entrusted themselves and the protection of all their worldly goods to me alone; they look upon me as a father. I can do good to these great numbers if I prove myself a good prince. I will bring harm upon even more if I am a bad prince. I must certainly exercise great care not to be unjust, lest I bring tribulation upon such vast numbers." Never forget that "dominion," "imperial authority," "kingdom," "majesty," "power" are all pagan terms, not Christian. The ruling power of a Christian state consists only of administration, kindness, and protection.

But if these words were to your liking, remember this idea also, which was known and handed down by the pagan philosophers, that the rule of a prince over his people is no different from that of the mind over the body. The mind dominates THE MIND the body because it knows more than the physical body, but it IN THE BODY does so to the great advantage of the latter rather than to itself.[109] The blessed fortune of the physical form is this rule of the mind. What the heart is in the body of a living creature,

[109] Cf. Aristotle *Pol.* I. 5; Plato *Rep.* IV. 441; Seneca *De clementia* I. 3. 5; Augustine *Civ. Dei.* IX. 9.

THE HEART
IN THE BODY

that the prince is in the state. If the heart is sound, it imparts life to the whole body, since it is the fountain of the blood and life spirit; but if it has been infected, it brings utter collapse to every part of the body. The heart is the last part of a living body to be broken down, and the very last traces of life are thought to survive in it. Consequently the prince should keep himself clean and undefiled from all corrupting folly whenever any such disease lays hold of the people. In a man it is the finely organized part (namely, the mind) that exercises the control. Likewise, in the mind it is its finest element, reason, that asserts itself. And God, who rules the universe, is the very essence of all things. Therefore, whosoever assumes the functions of rule in a state, as in a sort of great body, should excel all others in goodness, wisdom, and watchfulness. The prince should be superior to his officers in the same degree that they are to the common people. [B 447] If there is any evil in the mind it springs from infection, and contact with the body, which is subject to the passions. Any good that the body

RIDICULOUS
FOR THE
STATE TO BE
HARASSED BY
THE PRINCE

possesses is drawn from the mind as from a fountain. How unbelievable it would be and how contrary to nature, if ills should spread from the mind down into the body, and the health of the body be corrupted by the viscious habits of the mind. It would be just as absurd for wars, seditious uprisings, profligate morals, debased laws, corrupt officials, and every similar curse to a state, to spring from the prince whose wisdom should lay the storms stirred up by the folly of the common folk. But we often see states (*civitates*),[110] well established and flourishing under the diligent activity of the people, overthrown by mismanagement of the princes. How unlike a Christian it is to take pleasure in the title "Master," which many who were not in the fold of Christ have shunned; that which in their ambition they desire to be but do not want to be called because of the odium attached to the name. Yet will a

THE PRINCE
IS A FATHER,
NOT A
MASTER

Christian prince think it just in the eyes of God for him to be the same [sort of man] and be called "The Magnificent?" The emperor Augustus, even though he had gained the im-

110 The translation "cities" is also possible here.

perial throne through foul intrigue, considered it an insult to be called "Master;" and when this title was used by an actor before all the people, he showed his disapproval by his facial expression and his remarks, as if it were a term of reproach applied to tyrants.[111] And shall the Christian prince not imitate this propriety of the pagan? If you are master of all your subjects, they must of necessity be your slaves. Then have a care that you do not fulfill the ancient proverb: [112] "You have as many enemies as you have slaves."

Nature created all men equal, and slavery was superimposed on nature, which fact the laws of even the pagans recognized. Now stop and think how out of proportion it is for a Christian to usurp full power over other Christians, whom the laws did not design to be slaves, and whom Christ redeemed from all slavery. Recall the instance when Paul [113] called Onesimus (who was born a slave) the brother of his former master Philemon, from the time of his baptism. How incongruous it is to consider them slaves whom Christ redeemed with the same blood [as He did you]; whom He declared free along with all others; whom He fostered with the same sacraments as He did you; whom He calls to the same heritage of immortality! And over them, who have the same Master as you, the Prince, Jesus Christ, will you impose the yoke of slavery?

A PRINCE RULES FREE MEN

There is only one Master of Christian men.[114] Why, then, do those who assume His functions, prefer to take their pattern of government from anyone except Him, who alone is in all ways to be imitated? It is proper enough to gather from others whatever virtues they have; but in Him is the perfect example of all virtue and wisdom. This seems the [essence of] foolishness to those outside the faith, but to us, if we are really faithful, He is the goodness of God and the wisdom of God. Now I do not want you to think that this means that

CHRIST IS THE PERFECT PATTERN

---

[111] Cf. Suetonius *op. cit., Aug.* 53.

[112] Quoted in Macrobius *Sat.* I. 11. 13; Seneca *Ep. Mor.* XLVII. 5; Quintus Curtius Rufus VII. 8. 28; and Festus, *s. v. quot.*

[113] *Col.* 4:9.

[114] Cf. *Matt.* 23:10.

you should be a slave, not a ruler. On the contrary, it illustrates the finest way to rule, unless, of course, you think God is only a bondsman because He governs the whole universe without recompense, because everyone and everything has felt His kindness, although they give Him nothing in return, and unless the mind seems a slave because it looks out so zealously for the welfare of the body, which it does not need, or unless you think the eye is a slave to all the other parts of the body because it sees for them all. You may well consider this: if someone should turn all these men whom you call your own

AN ARGU-
MENT FROM
MYTHOLOGY

into swine and asses by the art of Circe, would you not say your ruling power had been reduced to a lower level? I think you would. And yet you may exercise more authority over swine and asses than over men. You may treat them as you please, divide them off as you will, and even kill them. Surely he who has reduced his free subjects to slaves has put his power on a meaner level. The loftier the ideal to which you fashion your authority, the more magnificently and splendidly will you rule. Whoever protects the liberty and standing of your subjects is the one that helps your sovereign power. God gave the angels and men free will so that He would not be ruling over bondsmen, and so that He might glorify and add

GOD WISHED
TO RULE
FREE MEN

further grandeur to His kingdom. And who, now, would swell with pride because he rules over men cowed down by fear, like so many cattle?

Do not overlook the words of the Gospels or of the writings of the Apostles on the toleration of a master, on obeying the prefects, on honoring kings, and on paying tributes. These must have been directed to pagan princes because at that time

INTERPRETA-
TION OF THE
COMMAND,
"OBEY THOSE
SET OVER
YOU," ETC.

there were no Christian princes. The people are bidden to endure worthless magistrates, so as not to disrupt the order of the state, provided that they perform their duties and do not give orders that are opposed to God. If the pagan prince demands honor, Paul [115] bids him be honored; if he demands that taxes be paid, Paul desires the taxes to be paid; if he demands tribute, Paul orders the tribute paid. For a Christian

[115] *Rom.* 13:1-7.

is not lowered by such acts, and the princes have certain peculiar rights and are not to be angered just because there is an opportunity. But what does he add about Christians? [116] Do not owe anything to one another unless it be in such a way that you may still love one another. Surely you do not believe that Christ really owed tribute to Caesar just because He is said to have paid him a didrachma! [L 580] According to the Gospel,[117] when He was treacherously asked whether a people which had been dedicated to God should pay tribute to Caesar, He bade them bring Him a coin. He did not recognize it, and as if He did not know, He asked: "Whose is this image and superscription?" [B 448] When they told Him it was Caesar's, He gave His ambiguous answer to those who were tempting Him in their wickedness: "Render therefore unto Caesar the things which are Caesar's; and unto God, the things that are God's." Thus He outwitted them in their treacherous questioning and took the opportunity of calling all to devotion to God, to whom we owe everything. This is really what He meant: "You see what you owe to Caesar, whom I do not know; see rather what you owe to God. It is His work I am carrying out, not Caesar's." I hope that my remarks have not caused any such questions as this to arise in the minds of anyone: "Why do you deprive the prince of his own rights, and grant more to a pagan than to a Christian?" That is not so. I defend the rights of the Christian prince. To subject his people through fear, to make them perform servile tasks, to drive them from their possessions, despoil them of their goods, and finally, even to martyr them — those are the rights of a pagan prince. You certainly do not want the same things in a Christian, do you? Or will his rights seem diminished if these same privileges are not allowed him?

THE RIGHT OF CAESAR ACCORDING TO THE GOSPEL

He does not lose his prerogatives, who rules as a Christian should; he has them in a different way and is as much more distinguished as he is safe. The following arguments will make that clear. First, those are not really yours whom you oppress in slavery, for common agreement makes princes. But they are

TRUE RIGHTS OF A PRINCE

[116] Rom. 13:8.     [117] Matt. 22:17-22.

really yours who yield obedience to you willingly and of their own accord. Secondly, when you hold people bound to you through fear, you do not possess them even half. You have their physical bodies, but their spirits are estranged from you. But when Christian love unites the people and their prince, then everything is yours that your position demands, for a good prince does not demand anything for which service to his country does not call. On the other hand, when he uses the authority of a master instead of kindness, however much he may exact certainly he has less than if he had everything. No one gets more than he who makes no levies but gets everything as his just due. According to these standards, the honor which is shown a tyrant is no honor at all but either flattery or dissembling; and he gets no obedience, but slavish compliance. His is not real splendor, but only arrogance. He does not possess authority, but only force. All these things in their true form are possessed by the really Christian prince. No one gets

TRUE HONOR more honor than the man who does not exact it. To no one are men more willingly obedient than to him who does not seek such attention. To no one do they more willingly pour out their wealth than to him whom they know will expend it for the development of the state and return it with interest.

There is a common relation between the prince and the
THE people. To you the people owe money, allegiance, and honor.
MUTUAL That is all very well; but you in turn owe the people a good
RIGHTS OF
THE PEOPLE and careful prince. Before you exact taxes from your subjects
AND THE as your due, question yourself first whether you have fulfilled
PRINCE your obligation and duties toward them. Aristotle [118] says clearly that the theory of supreme authority is not in the possession, but rather in the use of slaves. Very well; but much
FROM less does the principate consist of titles and statues and the
ARISTOTLE'S collection of moneys than in giving thought for others.
POLITICS
Since the state is a sort of body, composed of various members including the prince himself, it befits him, although different [from the others], to use moderation so that things will go well for everyone and not [to act] in such a way that when

[118] *Pol.* I. 7.

all others have been reduced to weakness, one or two healthy and strong members may be developed. But if the prince rejoices in, and is supported by, evils he is not part of the state. He is no prince; he is a brigand.

Aristotle [119] says that the slave is a living part of the master if the latter is the right kind of master. At any rate there is a friendly relationship of the part and the whole and a mutual need each for the other. If this is true between a master and a slave bought at the block, as they say, how much more true should it be between a Christian who is of poor birth and a Christian prince? As for the prince who can think of nothing else and do nothing else except to extort as much money as possible from his subjects, to see how much more he can gather in by his laws and for how much he can sell his magistracies and offices — is he really to be called a prince, or should he be called a business agent, or, to speak more to the point, a robber?

When Croesus saw the soldiers of Cyrus running madly and with wild tumult through the captured city, he asked what they were doing. When told by Cyrus that they were following the custom of the victorious army and were plundering the goods of the people, he said, "What is this I hear? Do not all these things belong to you who have conquered me? Why, then, are your men despoiling your own possessions?" Acting on this thought, Cyrus checked his soldiers in their plundering.[120] It will be well for the prince to keep this same idea in mind [and say to himself], "Those things which are being extorted, are really mine. Those people who are being despoiled and weakened are really my subjects. Whatever sins I commit against them, I commit against myself." See that you conduct your rule so that you may readily give account of your acts. You should be more exacting of yourself if no one else is going to call you to account, for it will shortly happen that He will demand account of you. With Him the only effect of your being a prince will be [the fact] that you will be judged more severely in proportion to the great power entrusted to you.

THE PRINCE HURTS HIMSELF WHEN HE INJURES THE PROPERTIES OF HIS PEOPLE

[119] *Pol.* I. 6.        [120] Cf. Herodotus I. 88.

Even if you were monarch of the whole world, you could not deceive this Judge, nor escape Him, nor frighten Him, nor bribe Him.

After you have once dedicated yourself to the state, you are no longer free to live according to your own ways. You must keep up and preserve the character which you have assumed. No one enters the Olympic games without first considering what the rules of the contest demand. [B 449] And he does not complain that the sun is bothersome, or the dust, or the perspiration, or any of the other things of this sort. All these are included in the general conditions of the sport. Likewise the man who undertakes to rule should first consider what the position of prince demands. He must give his thought to the best advantage of others and neglect his personal interests. He must always be alert so that others may sleep. He must

toil so that others may rest. He must exhibit the highest moral integrity, while in others a general appearance of uprightness is enough. His mind must be divested of all private emotions. He who is carrying on the offices of the state must give his attention to nothing but that. He must perform kindnesses even to those who are ungrateful, to those who do not understand, and to those who are opposed. If these conditions are not to your liking, why do you desire the burden of ruling? Or if you inherited this authority, why do you not yield it to another? But if this is not possible, at least put the actual execution of the duties in the hands of some one who meets the requirements you should have.

A philosopher [121] among the Greeks very wisely said that

IT IS A
MATTER OF
GREAT DIFFI-
CULTY, BUT
OF GREAT
HONOR, TO
RULE WELL

the best things are the difficult ones. Accordingly you should remember that it is alike the honorable and the most difficult thing to stand out as a good prince. And do not be concerned if at this time you see some princes living in such a way that it would be harder to be an average *paterfamilias* than a prince of that sort. The old proverb [122] is by no means without foundation: "He ought to have been born either a king or a

[121] Plutarch *Training of Children* 9; cf. also Plato *Rep.* VI. 497.
[122] Quoted in Seneca *Apocolocyntosis* 1.

fool." All other men take great pains to get previous knowledge of the profession which they follow. How much more care should the prince take to get an early knowledge of the theory of government! Other arts are developed from four main essentials: inherent nature, instruction, precedent, and experience. Plato [123] demands a quiet and mild nature in a prince. He says that men of sharp and excitable nature are suited to a military career, but they are entirely unfit for governing. There are certain moral defects of nature which can be corrected by training and care. But it is conceivable to find a character either so dull, or else so wild and untractable, that it would be a fruitless task for anyone to attempt to develop it. The character of Nero was so corrupt that even Seneca, who was a most august and remarkable teacher, could not prevent him from becoming the most ruinous of princes. As we have already said, sound doctrines suitable to a prince should be implanted at once. It was to this same end that Plato [124] wanted his guardians to take up dialectic at a late period, for that subject deals with every sort of question and tends to shape one's opinions with regard to true virtue and the dishonorable. The model in government is to be taken from God himself and from Christ who was both God and man. From His teachings there are many principles to be gathered. Trial practice, which is the last resort, is not a safe thing in the case of a prince. It is not a matter of great consequence if a young man who wants to be a great lute-player breaks several instruments [in his practice]. But it would be a serious matter for the state to be ruined while the prince is learning. Let the prince be accustomed from boyhood to be present at consultations, attend trials, to be present at the creation of magistrates, and hear the demands of kings [L 582]. But he should be instructed first so that he may better judge [of what is taking place]. He should not be allowed to make any decisions unless they are approved by the judgment of many men, until his age and experience have provided him with a more trustworthy judgment.

YOU MUST LEARN TO RULE BEFORE RULING

[123] *Rep.* VIII. 547, 48; see also *ibid.*, III. 410; VI. 503.
[124] *Rep.* VII. 539; cf. *Laws* VII. 808.

If Homer [125] was right when he said that the prince, to whom so many thousand souls and so many burdensome tasks are entrusted, should not sleep through the whole night, and Vergil [126] was not erring in judgment when he made his Aeneas the character that he did, whence, I ask you, does the prince

WATCHFUL-<br>NESS OF A<br>PRINCE get the leisure time to remain secluded for whole days, to waste the greatest part of his life in playing at dice, in dancing, in hunting, in associating with utter fools, and in [other forms of] idle nonsense, even more frivolous than these? The state is overthrown by party factions and sorely tried with wars; robbery is rife everywhere; the poor people are driven to starvation and the gallows through unrestrained despoliation [of their goods]; the weak are downtrodden by the iniquitous nobility; the civil officers are corrupt and do whatever they please, not what is according to law. In the midst of all this, as if he had no cares in the world, does the prince have time for gaming?

The man at the wheel cannot be a sleepy-headed fellow. Can the prince in such times of danger snore [soundly on]? No sea ever has such dreaded storms as constantly beset every kingdom. So it is that the prince must ever be on his guard against any mistake at all, for he cannot make an error without great loss to many people.

The size of his ship, the value of his cargo, the number of his passengers does not make the good master merely swell with pride, but it makes him all the more concerned in his responsibility. So it is with a good king; the more people he rules over, the more watchful he should be, not the more arrogant. If you will only think of the great task you have undertaken, you will never be at a loss for something to do. If you

IN WHAT THE<br>LEISURE AND<br>WORK OF A<br>PRINCE<br>CONSIST are accustomed to take your pleasure in the progress of your people, you will never be at a loss for a source of enjoyment. In this way there is no chance for ennui to trick the good prince with the gay pleasures of leisure.

A prince should first be taught that principle which has been given to the wisest men: Choose the best plan of life, not the

[125] *Iliad* V. 490.     [126] *Aeneid* I. 305.

pleasantest. Continued habit finally makes these best principles
the most delightful. The painter gets pleasure from a picture
beautifully executed [B 450]. The farmer, the truck gardener,
the smith, all get pleasure from their work. What should
bring more enjoyment to the prince than the contemplation of
his country, improved and more flourishing as a result of his
efforts? No one can deny that it is an onerous task [to try] to
be a good prince; but it is far more troublesome to be a really
wicked one. There is far less for the man who follows the
course of nature and of honor to do, than for him who owes his
existence to trickery and deceits.[127] If you are a real prince, it
will be most unusual if you do not feel a great source of pride THE
in your heart when you recall in your mind how, in one in- PLEASURES
stance, a war was wisely avoided; in another, how an uprising OF THE
was effectively suppressed, and with very little bloodshed; and PRINCE
again, the election of some particular man to office; and finally,
your own conscious plans for the state and your own name.
This sort of pleasure becomes a Christian prince.[128] Store up
the basis of it for yourself by acts of goodness every day. Leave
those empty pleasures of the common folk to the rabble.

Solomon [129] was praised by all because at a time when he
was free to ask whatever he wanted and would have instantly
received whatever he asked for, he did not ask for great THE
wealth, nor world empire, nor the destruction of his enemies, DIFFERENCE
nor great honor and fame, nor worldly pleasures, but he BETWEEN
asked for wisdom. And not just an indifferent sort of wisdom THE PRAYER
either, but such as he could use to govern with credit the OF MIDAS
kingdom which had been entrusted to him. Just the opposite AND SOLOMON
is true of Midas, who is condemned by everyone because nothing was more precious to him than gold. But why should we
have one judgment for facts of history and another for actual
life? We pray that our prince will have good fortune, and
victories, and glory, and long life, and riches. If we really are
devoted to our prince, why do we not ask for that one thing
which Solomon asked for? And do not think his request was ill

[127] Cf. Seneca De ira II. 13. 1-2.
[128] Cf. Aristotle Pol. VII. 1; Ethics VII. 13.
[129] I Kings 3:5-12.

advised. He was praised by God because of it. Why should we say that that quality which alone is important has nothing to do with the matter? Yet there are plenty who believe that this one thing alone, wisdom of the prince, is a stumbling block to actual rule. They say that a vigorous spirit weakens and becomes faint hearted. But it is only rashness, not boldness, only foolishness, not alertness, to have no fear for that which you consider nothing. The firm resolution of the prince must be sought from other sources. Young men very often take a chance after this fashion, but even more do those who act in a fit of anger. A sense of fear is an advantageous quality which points out danger, teaches one to avoid it, and restrains one from wicked and pernicious ways. The one man who has to look out for everyone must especially examine things. Whoever has to plan for everyone and everything must have an especial store of wisdom. What God is in the universe, what the sun is in the world, what the eye is in the body, that the prince should be in his state.

THE ALLEGORY OF A KING

Those wise men of old who used to employ hieroglyphs and to throw a shadowy veil over the scheme of life with their symbolism, used to depict a king in this fashion: they added a scepter to the eye, symbolizing an upright life, a spirit that cannot be turned by any conditions from right, and inherently connected with prudence and the essence of watchfulness.[130] Some represent the king's scepter in this fashion: on the top is a stork, the symbol of devotion, and on the other end is that wild and dreadful creature, the hippopotamus. This means that if any fierce passions, such as wrath, vengefulness, greediness, and violence rage within the prince, devotion to his country will overcome and suppress these emotions.[131] License, born of good fortune, and worldly success lead to insolent arrogance, but patriotism should be stronger.

STATUES OF THE PRINCE

According to Plutarch [132] the ancient Thebans used to have certain seated figures without hands among their sacred images. The first of these also was without eyes. The fact

130 Cf. Plutarch *Of Isis and Osiris* 10.
131 Cf. Plutarch *Water and Land Animals* 4.
132 Plutarch *Of Isis and Osiris* 10.

that they are seated means that magistrates and judges ought to be of a stable character not disturbed by any personal emotions. Their lack of hands clearly means that they should be pure and free from all corrupting bribes. The prince without eyes means that the [true] king is not to be led astray from the course of honor by bribes; is not to be affected by regard for someone else; but is only to learn from what he hears. There is more along this line. The prince should learn to philosophize about those very decorations with which he is adorned. What does the anointing of the king mean, unless the greatest mildness of spirit? What significance has the crown on his head, if not wisdom that is absolute? What is the meaning of the collar of plaited gold around his neck, except the union and harmony of all virtues? What is symbolized by the bright rays of gems shining with many colors, if not the highest degree of virtue and that whatever is honorable ought to be found in a special degree in the prince? What does the rich purple mean, except an ardent love toward his subjects? What do his various decorations mean, except that he should either equal or exceed the glorious deeds of his ancestors? What is the significance of the sword that is carried before him, unless that his country ought to be safe under the protection of this man, safe both from outside enemies and those within?

THE DRESS AND INSIGNIA OF THE PRINCE

The first duty of a good prince is to desire the best things possible. The second duty, to see by what means all things that are evil can be avoided or removed; and on the other hand, how good conditions can be gained, developed, and strengthened. In the case of a private citizen it is perhaps quite enough that he should have a good mind, since he is directed by the laws, and the public officials set forth what he shall do. But in the case of the prince, it is of little help that he shall have been endowed with a good mind that desires the best things if there is not also present wisdom which points the way to gain that which the prince desires. How little difference there is between a marble statue inscribed with the names of Croesus or Cyrus, magnificently set off with diadem and scep-

A GOOD MIND COUPLED WITH PRUDENCE

ter, and a prince without a heart — unless you say that the senseless state of the one does no harm, while the latter's folly operates to the great misfortune of everyone.[133]

[B 451] Judge yourself, not on your physical appearance or by your good fortune, but on the qualities of your spirit. Measure yourself, not by the commendations of others, but by the standard of your own deeds. Since you are a prince, do not admit of any commendations which are not worthy of a prince. If anyone speaks about your appearance, remember that women are praised after that fashion. If anyone praises your easy flowing speech, remember that such terms of commendation are applied to the sophists and rhetoricians. If anyone calls attention to your bodily strength and vigor, remember that that sort of praise is to be applied to athletes, not princes. If anyone extols your lofty station, this should be your thought: "He would praise me rightly if there were something to be taken from my high place." If there is someone who praises your wealth, remember that such praise is for the bankers. So far, while you have been listening to such laudatory remarks as the preceding, you have heard nothing that fits a prince.

What then is fitting praise for a prince? If he has eyes to the back as well as to the front (as Homer [134] says, *qui voit devant et derrière*), that is, if he can look back on what has already happened and ahead to the future, thereby having the greatest knowledge possible, his wisdom will be used for the good of his country, not for himself. In no other way can his wisdom be turned to his own good than by using it for his country. If any one should praise a physician because he is handsome, well-built, of good connections, possessed of plenty of money, and because he plays handsomely at dice, dances with skill, sings well, and plays a good game of ball, would you not immediately say to yourself: [L 584] "What has all this to do with a physician?" When you hear the same sort of thing from foolish eulogizers, there is even more reason for

---

133 Cf. Plutarch *Discourse to an Unlearned Prince* 2.

134 *Iliad* III. 109, 10. The original text of Erasmus reads βλέπων πρόσσω καὶ ὀπίσσω.

you to say, "What has this to do with a prince?" There are three essentials that are sought in a physician. First, he must thoroughly know the practice of medicine, the relative powers of the body and of diseases, and the proper treatment of each malady. Secondly, he must be reliable, and have no interest other than the health of the patient, [although] some are moved by ambition or [lust for] wealth to administer a drug instead of a remedy. Thirdly, he must exercise all due care and diligence. For a prince, these same points are even far more important.

In his *Politics*, Aristotle[135] asks the question, "What does the average man demand in his prince?" Is it the figure of Nereus, or the strength of Milo, or the stature of Maximinus, or the wealth of Tantalus? No; it is none of these things. What is the answer then? He must have virtue in its highest and purest form and he must be content with a golden mean in his private affairs.

If you can be at the same time a prince and a good man, you will be discharging a handsome service. If you cannot, then yield the [chance to be] prince, rather than become a wicked man merely to enjoy it. It is quite possible to find a good man who would not make a good prince; but there can be no good prince who is not also a good man. Yet the ways of some princes have slipped back to such a point that the two ideas of "good man" and "prince" seem to be the very antitheses of one another. It is obviously considered foolish and ridiculous to mention [the idea of] a good man in speaking of a prince.

NO ONE CAN BE A GOOD PRINCE UNLESS HE IS ALSO A GOOD MAN

But you cannot be a king unless reason completely controls you; that is, unless under all circumstances you follow [the course of] advice and judgment. You cannot rule over others, until you yourself have obeyed the course of honor.[136]

Those expressions of a tyrant, "Such is my will," "This is my bidding," "Let will replace reason," should be far removed from the mind of the prince. And far more that other one [137] which already has come into the open malediction of men,

WORDS THAT ARE UNSUITED TO A PRINCE

135 *Pol.* III. 17; cf. *ibid.*, I. 13.
136 Cf. Plato *Laws* VI. 762; Cicero *Laws* III. 2. 5.
137 Quoted in Seneca *De clementia* I. 12. 4; Cicero *De off.* I. 28. 97; *et al.*

"Let them hate, if only they fear." It is the mark of a tyrant
— and womanish, too — to follow the unbridled will of your
mind; and fear is the poorest surety for a long duration of
office. Let this be the permanent policy of the prince: to harass
no one, to help everyone, especially his own subjects; to tolerate evils, or else to remedy them, as he will judge expedient
for the common good. Whoever does not take this attitude
toward the state is a tyrant, not a prince. If anyone would call
you a tyrant and a robber, instead of a prince, would you not
be greatly aroused and prepare severe penalties [for him]?
You would, and rightly so, for insult is bitter and should not
be borne under any condition. I wish you would think this
over: "How much more abusive is that charge to one who is
willingly the sort of man that he is charged with being." For
it is a more serious matter to be a thief than to be called one,
and it is more hideous to violate a maiden than to upbraid
her for her sin.

If you want to be called just what you are, then see that
you conduct yourself in such a manner that you enjoy an
excellent reputation, and you will follow the surest road.[138]
A Good For that is no true praise which is extorted through fear or
Reputation is paid by flatterers. It is bad when the reputation of the prince
Springs from
Good Deeds and its protection lie in silence imposed through threats. Although your own age may maintain perfect silence, posterity
will surely talk. Who was ever so formidable a tyrant that he
could check the tongues of everyone? The first caution of a
Christian prince must be exercised on the point upon which
Seneca [139] has impressively discoursed. Among those who are
called "king," there are found some who, by comparison
with Phalaris, Dionysius, Polycrates (the very names of all
of them have become an abomination in all ages) are unworthy
even to be called "tyrants." It does not matter by what road,
but it does matter to what end, you are tending. He who looks
to the good of his people is a king; he who is concerned for
himself is a tyrant. But now what terms shall we apply to

138 Xenophon *Cyropaedia* I. 6. 22.
139 *De clementia* I. 12. 1; *ibid.*, II. 4. 3.

those who increase their own good fortune by the misfortunes of their country and are, in practice, robbers? Shall it be "prince," but falsely?

In his *Laws* Plato [140] forbade any one to name God as the cause of any evil, because by nature He is good and kind. [B 452] But the prince (if he is a real prince) is a sort of likeness of God.[141] How inconsistent with this prototype are they who manage things in such a way that whatever evils spring up in the state arise from their misdeeds?

No attention should be given to any chance flatterer who says, "But that is only to reduce the station of the prince." On the contrary, he who wants to permit the prince what is not honorable is really lowering the prince! In what else does lowering a prince consist than in making him like the common run of men; to be a slave to anger, lust, ambition, avarice, and beholden to folly? Would it be a shameful outrage and one not to be tolerated if that were not granted to a prince which is not granted God himself? God does not demand that He be allowed to act contrary to the course of propriety. But if He did, He would no longer be God! Consequently, whoever wants to grant the prince those things which will act contrary to the nature and reason of a prince despoils him of the honor of a prince and makes him one of the common throng. A prince should be unashamed to owe allegiance to honor, when God himself obeys it. And let him not think he is any less a prince if he approach the very image of the greatest Prince with his every effort.

Such seeds as all these should be sown in the young heart of the boy by his parents, his nurses, and his tutor in order to make him a prince. These principles he should learn willingly, not under compulsion. In this manner it is fit for a prince who

AN ARGUMENT ADMIRABLY RETURNED

[140] Although Erasmus distinctly refers to the *Laws* here, I can find no passage in that work which compares to *Rep.* II. 380 which is a perfect parallel. It is quite possible that Erasmus was quoting from memory and confused the title. The thought of *Laws* X. 901 is only vaguely suggestive of his statement. Cf. also Plutarch *According to the Doctrines of Epicurus* 22.

[141] This idea, already encountered, is found in several ancient writers (see above, chap. iii) and is very common in the medieval period (see above, chap. v).

is to rule over free and willing subjects to be developed. Let him learn to love morality and loath dishonor; let him be restrained from shameful acts by a sense of shame, not of fear. Although there is some hope of a good prince to be found in changed ways and tempered passion, the main hope lies in sound ideas; for sometimes shame corrects wicked morals and maturer age or correction changes depraved desires. But when the argument is brought forth that that which is foreign to honor is joined with virtue and that that which is far more fitting a tyrant is an excellent function of a prince, that is, when the fountain from which all actions of life flow are polluted, then correction will be a very difficult matter. Therefore, in this matter of instruction, as has been said, the first and foremost care should be to see that all low ideas of the common folk are pulled out by the roots from within the prince's spirit, if by any chance they have gained root there, and that they are replaced by salutary thoughts, worthy of a Christian prince.

# II

## THE PRINCE MUST AVOID FLATTERERS

But the objective [just mentioned above] cannot be accomplished, unless every means is used to stave off abject flatterers. To this malicious tribe the good fortune of great princes is especially exposed. The very innocence of the prince's age makes it vulnerable to attacks of this evil, partly because by natural inclination it takes more pleasure in blandishments than in truth, and partly because of inexperience. The less one suspects trickery, the less one knows how to avoid it. Let no one think that the evil of flatterers (being a sort of minor evil) should be passed over: the most flourishing empires of the greatest kings have been overthrown by the tongues of flatterers. Nowhere do we read of a state which has been oppressed under a great tyranny in which flatterers did not play the leading rôles in the tragedy. Unless I am mistaken Diogenes [1] had this clearly in mind. When asked what animal was the most dangerous of all, he said "If you mean among the wild beasts, I will say the tyrant; if among the tame ones, the flatterer." This pest has a pleasing sort of poison, but it is instantaneous, so that once demented by it, princes who were conquerors of the world allowed utterly worthless flatterers to sport with them and ride them roughly. Those abominable wretches of society, libertines and sometimes even slaves, dominated the masters of the world!

A WISE
SAYING

In the first place, care must be taken to have nurses that are either immune from this disease or else subject to it only in

[1] Cf. Plutarch *How to Distinguish between a Friend and a Flatterer* 19, where the thought is attributed to Bias, another of the seven sages of Greece. Since Erasmus translated the particular essay of Plutarch in which this passage is found, he must have been familiar with it. The interchange of names, Diogenes and Bias, can easily be explained if Erasmus was quoting from memory, and this situation seems likely from the words "unless I am mistaken."

THE NURSE OF THE PRINCE — its very mildest form. That particular sex is especially subject to this malady. Besides that, most nurses have the same fault that mothers have — the greater number of them spoil the characters of their children through indulgence. All of this group should be kept away from the future prince in so far as is possible, because they seem by their very nature to be subject to the two great faults — folly and flattery. The next concern is to add companions of an honest character — in addition to the training from the tutor — so that they will be affable without using flattery, [L 586] will be accustomed to speak elegantly, and will not deceive or lie merely to curry favor. On the matter of choosing a teacher I have already expressed myself.

ATTENDANTS OF THE PRINCE — The matter of the prince's ministers is of no small moment, for they frequently favor the rash desires of youth, either because of stupidity or because they hope some gain will be theirs as a result. It will be well to select men for this duty, in so far as it is possible, who are sagacious and trustworthy, and in addition, to impose a restraint upon them in their assent by means of warnings and threats and also to use rewards to urge them to discharge their office honorably. This will be greatly helped if anyone who is caught perverting the mind of the prince with biased talk and ignoble complaisance to those things which are unworthy of a prince, [B 453] would have publicly to suffer punishment (even death, if the crime should call for it) as an example to others. This should not seem cruel to anyone, since we inflict the death penalty (and that quite beyond the example of all the laws of the ancients) on a thief who has chanced to steal a few dollars. The supreme penalty should be paid by him who wishes to corrupt the best and most precious thing the country has. If the novelty of the idea presents an obstacle to its adoption (although the Roman emperor Alexander [2] ordered a vain boaster of Thurium bound to a stake, heaped about with green logs, and suffocated from their smoke) an example can be cleverly arranged in another way: if some one is convicted of any other capital offense, still

---

[2] *Scriptores historiae Augustae, Alex. Sev.* XXXVI. 2, 3.

let him be punished on the charge of corrupting the mind of the future prince by malicious flattery. If one is going to weigh the relations of crimes in the matters of punishment, a malicious flatterer who corrupts and biases the early years of the prince's life with tyrannical ideas does more harm than one who plunders the public treasury. Whoever tampers with the coinage of the prince is visited with elaborate punishment; for those who corrupt the character of the prince there is almost a reward!

If only that statement of Carneades [3] were less true among us Christians! He said that the sons of kings could not properly learn anything except the art of horsemanship, because in all other matters everyone humored them and obsequiously agreed; but a horse, since he does not know whether his rider is a nobleman or a commoner, a rich man or a poor man, a prince or a subject, throws any unskilled rider who mounts him. Frequently we see it happen that not only the nurses and companions and ministers flatter the sons of princes, but even the tutor and preceptor of his youth who only wishes to gain further riches for himself, manages his duties without a thought to making a better prince. At no infrequent intervals do those who are assembled on holy matters speak graciously, seeking after the favor of princes and courtiers; and if they have any reproach to make, their correction is so phrased that even then they seem most flattering. I do not speak in this fashion because I believe approval should be given those who madly rage with turbulent clamors against the lives of princes, but because I desire the example of a good prince to be set forth by them without abuse, so that those matters which the pagans condemned in their pagan rulers should not be approved by flattering adulation in a Christian prince. I mean that magistrates do not frankly give their advice, and that the counselors do not amicably confer together. The nobility dissent from one another in their interests, and consequently they all zealously court the favor of the prince, but only to vanquish a rival or to give an enemy no chance for doing harm.

EVERYONE
FLATTERS
THE PRINCE

[3] Plutarch *How to Distinguish between a Friend and a Flatterer* 16.

The priests flatter the prince, the physicians slavishly agree with him. Now and then to listen to true words of praise from orators come from abroad is perfectly proper. There still remains one holy stay — and even that often fails. I refer to those whom the common folk call the "royal confessors." If they would be impartial and prudent, surely in that most intimate confidence they could help the prince with loving and frank advice. But it very often happens that while each one is watching out for his own interests he neglects the welfare of the state. Less harm is done by the poets and rhetoricians, to none of whom is unknown the scheme of measuring the praises of the princes not by the princes' merits, but by their own genius. Far more dangerous is that group of magicians and soothsayers who promise long life, victories, triumphs, pleasures, and empires to some kings and again to others threaten sudden death, downfall, misfortune, and exile, thereby abusing the two principle tyrants of human life, hope and fear. To this class belong the astrologers who foretell the future from the stars. Whether they have any real skill or not, it is not for me to discuss here. As they now have a hold on the common people, they are causing no small trouble to humanity.

The most deadly of all flatterers are those who under a guise of candor assent, and by a wonderful artifice are able to urge one rigorously on while they are putting up a resistance, DISGUISED and to praise while scolding. Plutarch [4] has admirably deFORMS OF picted them in his little essay entitled How to Distinguish ADULATION a Friend from a Flatterer.

There are two periods of life which are especially susceptible to flattery: extreme youth because of its inexperience, and old age because of its weakness. However, folly is found in every period and brings its handmaiden, conceit. Plato [5] is right in his warning that the most dangerous type of flattery is flattery of one's self, which consequently makes one ready game for others who do just what he does of his own accord.

There is a tacit sort of adulation in pictures, statues, and

[4] Ibid., 18, 19.     [5] Laws V. 731, 32.

honorary titles. Apelles [6] flattered Alexander the Great in this manner by painting him hurling a thunderbolt; and Octavius took great pleasure in being painted in the likeness of Apollo.[7] The same thing applies to those huge statues of colossal proportion, far greater than human size, which were formerly set up to the emperors. Perhaps this next point will seem trivial to some, but it really is of some consequence that artists should represent a prince in the dress and manner that befits a wise and serious prince. It is better to represent the prince as doing something in connection with state business, than as in a position of idleness; for example, [the statue of] Alexander holding his hand over one ear as he heard a case [tried before him], [B 454] or that of Darius holding a pomegranate, or that of Scipio restoring to a youth his promised bride unharmed and rejecting the gold that had been offered. The princely halls should be adorned with wholesome pictures of the sort just suggested instead of those which inculcate wantonness, vain glory, or tyranny.

FLATTERING PICTURES

Now in the matter of titles I would not say that his due honor should not be shown the prince, but I should prefer the titles to be of the sort that would remind the prince of his duties; that is, I should prefer to have him called, "The Honorable," "The Incorruptible," "The Wise," "The Clement," "The Kind," "The Judicious," "The Watchful," "The Temperate," "The Zealous," rather than "The Exalted," "The Invincible," "The Triumphant," "The Ever August," so as not to recount thereby exalted position, inviolate majesty, divinity, and even more flattering titles than these. I approve the custom by which they now call the Roman Pontiff "His Holiness," for by hearing this title constantly he is advised what qualities he should show and what is most becoming in him: not great wealth or rule over a very wide domain, but distinction for his moral purity. But if the prince cannot avoid hearing these usual titles at times, even against his own desires, still he should not refrain from showing by what kind

TITLES OF THE PRINCE

HOW THE USUAL TITLES MUST BE TREATED

[6] Cf. Plutarch *Alex*. IV. 2.
[7] Cf. Suetonius *Aug*. 70.

he is more pleased. Alexander Severus [8] is said to have considered all flatterers distasteful to such a degree that if anyone saluted him in too humble a manner or bowed his head with too great a show of reverence, straightway he upbraided him with vehement reproach; or if the subject's position or office prevented open reproach, he was censured by a severe scowl.

THE "FATHER OF HIS COUNTRY"

The boy should be instructed to turn to his own advantage those titles to which he is forced to listen. He hears [himself called] "Father of his Country": let him think that no title could ever be given to princes which more perfectly accords [with the nature of] a good prince than does that of "Father of his Country." He must then act in such a way as to appear worthy of that title. If he thinks of it in that way, it will be a warning; but if he takes it otherwise, it will be fawning adulation.

If the prince is called "The Unconquerable," let him think how ridiculous it is for one to be called unconquerable who is conquered by wrath, who daily is a slave to passion, and whom ambition pulls and leads as a captive whither she will. He is truly unconquerable who gives way to no passion and under no pretext can be deflected from the course of honor.

When the prince is referred to as "The Serene," let it occur to him that it is the duty of the prince to keep everything peaceful and composed. But if anyone disturbs and confuses the order of things through his ambitions or his anger, by seditions and the upheavals of wars, the title of "The Serene" does not add honor to him, [L 588] but mockingly flings his shortcomings hard at him. When he is called "The Exalted," let him understand that there is no real honor except that which springs from virtue and good deeds. If anyone is defiled by license, contaminated by greed, sullied by ambition — what then is the title of "The Exalted," if not an admonition if he who has erred was an impudent man, or an open reproach, if the sinner should have known better? When the prince hears

FLATTERY OF TITLES

his various titles from the provinces, let him not immediately swell with conceit as if he were the absolute master of so many

[8] *Scriptores historiae Augustae, Alex. Sev.* 18. 1.

affairs, but let him think to how many he is morally obliged to be a good prince. If anyone should offer the title of "Your Highness," "Your Majesty," "Your Divine Excellence," let the prince remember that they are not appropriate unless he governs his kingdom after the fashion of God, with a sort of celestial magnanimity. When the prince listens to the usual panegyrics, let him not straightway believe them or be well disposed toward praises of himself, but if he is not yet such an one as his praises proclaim him, let him take that as advice and give his attention to making his acts correspond to his praises. If he already fulfills them, then he should strive to be better.

The very laws will also have to be under suspicion. Even these sometimes yield openly to the prince, for they are either compiled or established by the closest adherents of the kings and emperors. When they tell the prince that he is not bound by the laws, they yield themselves to him; when they ascribe to him power over everything, he must be careful not to think immediately that he may do anything that suits his fancy. To a good prince everything can be entrusted with safety; to a mediocre one, some things; to a bad one, nothing.

Demetrius Phalareus [9] wisely urges the reading of books, because the prince may frequently learn from them things which his friends would not dare to advise. But the prince must be forearmed with an antidote, after this fashion: [10] he whom you are reading is a pagan; you who are reading, are a Christian. Although he speaks with authority on many subjects, yet he by no means gives an accurate picture of the good prince. Look out that you do not chance upon something in his works which you think you must therefore imitate directly. Measure everything by the Christian standard.

*BOOKS FREELY GIVE ADVICE*

The first matter is the selection of authors, for the sort of books the boy first reads and absorbs is of prime importance. Wicked conversations ruin the mind, and in no less a degree do wicked books. Those mute letters are transformed into manners and moods, especially if they come upon a native

*IMPROPER READING RUINS CHARACTER*

[9] Plutarch *Apophthegmata*, s. v. Demetrius Phalareus.
[10] Cf. Plutarch *How a Young Man Ought to Hear Poetry* 8.

character that is prone to some weakness. A boy that is wild and impetuous by nature would easily be incited to tyranny, if without forewarning he should read about Achilles, Alexander the Great, Xerxes, or Julius Caesar. But today we see many a one taking delight in the tales of Arthur and Lancelot, and other tales of similar nature [B 455] which are not only about tyrants but are also very poorly done, stupid, and fit to be "old wives' tales," so that it would be more advisable to put in one's time reading the comedies or the legends of the poets instead of nonsense of that sort. But if any should desire to make use of my plan, as soon as the elements of language have been taught, he should set forth the *Proverbs* of Solomon, *Ecclesiasticus*, and the *Book of Wisdom*, not with the idea that the boy may be tormented with the four senses (*sensus*) of the theologian by a vaunting interpreter, but that he may fitly show in a few words whatever pertains to the functions of a good prince. First a love for the author and his work must be inculcated. You are destined to rule, he [the author] explains the art of ruling. You are the son of a king, yourself a future king you will hear what the wisest king of all teaches his own son, whom he is preparing to be his successor. Later take the Gospels. There the means by which the spirit of the boy is kindled with a love for the writer and his work is of great importance, for no small part will depend upon the cleverness and opportunism of the one interpreting, to explain briefly, clearly, plausibly, and vividly, not everything, but just those points which have most to do with the office of the prince and those that will cause [the young prince] to rid his mind of the undermining ideas common to the general run of princes. In the third place, read the *Apophthegmata* of Plutarch and then his *Morals*, for nothing can be found purer than these works. I should also prefer his *Lives* to those of anyone else. After Plutarch, I would readily assign the next place to Seneca, whose writings are wonderfully stimulating and excite one to enthusiasm for [a life of] moral integrity, raise the mind of the reader from sordid cares, and especially decry tyranny everywhere. From the *Politics* of Aristotle and from the

WHAT THE
PRINCE
SHOULD
READ FIRST

*Offices* [11] of Cicero many pasages that are worth knowing can well be culled out. But Plato is the most venerable source of such things — in my opinion at least. Cicero has followed him in part in his work *The Laws*; that entitled *The Republic* is lost.

Now I shall not deny that a great fund of wisdom may be gathered from reading the historians, but you will also draw out the very essence of destruction from these same sources unless you are forearmed and read with discretion. Be on guard lest the names of writers and leaders celebrated by the approval of centuries deceive you. Herodotus and Xenophon were both pagans and often set forth the worst types of prince, even if they did write history, the one to give pleasure through his narrative, the other to show the picture of an exceptional leader. Sallust and Livy tell us many things very clearly and everything very learnedly to be sure, but they do not weigh all that they tell, and they approve some things which are by no means to be approved for a Christian prince. When you hear about Achilles, Xerxes, Cyrus, Darius, and Julius Caesar, do not be carried away and deluded by the great names. You are hearing about great raging robbers, for that is what Seneca [12] has called them on various occasions.

But yet, if you happen upon anything in these works that is worthy of a good prince, take care to rescue it as you would a jewel from a dung heap. There never was a tyrant so detestable that he did not do some things which, if they were not done in the cause of virtue, at least may be fitted to the example of such a quality. There are many things in the letters of Phalaris which are not unworthy of any excellent king, and his own creation reacted despotically enough on Perillus, the instigator of cruelty.[13] Alexander did many thinks like a madman, but he acted honorably in keeping aloof from the captured women of Darius, and equally so when he ordered a woman

*(margin note:* How Bad Examples Are to Be Turned into Good Ones*)*

[11] This erroneous translation of the title to Cicero's work *De officiis* (On Duty) is kept because of its established usage.

[12] *De ira* III. 16. 3, 4; *ibid.*, II. 2. 3; *ibid.*, III. 21. 1. I cannot find a specific passage on Julius Caesar; Gaius Caesar (Caligula) is mentioned in a context fitting our reference in *De ira* III. 19.

[13] Cf. Plutarch *Parallels* 39.

sent back upon learning that she was married.[14] [Such things as]
these are to be selected; then the examples of pagan or bad men
have a great stimulus. [Ask yourself this:] if a tyrant and a
pagan showed this self-restraint; if this youthful conqueror
showed this honorable attitude toward the women of the enemy,
what should I, as a Christian prince do toward mine? If there
was so much soul in a mere chit (*muliercula*), what should a
man show? If that was set down as a disgrace for a pagan
prince by a pagan, how much zeal must I apply to keep a
straight course, I, who profess Christianity!

How one may pile up examples by expansion I believe I
have pointed out clearly enough in my book *De copia rerum*.
But even the examples of evils can be turned to good. Great
application and loftiness of spirit such as Julius Caesar used
to favor his ambitions you should expend to the general good
of your country. The clemency such as he feigned for preparing and bolstering up his tyrannical sway you should earnestly
use to win for yourself the love of your subjects.

The examples of very depraved princes sometimes incite
one to a higher standard than do those of the mediocre princes,
or even the best, for who is not checked in his avaricious desires by the story of Vespasian's [15] tax on urine, and his statement, equally as disgusting as the tax, "Money has a good
smell, whatever its source;" and that detestable phrase of
Nero,[16] with which he regularly instructed his officers, "You
know what I want, and see that no one has anything." By this
method, whatever is found in the historian may be turned into
an example for conducting one's self well. See that you choose
THE BEST for yourself only the best of the leaders from the whole throng
OF THE BEST — such men as Aristides, Epaminondas, Octavius, Trajan,
ARE TO BE
IMITATED  Antoninus Pius, Alexander Mammeas. Nor yet should you
take them in their entirety, but you should choose the
best from the best, just as there are some things in David
and Solomon (both kings who were praised by God) which you
avoid.

14 Cf. Plutarch *Alex.* xxi. 3; see also xii.
15 Suetonius *Vesp.* 23. 3.        16 Suetonius *Nero* 32-4.

[B 456] Now what could be more senseless than for a man who has received the sacraments of the Christian church to set up as an example for himself Alexander, Julius Caesar, or Xerxes, for even the pagan writers would have attacked their lives if any of them had had a little sounder judgment? As it would be most disgraceful to be surpassed by them in any honorable deed of theirs, so it would be the last degree of madness for a Christian prince to wish to imitate them without change.

The prince should have thorough warning that not all of the things that he reads in the Holy Scriptures are to be straightway imitated. Let him learn that the battles and the butcheries of the Hebrews, and their barbarity toward their enemies, are to be interpreted allegorically; otherwise it would be most disastrous to read them. [L 590] One course was allowed that people because of the standards of the time; quite a different one is laid down for the heaven-blessed Christian peoples. *How the Old Testament Is to Be Read*

Whenever the prince picks up a book, he should do so not with the idea of gaining pleasure but of bettering himself by his reading. He who really wants to be better can easily find the means of becoming better. A great part of goodness is the desire to be good; for example, anyone who knows and hates the disease of political ambition, irascibility, or passionate desire, and opens a book [to find something] by which he may cure his malady, easily finds a remedy that will either remove the cause or [at any rate] lessen it.

From no source is the truth more honestly and advantageously gained than from books; but the prince should accustom his friends to believe that they will gain favor by giving frank advice. It is the part of those who are closely associated with the prince to give him counsel that is seasonable, appropriate, and friendly. It will be well for the prince to pardon those whose counsel is crudely given, so that there may be no example to deter his good counselors from their duty. *How the Prince Should Be Warned*

During a great tempest even the most skillful navigators will listen to advice from a layman. But the ship of state is never without a storm. Who could pay sufficient praise to the prudence in public matters which was displayed by Philip, king of Macedon, who freed the man by whom he was privately advised that he looked ungraceful when seated with his cloak pulled up to his knees.[17] What he did in a trivial matter should be done much more by a prince for his country during stirring events; for example, in undertaking a journey to foreign lands, in revising the laws, in establishing treaties, in beginning war.

[17] Plutarch *Apophthegmata, s. v.* Philip.

# III

## THE ARTS OF PEACE

Although the writers of antiquity divided the whole theory of state government into two sections, war and peace, the first and most important objective is the instruction of the prince in the matter of ruling wisely during times of peace, in which he should strive his utmost to preclude any future need for the science of war. In this matter it seems best that the prince should first know his own kingdom. This knowledge is best gained from [a study of] geography and history and from frequent visits through his provinces and cities. Let him first be eager to learn the location of his districts and cities, with their beginnings, their nature, institutions, customs, laws, annals, and privileges. No one can heal the body until he is thoroughly conversant with it. No one can properly till a field which he does not understand. To be sure, the tyrant takes great care in such matters, but it is the spirit, not the act, which singles out the good prince. The physician studies the functions of the body so as to be more adept in healing it; the poisoning assassin, to more surely end it! Next, the prince should love the land over which he rules just as a farmer loves the fields of his ancestors or as a good man feels affection toward his household. He should make it his especial interest to hand it over to his successor, whosoever he may be, better than he received it. If he has any children, devotion toward them should urge him on; if he has no family, he should be guided by devotion to his country; and he should always keep kindled the flame of love for his subjects. He should consider his kingdom as a great body of which he is the most outstanding member and remember that they who have entrusted all their fortunes and their very safety to the good faith of one man are deserving of consideration. He should keep constantly in mind the example of those rulers to whom the welfare of their people was dearer than their own lives; for it is obviously impossible for a prince to do violence to the state without injuring himself.

In the second place the prince will see to it that he is loved by his subjects in return, but in such a way that his authority is no less strong among them. There are some who are so stupid as to strive to win good will for themselves by incantations and magic rings, when there is no charm more efficacious than good character itself; nothing can be more lovable than that, for, as this is a real and immortal good, so it brings a man true and undying good will. The best formula is this: let him love, who would be loved, so that he may attach his subjects to him as God has won the peoples of the world to Himself by His goodness.[1]

THE GOOD
WILL OF THE
CITIZENS
TOWARD
THEIR PRINCE

They are also wrong who win the hearts of the masses by largesses, feasts, and gross indulgence. It is true that some popular favor, instead of affection, is gained by these means, but it is neither genuine nor permanent. In the meanwhile the greed of the populace is developed, which, as happens, [B 457] after it has reached large proportions thinks nothing is enough. Then there is an uprising, unless complete satisfaction is made to their demands. By this means your people are not won, but corrupted.[2] And so by this means the [average] prince is accustomed to win his way into the hearts of the people after the fashion of those foolish husbands who beguile their wives with blandishments, gifts, and complaisance, instead of winning their love by their character and good actions. So at length it comes about that they are not loved; instead of a thrifty and well mannered wife they have a haughty and intractable one; instead of an obedient spouse they find one who is quarrelsome and rebellious. Or take the case of those unhappy women who desperately try to arouse love in their husbands' hearts by giving them drugs, with the result that they have madmen instead of sane lovers.

The wife should first learn the ways and means of loving

[1] Cf. Cicero *De off.* II. 6. 22-7. 23; Xenophon *Cyropaedia* VIII. 2. 1.
[2] Cf. Cicero, *op. cit.*, II. 15. 53.

her husband and then let him show himself worthy of her
love. And so with the people — let them become accustomed
to the best, and let the prince be the source of the best things.
Those who begin to love through reason, love long.

In the first place, then, he who would be loved by his people
should show himself a prince worthy of love; after that it will
do some good to consider how best he may win his way into
their hearts. The prince should do this first so that the best
men may have the highest regard for him and that he may be
accepted by those who are lauded by all. They are the men
he should have for his close friends; they are the ones for
his counselors; they are the ones on whom he should bestow his
honors and whom he should allow to have the greatest influence with him. By this means everyone will come to have an
excellent opinion of the prince, who is the source of all good
will. I have known some princes who were not really evil
themselves who incurred the hatred of the people for no other
reason than that they granted too much liberty to those whom
universal public sentiment condemned. The people judged the
character of the prince by these other men.

For my part, I should like to see the prince born and raised
among those people whom he is destined to rule, because
friendship is created and confirmed most when the source of
good will is in nature itself. The common people shun and hate
even good qualities when they are unknown to them, while
evils which are familiar are sometimes loved. This matter at
hand has a twofold advantage to offer, for the prince will be
more kindly disposed toward his subjects and certainly more
ready to regard them as his own. The people on their part
will feel more kindness in their hearts and be more willing to
recognize his position as prince. For this reason I am especially
opposed to the accepted [idea of] alliances of the princes with
foreign, particularly with distant, nations.

The ties of birth and country and a mutual spirit of understanding, as it were, have a great deal to do with establishing
a feeling of good will. A goodly part of this feeling must of
necessity be lost if mixed marriages confuse that native and

inborn spirit. But when nature has laid a foundation of mutual
affection, then it should be developed and strengthened by
every other means. When the opposite situation is presented,
then even greater energy must be employed to secure this feeling of good will by mutual obligations and a character worthy
of commendation. In marriage, the wife at first yields entirely
to the husband, and he makes a few concessions to her and
indulges her whims until, as they come really to know one
another, a firm bond unites them; so it should be in the case
of a prince selected from a foreign country. Mithridates
learned the languages of all the peoples over whom he ruled,
and they were said to be twenty in number.[3] Alexander the
Great,[4] however barbarous the peoples with whom he was
dealing, at once used to imitate their ways and customs and by
this method subtly worked himself into their good graces.
Alcibiades has been praised for the same thing.[5] Nothing so
alienates the affections of his people from a prince as for him
to take great pleasure in living abroad, because then they seem
to be neglected by him to whom they wish to be most important. The result of this is that the people feel that they are not
paying taxes to a prince [L 592] (since the moneys are spent
elsewhere and totally lost as far as they are concerned) but
that they are casting spoils to foreigners. Lastly, there is
nothing more harmful and disastrous to a country, nor more

THE LONG dangerous for a prince, than visits to far-away places, espe-
ABSENCE cially if these visits are prolonged; for it was this, according
OF PHILIP to the opinion of everyone, that took Philip from us and
injured his kingdom no less than the war with the Gelrii, which
was dragged out for so many years. The king bee is hedged
about in the midst of the swarm and does not fly out and away.
The heart is situated in the very middle of the body. Just so
should a prince always be found among his own people.

There are two factors, as Aristotle [6] tells us in his *Politics*,
which have played the greatest rôles in the overthrow of em-

---

[3] Aulus Gellius *N. A.* XVII. 17. 2; Valerius Maximus VIII. 7. 16. On page
245 Erasmus gives the number as 22.

[4] Cf. Plutarch *Alex.* XLVII. 3.

[5] Plutarch *Alcibiades* XXIII. 3.          [6] *Pol.* V. 10.

pires. They are hatred and contempt. Good will is the opposite of hatred; respected authority, of contempt. Therefore it will be the duty of the prince to study the best way to win the former and avoid the latter. Hatred is kindled by an ugly temper, by violence, insulting language, sourness of character, meanness, and greediness; it is more easily aroused than allayed. A good prince must therefore use every caution to prevent any possibility of losing the affections of his subjects. You may take my word that whoever loses the favor of his people is thereby stripped of a great safeguard.[7] On the other hand, the affections of the populace are won by those characteristics which, in general, are farthest removed from tyranny. They are clemency, affability, fairness, courtesy, and kindliness. This last is a spur to duty, especially if they who have been of good service to the state, see that they will be rewarded at the hands of the prince. Clemency inspires to better efforts those who are aware of their faults, [B 458] while forgiveness extends hope to those who are now eager to make recompense by virtuous conduct for the shortcomings of their earlier life and provides the steadfast with a happy reflection on human nature. Courtesy everywhere engenders love — or at least assuages hatred. This quality in a great prince is by far the most pleasing to the masses.

    Contempt is most likely to spring from a penchant for the worldly pleasures of lust, for excessive drinking and eating, and for fools and clowns — in other words, for folly and idleness. Authority is gained by the following varied characteristics: in the first place wisdom, then integrity, self-restraint, seriousness, and alertness.[8] These are the things by which a prince should commend himself, if he would be respected in his authority over his subjects. Some have the absurd idea that if they make the greatest confusion possible by their appearance, and dress with pompous display, they must be held in high esteem among their subjects. Who thinks a prince great just because he is adorned with gold and precious stones? Everyone

ON THE PRESERVATION OF THE KINGDOM

KINDLINESS

CLEMENCY

COURTESY

THE CAUSE OF CONTEMPT

---

[7] Cf. Isocrates *To Nicocles* 21.
[8] Cf. Cicero *De off*. II. 9. 32, 33.

knows he has as many as he wants. But in the meanwhile what else does the prince expose except the misfortunes of his people, who are supporting his extravagance to their great cost? And now lastly, what else does such a prince sow among his people, if not the seeds of all crime? Let the good prince be

**THE LIFE OF THE PRINCE** reared in such a manner and [continue to] live in such a manner that from the example of his life all the others (nobles and commoners alike) may take the model of frugality and temperance. Let him so conduct himself in the privacy of his home as not to be caught unawares by the sudden entrance of anyone. And in public it is unseemly for a prince to be seen anywhere, unless always in connection with something that will benefit the people as a whole. The real character of the prince

**THE SPEECH OF THE PRINCE** is revealed by his speech rather than by his dress. Every word that is dropped from the lips of the prince is scattered wide among the masses. He should exercise the greatest care to see that whatever he says bears the stamp of [genuine] worth and evidences a mind becoming a good prince.

Aristotle's [9] advice on this subject should not be overlooked. He says that a prince who would escape incurring the hatred of his people and would foster their affection for him should delegate to others the odious duties and keep for himself the tasks which will be sure to win favor. Thereby a great portion of any unpopularity will be diverted upon those who carry out the administration, and especially will it be so if these men are unpopular with the people on other grounds as well. In the matter of benefits, however, the genuine thanks redound to the prince alone. I should like to add also that gratitude for a favor will be returned twofold if it is given quickly, with no hesitation, spontaneously, and with a few words of friendly commendation. If anything must be refused, refusal should be affable and without offense. If it is necessary to impose a punishment, some slight diminution of the penalty prescribed by law should be made, and the sentence should be carried out as if the prince were being forced [to act] against his own desires.

[9] *Pol.* V. 11.

It is not enough for the prince to keep his own character pure and uncorrupted for his state. He must give no less serious attention, in so far as he can, to see that every member of his household — his nobles, his friends, his ministers, and his magistrates — follows his example. They are one with the prince, and any hatred that is aroused by their vicious acts rebounds upon the prince himself. But, someone will say, this supervision is extremely difficult to accomplish. It will be easy enough if the prince is careful to admit only the best men into his household, and if he makes them understand that the prince is most pleased by that which is best for the people. Otherwise it too often turns out that, due to the disregard of the prince in these matters or even his connivance in them, the most criminal men (hiding under cover of the prince) force a tyranny upon the people, and while they appear to be carrying out the affairs of the prince, they are doing the greatest harm to his good name. What is more, the condition of the state is more bearable when the prince himself is wicked than when he has evil friends; we manage to bear up under a single tyrant. Somehow or other the people can sate the greed of one man without difficulty: it is not a matter of great effort to satisfy the wild desires of just one man or to appease the vicious fierceness of a single individual, but to content so many tyrants is a heavy burden. The prince should avoid every novel idea in so far as he is capable of doing so; for even if conditions are bettered thereby, the very innovation is a stumbling block. The establishment of a state, the unwritten laws of a city, or the old legal code are never changed without great confusion. Therefore, if there is anything of this sort that can be endured, it should not be changed but should either be tolerated or happily diverted to a better function. As a last resort, if there is some absolutely unbearable condition, the change should be made, but [only] gradually and by a practiced hand.[10]

The end which the prince sets for himself is of the greatest consequence, for if he shows little wisdom in its selection he

MINISTERS AND FRIENDS OF THE PRINCE

EVERY CHANGE IS DANGEROUS

[10] Cf. Aristotle *Pol.* II. 8.

must of necessity be wrong in all his plans. The cardinal principle of a good prince should be not only to preserve the

THE GOAL OF THE PRINCE

present prosperity of the state but to pass it on more prosperous than when he received it. To use the jargon of the Peripatetics, there are three kinds of "good" — that of the mind, that of the body, and the external good.[11] The prince must be careful not to evaluate them in reverse order and judge the good fortune of his state mainly by the external good, for these latter conditions should only be judged good in so far as they relate to the good of the mind and of the body; that is, in a word, the prince should consider his subjects to be most fortunate not if they are very wealthy or in excellent bodily health but if they are most honorable and self-controlled, if they have as little taste for greed and quarreling as could be hoped for, and if they are not at all factious but live in complete accord with one another. He must also beware of being deceived by the false names of the fairest things, for in this deception lies the fountainhead from which spring practically all the evils that abound in the world.[B 459] It is no true state of happiness in which the people are given over to idleness and wasteful extravagance, any more than it is true liberty for everyone to be allowed to do as he pleases. Neither is it a state of servitude to live according to the letter of just laws. Nor is that a peaceful state in which the populace bows to every whim of the prince; but rather [is it peaceful] when it obeys good laws and a prince who has a keen regard for the authority of the laws.[12] Equity does not lie in giving everyone the same reward, the same rights, the same honor; as a matter of fact, that is sometimes a mark of the greatest unfairness.

PUBLIC SCHOOLS AND EDUCATION

A prince who is about to assume control of the state must be advised at once that the main hope of a state lies in the proper education of its youth. This Xenophon [13] wisely taught in his *Cyropaedia*. Pliable youth is amenable to any system of training. Therefore the greatest care should be exercised over public and private schools and over the education of the girls,

---

11 *Ibid.*, VII. 1; cf. Plato *Laws* III. 697; *Phil.* 48, 49; Aristotle *Ethics* I. 8.
12 Cf. Plato *Laws* IV. 715.      13 *Cyropaedia* I. 2. 2-14.

so that the children may be placed under the best and most trustworthy instructors and may learn the teachings of Christ and that good literature which is beneficial to the state.[14] As a result of this scheme of things, there will be no need for many laws or punishments, for the people will of their own free will follow the course of right.

Education exerts such a powerful influence, as Plato [15] says, that a man who has been trained in the right develops into a sort of divine creature, while on the other hand, a person who has received a perverted training degenerates into a monstrous sort of savage beast. Nothing is of more importance to a prince than to have the best possible subjects.

The first effort, then, is to get them accustomed to the best influences, because any music has a soothing effect to the accustomed ear, and there is nothing harder than to rid people of those traits which have become second nature to them through habit. None of those tasks will be too difficult if the prince himself adheres to the best manners. [L 594] It is the essence of tyranny, or rather trickery, to treat the common citizen as animal trainers are accustomed to treat a savage beast: first they carefully study the way in which these creatures are quieted or aroused, and then they anger them or quiet them at their pleasure. This Plato [16] has painstakingly pointed out. Such a course is an abuse of the emotions of the masses and is no help to them. However, if the people prove intractable and rebel against what is good for them, then you must bide your time and gradually lead them over to your end, either by some subterfuge or by some helpful pretence. This works just as wine does, for when that is first taken it has no effect, but when it has gradually flowed through every vein it captivates the whole man and holds him in its power.

THE BEST INFLUENCES MUST BE MADE FAMILIAR

AT TIMES THE POPULACE MUST BE HUMORED

If sometimes the whirling course of events and public opinion beat the prince from his course, and he is forced to obey

[14] Cf. Plato *Laws* VII. 794, 804, 813; Plato provides for the education of girls as well as boys.

[15] *Laws* VI. 766.

[16] *Rep.* VI. 493.

the [exigencies of the] time, yet he must not cease his efforts as long as he is able to renew his fight, and what he has not accomplished by one method he should try to effect by another.

# IV

## ON TRIBUTES AND TAXES

If anyone will merely glance through the annals of the Unjust ancients he will discover that a great many seditions have Taxation Must Be Avoided arisen from immoderate taxation. The good prince must be careful that the feelings of the commoners be not aroused by such actions. He should rule without expense if he possibly can. The position of the prince is too high to be a mercenary one; and besides, a good prince has all that his loving subjects possess. There were many pagans who took home with them only glory as a result of their public activities which they had honorably discharged. There were one or two (for example, Fabius Maximus and Antoninus Pius) who spurned even this.[1] How much more should a Christian prince be content with a clear conscience, especially since he is in the service of Him who amply rewards every good deed! There are certain ones in the circles of princes who do nothing else Evil Advisors except extort as much as possible from the people on every new pretext they can find and then believe that they have properly served the interests of their princes, as if they were the open enemies of their subjects. But whoever is willing to hearken to such men, should know that he by no means comes under the title of "prince"!

A prince should studiously endeavor to minimize his demands on the people. The most desirable way of increasing the revenue is to cut off the worse than useless extravagances, to abolish the idle ministries, to avoid wars and long travels, which are very like wars [in their bad effects], to suppress graft among the office holders, and to be interested in the proper administration of the kingdom rather than in the extension

---

[1] Cf. Ennius, quoted in Cicero *De senec.* IV. 10, and *Scriptores historiae Augustae, Ant. Pius* 9. 10; 10. 1 .

of its boundaries. But if the prince is going to measure the amount of taxes by his greed or ambitions, what bounds or GROSS limits will there be to his demands? Greed knows no end and GREEDINESS continually presses and extends what it has started until, as the old proverb [2] goes, too great a strain breaks the rope, and finally the patience of the people is exhausted and they break into an uprising, which is the very thing that has been the undoing of kingdoms that once were most prosperous. If, however, circumstances force the levying of taxes on the people, then it is the part of a good prince to raise them according to such a system that as little as possible of the hardships will fall upon the poor. It is perhaps desirable to bring the wealthy to a simple life, but to reduce the poor to starvation and chains is most inhuman, as well as extremely dangerous.

THE EX-
TRAVAGANT
EXPENDI-
TURES OF
THE PRINCE
FOR POM-
POUS DIS-
PLAY AND
SENSUAL
PLEASURES

[B 460] The conscientious king, at the time when he wants to increase his court, to obtain an excellent alliance for his grand-daughter or his sister, to raise all his children to rank with him, to fill the coffers of the nobility, to flaunt his wealth in the face of other nations by extended travels, should ponder again and again in his own mind how inhuman it is for so many thousands of men with their wives and children to starve to death, to be plunged into debt and driven to the last degrees of desperation, so that he can accomplish these ends. I should not even consider such persons under the class of human beings — much less princes — when they extort from the lowest paupers what they sinfully squander on lewd women and on gambling. And yet we hear of some men who think that even such actions come under their rights.

The prince should also give a good deal of thought to this fact, that whatever is once introduced as a temporary expedient and appears to be connected with the purse strings of prince or nobles, can never be set aside. When the occasion for the taxation is removed, not only should the burden be removed from the people, but recompense made by replacing, as far as possible, the former expenditures. He who has his

[2] Lucian *Dialogi meretricii* III. 286; quoted in Erasmus *Adages* LXVII.

people's interests at heart will avoid introducing a calamitous precedent; but if he takes pleasure in the disasters of his subjects, or even disregards them, he is in no way a prince, regardless of his title whatever it may be.

The prince should try to prevent too great an inequality of wealth. I should not want to see anyone deprived of his goods, but the prince should employ certain measures to prevent the wealth of the multitude being hoarded by a few. Plato [3] did not want his citizens to be too rich, neither did he want them extremely poor, for the pauper is of no use and the rich man will not use his ability for public service. <sub>EQUALITY OF FORTUNES</sub>

It happens that princes like those [which I have just described] are sometimes not even enriched by these levies. Whoever would like to find out for himself has only to recall how much less our ancestors received from their peoples and how much more beneficent they were and how much more they possessed in every way, because a great part of this money slips through the fingers of the collecting and receiving agents and a very small portion gets to the prince himself.

A good prince will tax as lightly as possible those commodities which are used even by the poorest members of society; e.g., grain, bread, beer, wine, clothing, and all the other staples without which human life could not exist. But it so happens that these very things bear the heaviest tax in several ways; in the first place, by the oppressive extortion of the tax farmers, commonly called *assisiae*,[4] then by import duties which call for their own set of extortionists, and finally by the monopolies by which the poor are sadly drained of their funds in order that the prince may gain a mere trifling interest.

As I have brought out, the best way of increasing the prince's treasury is to follow the old proverb,[5] "Parsimony is a great revenue," and carefully check expenditures. However, if some taxation is absolutely necessary and the affairs of the <sub>PARSIMONY IS A GREAT SOURCE OF REVENUE</sub>

---

[3] *Rep.* IV. 421, 22; cf. also Aristotle *Pol.* IV. 11.

[4] This word (spelled *asisiae* by Erasmus) has many meanings; from the name of the council which imposed a tax it came to mean the tax itself. Cf. Du Cange *Glossarium mediae et infimae latinitatis.*

[5] Quoted in Cicero *Parad.* VI. 3. 49; Pseudo-Seneca *Monita* 22.

people render it essential, barbarous and foreign goods should
be heavily taxed because they are not the essentials of livelihood but the extravagant luxuries and delicacies which only
the wealthy enjoy; for example, linen, silks, dyes, pepper,
spices, unguents, precious stones, and all the rest of that same
category. But by this system only those who can well afford
it feel the pinch. They will not be reduced to straightened circumstances as a result of this outlay but perchance may be
made more moderate in their desires so that the loss of money
may be replaced by a change for the better in their habits.

In the minting of his money the good prince should observe
that faith which he owes to God and his own people and not
allow himself a liberty by which he inflicts the direst penalties
ON THE on others. In this matter there are four ways of robbing the
COINAGE OF people, a fact which was only too clearly brought before us at
THE PRINCE the death of Charles, when a long period of anarchy more
blighting than any tyranny you could name afflicted your kingdom. The first way is to debase the coinage with alloys, the
second is to make them short weight, the third is to clip them,
and the fourth is to bring about intentional fluctuation of value
to suit the needs of the prince's treasury.

# V

## ON THE BENEFICENCES OF THE PRINCE

[L 596] The appropriate honor for good princes comes from their kindliness and their beneficence. How, then, can some men claim this title of "prince" for themselves, when they turn every thought to the improvement of their own affairs and to the ruin of everyone else. The mark of an ingenius and acute prince is [the ability] to assist everyone by every means he has available — and that does not merely mean by giving. Some he will help through his liberality, some he will assist by his favor, some who are downtrodden he will free from their difficulties, and some he will help by friendly advice. Let him count that day lost, I say, on which he has benefited no one.

Yet the prince's liberality should by no means be promiscuous. There are some who heartlessly extort from the good citizen what they squander on fools, court informers, and panderers. Let the state see that the rewards of the prince are most ready for those who have used every means to do good for the state. Let merit, not fancy, be the basis for reward. The Staunch Supporters of the State Must Be Awarded

[B 461] The prince should be most liberal with those benefits which will cause no hurt or injury to anyone, for to despoil some to enrich others, to ruin one group to elevate another, is certainly no real benefit. It is really a twofold source of evil, especially if anything be taken from the deserving to be transferred to the unworthy.

In the mythical stories of the poets it has been truly shown that the gods never made a visit to any place without conferring great benefit upon those by whom they were received. But when on the arrival of a prince his subjects hide any rather elaborate piece of furniture, keep their comely daugh- The Advent of a Good Prince Is Beneficial to Everyone ters out of sight, send away their young sons, lie about their wealth, and in every way reduce their real position, is it not then self-evident that they hold the same opinion of the prince as they would hold of an invading enemy or a brigand, since on his arrival they fear for those things which it should be his duty to protect if there were any hidden plot or violence on foot? They fear treachery from others, but from him they fear violence also, since one complains that he has been beaten, another that his maiden daughter has been stolen, another that his wife has been seduced, another that his pittance has been withheld. What a tragic difference between the picture of this arrival and that of the gods! Each of his cities holds the prince under suspicion in direct proportion to its own prosperity; on the coming of the prince the opportunists push themselves to the fore and all of the worthy men of parts are on their guard and draw away. Tacitly by their actions they show how they regard the prince. Some one may say, "I cannot control the hands of all my court; I am doing all I can." Let your followers know that you are inflexibly firm in this matter. You will eventually get the people really to believe that this is done against your will, but only if you do not allow an offender to go unpunished. Perhaps it was enough for a pagan prince to be kind to his own people and merely just to foreigners, but it is the part of a Christian prince to regard no one as an outsider unless he is a nonbeliever, and even on them he should inflict no harm. His own subjects should naturally come first in his thought, but he should help everyone that he can.

JUSTICE FOR FOREIGNERS    Although the prince must ever try to see that no one suffers any harm, still, according to Plato,[1] in the case of strangers he should be even more careful than in the case of his own subjects to see that no harm befalls them, for strangers are deprived of all their friends and relatives and are consequently more susceptable to mishaps. For this reason they are said to have Jupiter as their special protector, who in this capacity was called "Xenius" [the wayfarer's god].

[1] *Laws* V. 729; cf. also Isocrates *To Nicocles* 22.

# VI

## ON ENACTING OR EMENDING LAWS

The best laws under the best princes make a city (*civitas*)
or a kingdom most fortunate. The most felicitous condition
exists when the prince is obeyed by everyone, the prince himself obeys the laws, and the laws go back to the fundamental
principles of equity and honesty, with no other aim than the
advancement of the commonwealth.[1]

A good, wise, and upright prince is nothing else than a sort
of living law.[2] He will make it his effort to pass not many laws
but the best possible ones that will prove most beneficial to the
state. A very few laws suffice for a well organized state
(*civitas*)[3] under a good prince and honorable officials. Under
any other conditions no number, however great, will be enough.
A sick person does not get along best with an unskilled physician
prescribing one medicine after another.

In the promulgation of laws, the first concern is to see that
they do not savor of royal financial plans nor of private gain
for the nobility but that they are drawn up on an honest plan
and that everything looks to the welfare of the people. This
welfare is to be judged not by the popular opinion but according to the dictates of wisdom, which should always be present
in the councils of the prince. Even the pagans admitted that a
law is really no law at all if it is not just, fair, and intended
for public benefit. That is not a law which merely pleases the
prince, but rather that which pleases a good and wise prince
who has no interest in anything which is not honorable and for

---

[1] Cf. Plato *Laws* IV. 715.

[2] Cf. Aristotle *Pol.* III. 13; Plutarch *A Philosopher Is to Converse with
Great Men* 4; Cicero *Laws* II. 5. 11; III. 1. 2; see also Suetonius *Julius* 77.

[3] I have rendered *civitas* as "city" the first time because it seemed to denote
something different from "kingdom"; in the second case, "state" seemed the
more probable meaning.

the good of his state. But if those standards by which evils
are to be corrected are themselves distorted, there can be only
one result from laws of this kind, namely, that even good
things are perverted to evil. Plato [4] desired that the laws
should be as few as possible, especially on the less important
matters, such as agreements, commercial business, and taxes;
for no more benefit accrues to the state from a mass of laws
than would come [to a person] from a multitude of medicines.
When the prince is a man of unquestioned character and the
officials fulfill their responsibilities, there is no need of many
laws. Under other conditions, however, the abuse of the laws
is turned into the destruction of the state, for even the good
laws are perverted into other meanings, due to the dishonesty
of these men.

Dionysus of Syracuse has been justly blamed for establishing most of his laws according to a tyrannical scheme, heaping
one upon the other and then, as it turned out, allowing his
people to disobey them so that by this means he could make
everyone liable to his punishments. That is not law making, it
is trapping.

Just condemnation has been brought on Epitadeus [5] who
passed a law to the effect that everyone should be free to leave
his property to anyone he wished. His one purpose in this was
that he himself might disinherit his son whom he hated. At
first the people did not see through the scheme of the man, but
the act itself eventually brought dire ruin on the state.

[B 462] Let the prince propose such laws as not only provide punishment in particular for the sources of crime but also
have influence against sin itself. Therefore, they are at fault
who think that laws should be framed in the briefest compass,
to be merely peremptory, not to instruct. [6] The main purpose
of law should be to restrain crime by reason rather than by
punishment. It is true, however, that Seneca [7] does not concur

[4] *Rep.* IV. 425-26.     [5] Cf. Plutarch *Agis and Cleomenes* 5.
[6] Cf. Plato *Laws* X. 890.
[7] Seneca *Ep. Mor.* XCIV. 37 which *agrees* with Plato's view. I cannot find
a passage in Seneca which expresses the opposite of this idea. This contradiction
of fact and statement is hard to explain; perhaps Erasmus has confused Seneca
with someone else, or there may be some passage which I have not located.

with Plato in his idea on this subject, but his dissent is a mark of daring rather than enlightenment.

Furthermore, young men should not be allowed to argue [at all] on the justice of the laws, and the older men but sparingly.[8] It is not the part of the common people to criticize rashly the laws of princes, but it is the province of the prince to see that he makes laws which will please all good citizens. He should remember that even the lowest members of society have some appreciation.[9] M. Antoninus Pius has been praised because he never promulgated any law which he did not try to justify to all by accompanying letters, in which he gave the reasons why he judged the measure expedient for the state.[10]

No One
Should
Discourse
Rashly on
the Laws

Xenophon[11] has cleverly set forth in his *Oeconomicus* that all other animals [except man], are mainly brought to obedience by [three] means: by food, if they are of the lower sort; by fondling if they are more intelligent, like the horse; or by beating if they are stubborn, like the ass. But since man is the highest of all animals, [L 598] he ought not to be so much coerced by threats and blows, as led to his duty by rewards. The laws should then not only provide punishments for the transgressors but also by means of rewards stimulate good conduct in the service of the state. We find many examples of this type among the ancients: whoever fought bravely in war, hoped for a reward; if he fell fighting, his children were reared by the state. Whoever saved a fellow citizen, whoever drove one of the enemy from the walls, whoever assisted the state by wise counsel, had his reward.

Although a good citizen should follow the path of honor even when no reward is offered, still inducements of that sort are desirable to spur on to an eagerness for good living the minds of those citizens who are still but little developed. Those who have more character are more interested in the honor; those who are on a lower level are influenced by the money also.

Rewards
Stimulate
the Unde-
veloped

---

[8] Cf. Plato *Laws* I. 634.
[9] Cf. *ibid.*, III. 684. If Erasmus had this passage in mind, he carefully omits reference to Plato's refutation of the statement.
[10] *Scriptores historiae Augustae, Ant. Pius* 12. 3.
[11] *Oecon.* XIII. 6-10.

A law should have its effect, then, in all these ways — honor and disgrace, profit and loss. Of course those who really are of a servile, or rather, beastial, character must be controlled by chains and floggings. Let your subjects grow up from childhood with this sense of honor and ignominy so that they will realize that rewards are not won through wealth or birth, but by good deeds. In a word, the watchful prince should use every means not only to see that offenses are punished but to look and reach much further back than that. He should see in the first place that no deed is committed which calls for punishment. The better physician is the one who prevents and wards off disease, not the one that cures the disease with drugs once it is contracted. Just so, it is not a little the more worth-while achievement to prevent the inception of crime than to inflict punishment once crime is committed. The former will be accomplished if the prince will discover the causes from which most crimes spring and then cut them out if he can, or at any rate, suppress them and deprive them of their force.

First, then, the majority of crimes arise, as I have said, from polluted ideas, as if from poisoned springs. Your first DEPRAVED course is to have your subjects grounded in the best principles, OPINIONS and secondly, to have as your officials men who are not only ARE THE FOUNTAINS wise but also incorruptible. Plato [12] is right in his advice that OF EVIL nothing should be left untried and, as the saying goes, no stone left unturned before making use of the supreme penalty. Try by teaching to prevent the desire to sin, then try to stop [the back-sliders] by [arousing] a fear of that divinity which takes vengeance on criminals and also by the threat of punishment. If no headway is made by these means, recourse must be had to punishments but only to those of the lighter sort which remedy the evil and do not destroy the whole being. As a last resort, if none of these efforts are fruitful, the incorrigible must be sacrificed by the law (just as a hopelessly incurable limb must be amputated) so that the sound part is not affected.

A reliable and skilled physician never resorts to an operation or cauterizes if he can stop the malady by plasters and

[12] *Laws* V. 731; cf. *ibid.*, IX. 862; *Rep.* III. 409-10.

strong medicines; and he never resorts even to those unless forced to do so by [the seriousness of] the disease. So a prince should try every remedy before resorting to capital punishment, keeping in mind that the state is a single body. No one cuts off a limb if [the patient] can be restored to health by any other means.[13] The honest physician has only one purpose in mind when he prepares his remedies and that is how to overcome the ailment with the very least danger to the patient; so it is with the good prince in passing laws. He has no other end in view than the advantage of his people and the remedying of their misfortunes with the least disturbance.

A goodly part of crime arises from the one fact that everywhere wealth is exalted and poverty is scorned. The prince will therefore make an effort to see that his subjects are rated according to their worth and character rather than their material wealth. He should exemplify this first in himself and in his household. If the people see the prince flaunting his riches, observe that with him the man who has the most money is rated the highest, and that money opens the way to magistracies, honors, and official positions, is it surprising that these injustices arouse the efforts of the masses to win wealth by fair means or foul?

Now, to speak in more general terms, [B 463] the great mass of the worthless crowd in every state is created through idleness, which they all seek in different ways. Those who have once become accustomed to [an idle] life will resort to any IDLERS MUST evil course, if they have no other means of supporting it. The BE EXPELLED prince will therefore always be on the lookout to keep the proportion of idlers down to the minimum among his courtiers, and either force them to be busy or else banish them from the country.

Plato [14] thinks that all beggars should be driven far from the boundaries of his state. But if there are any persons who are broken through old age or sickness and without any rela- BEGGARS tives to care for them, they should be cared for in public insti-

---

[13] Cf. Seneca *De clementia* I. 16. 2-4.
[14] *Laws* XI. 936.

tutions for the aged and the sick. Anyone who is well and content with little will have no need to beg.

The people of Marseilles did not admit into their city those priests who travel from town to town peddling pseudo-relics, **PRIESTS** so that under the guise of religion they might enjoy ease and luxury. Perhaps it would be to the advantage of the state if the number of monasteries were limited, for in them is found **MONASTERIES** a peculiar form of idleness, especially among those whose lives **AND** have little to be said for them and are spent in a lazy and **COLLEGES** sluggish fashion. What I say about monasteries, is also true of colleges.

To this class [i.e., the idlers] belong also contractors, street peddlers, money lenders, brokers, procurers, caretakers of country establishments, wardens of game preserves, and that troop of servants and attendants that some men keep in their service because of their ambitious pretenses. When they cannot get the things which extravagant waste, the companion of laziness, demands, they resort to wicked practices. And in the military service there is a busy sort of time wasting, and it is by far the most destructive, for from it result the complete **SOLDIERS** cessation of everything worth while and the source of all **ARE THE** things evil. If the prince will strike out these seed beds of **WORST** **OF ALL** crime from his kingdom, he will have much less to punish by law. I should merely like to add in passing that useful occupation should be respected and sluggish indolence not graced **THE REAL** with the title "nobility." I should not strip the well-born of **NOBILITY** their honors if they follow in the footsteps of their forefathers and excel in those qualities which first created nobility. But if we see so many today who are soft from indolence, effeminate through sensual pleasures, with no knowledge of any useful vocation, but only charming table fellows, ardent gamesters (I will not mention any of their obscene practices) why, I ask you, why should this class of persons be placed on a higher level than the shoemaker or the farmer? In former times leisure from the baser activities was granted the best families, not so that they might indulge in wanton nonsense, but so that they might learn the principles of government.

Let it then be no disgrace if the wealthy citizen or descendants of the old families teach their sons a sedentary vocation. In the first place, while the young men are engaged in such a study they will be restrained from many vices; in the second place, if there is no need to use their training, it burdens no one. But if they suffer reverses (such is the fickleness of man's fortune), then, according to the proverb, any land or any position will give opportunity for their trade.

The ancients, realizing that most evils arose from extravagant prodigality, passed sumptuary laws and created the office of censor to restrain immoderate expenditures on banquets, dress, or building.[15] Some one may think it is a severe course that does not allow a person to use or abuse his own possessions in accordance with his own unrestrained whims. Let him reflect that it is much worse for the morals of his subjects to become so depraved through this sort of extravagance that capital punishment is necessary. It is more in keeping for one to be forced into frugality than to be forced into utter ruin by vice.

There is nothing less helpful than for moneys to accrue to officials as a result of the offenses of the citizens; for who will turn his attention to reduce crime to the minimum, when it is to his advantage to have as many criminals as possible. It is an equitable arrangement, and one in common practice among the ancients, that fines should go largely to the injured party, then partly to the public treasury, and in the case of more outrageous crimes partly to the informer. This matter of outrage, however, must be adjudged in accordance with the harm done the state, not according to anyone's private prejudices. The laws should see in the main that no wrong is done any man, be he poor or rich, noble or commoner, servant or slave, official or private citizen. But they should lean more in the direc-

How the Fines Are to Be Distributed

[15] There were numerous sumptuary laws passed from time to time at Rome, and many of these were mentioned by writers with whom Erasmus was thoroughly conversant (e.g., Dio Cassius, Aulus Gellius, Macrobius, Valerius Maximus, and Suetonius). On the subject see Daremberg-Saglio, *Dictionnaire des antiquités grecques et romaines, s. v. sumptus*, and Pauly-Wissowa, *Realencyclopädie der classischen Altertumswissenschaft, s. v. sumptus*.

tion of leniency to the weaker, for the lot of those in the
lower stations is more exposed to injuries. What is lacking in
the protection of fortune, that the humanity of your laws
should equalize. Let them, then, punish more severely an outrage on a poor man than an offense against a rich man, and
provide a heavier penalty for a corrupt official than for a
faithless plebian, for the crimes of a man of rank than for
those of a commoner.

According to Plato [16] there are two kinds of penalty. The
first is a penalty not too severe in proportion to the offense
committed (consequently the supreme penalty must not be
resorted to except after careful thought), for the seriousness
of the crime must be judged not by our own eager desires
[L 600] but on the basis of justice and honesty. Why is it
that everywhere simple theft is punished by death and adul-
tery goes almost unscathed (which is in direct contradiction to
the laws of all the ancients), unless with everyone money is
held in too high esteem and its loss is measured not by the
facts but by their own feelings? But this is not the place to
reason out why at the present time there is little disturbance
made against adulterers, while formerly the laws were very
severe against them. The second class [of penalties] which
Plato designates as exemplary, [B 464] should but rarely be
resorted to, and then should only be employed in such a way
that all other men are restrained rather by the uniqueness of
the penalty than by its enormity, for there is nothing so awful
but that it is held in contempt through long familiarity. Nothing does less good than to make your subjects accustomed to
punishments.

In treating a disease, new remedies are not tried if the
malady can be cured by old ones. Just so new laws should not
be enacted if the old ones will suffice to remedy the troubles
of the state.[17] If useless laws cannot be repealed without causing a great deal of confusion, they should little by little be
allowed to fall into disuse or else should be emended. It is a
dangerous procedure to recast the laws promiscuously, but it is

How the
Laws
Should Be
Slipped
into Disuse

---

[16] *Laws* IX. 862.    [17] Cf. Aristotle *Pol.* II. 8.

necessary to suit the remedy to the condition of the body and likewise the laws to the present condition of the state. Therefore certain institutions that were once beneficial are [now] better repealed.

Many laws have been established with the best intentions but have been perverted to dishonorable uses by the wickedness of officials. Nothing is more ruinous than a just law which has been perverted to evil purposes. No possible loss to his purse should deter the prince from abolishing or emending such laws, for there is no gain which is not linked with a loss of honor, especially when the laws are in such a condition that their repeal will be readily applauded. Do not let the prince deceive himself, if such laws have become strongly established in some places and have become deeply rooted through long custom. Mere numbers in approval do not make for the justice of a measure, and the more deeply rooted an evil is, the more diligently should it be pulled out. I should like to mention one or two examples. It is the practice in some places for the prefect to take over in the king's name the effects of a deceased foreigner. That practice was started as a good measure to prevent those who had no right to the stranger's property from claiming it, and it remained in the hands of the prefect until the rightful heirs appeared. But now that [situation] has become disgracefully distorted, so that the property of a foreigner reverts to the treasury whether there be heirs or not. ESTABLISHED CUSTOM DOES NOT EXCUSE WRONG

That was once a good practice [which provided] that whatever was found on a thief was seized by the prince or an officer acting in his name to prevent, of course, the fraudulent assignation to an illegitimate owner, as would be the case if there were an indiscriminate right to claim it. As soon as the rightful owner was identified, the property was to be restored to him. But now there are some people who believe that whatever they find on a thief belongs to them just as much as if it had come to them by inheritance. Even they who do [so believe] are perfectly conscious that it is grossly unjust, but the sense of right is overcome by the desire for gain. THE ABUSE OF LAWS THAT WERE ESTABLISHED IN GOOD INTENTION

Long ago there was an excellent plan for the establishment

on the borders of the various kingdoms of officials who were
to supervise the imports and exports, with the special purpose
of guaranteeing passage safe from highwaymen to merchants
and travelers. The result was that if anything was stolen
within the confines of his territory, every prince saw to it that
the merchant suffered no loss and that the robber did not go
completely free. It was perhaps as a matter of courtesy that
the merchants started to give a small fee. But as it is now,
everywhere the traveler is stopped for his custom fee, the
stranger is bothered by it, the merchants are fleeced, and although the tax mounts from day to day, there is no suggestion
of protecting these peoples. The result is that the purpose for
which this institution was created is now completely lost and
a measure that was beneficial in its first stages has been completely transformed into a tyrannical institution by the vicious
practices of public officers.

There was in the past a law enacted that all property cast
up from a shipwreck should be held by the prefect of marine
affairs. This was not done so that this property should fall
into his or the prince's possession, but so as to prevent it from
being claimed by people without just title. It only became
state property if no one appeared with proper claim. But now
in some places, the prefect, more unrelenting than the sea
itself, seizes upon whatever is lost by any cause at sea as if it
were his own. What the storm has left the poor wretches, this
official, like a second tempest, sweeps away from them.

See how everything has gone wrong. The thief is punished
because he has stolen another man's property. But the magistrate who is appointed to prevent theft steals it over again,
and the owner is robbed a second time by him who was appointed for the specific purpose of preventing loss to anyone.
The merchant traders are harassed and plundered most by
those who were expressly created to prevent the traveler from
being annoyed and robbed. And those very men whom the law
established to see that property does not rest in illegal possession are the ones who prevent its reaching the rightful owner.
There are many provisions like these among many nations

which are no less unjust than injustice itself. It is not the purpose of this treatise to change any particular state. These practices are common to substantially all states, and they have been condemned by the judgment of everyone. I have brought them up for purposes of instruction. Of course there may be some of these institutions which could not be set aside without great confusion, but their abolition would win favor for the prince and a good reputation, which should seem greater than any pecuniary gain.

Nothing should be more democratic or just than the prince; [B 465] so with the law. Under any other conditions, you will have the situation which the Greek philosopher [18] well stated: "Laws are merely spider webs, which the birds, being larger, break through with ease, while the flies are caught fast." THE LAWS BIND EVERYONE EQUALLY

The law, like the prince, should always be more prone to pardon than to punish, either because it is more nearly according to the law of God — for His anger is but very slowly stirred to vengeance — or because a criminal who escapes can be brought back for punishment, but no help can be given an innocent man who has been condemned.[19] Even if he [the innocent man] does not lose his life, who can judge the suffering of another?

We read that there were formerly rulers (not princes, but tyrants) from whose example the Christian prince should be as different as possible, for they judged the crimes that were committed according to their own private discomfiture. Consequently, to them it was only a petty theft when a poor man was stripped of his goods and along with his wife and children driven into chains or beggary; but it was a very serious matter, deserving of all the tortures, if anyone defrauded the privy purse or a grasping collector of a penny. Likewise they would cry out that slander had been brought on their majesty if anyone should murmur against even the wickedest prince, or should speak a bit too freely of an oppressive official. Even the emperor Hadrian, a pagan and not to be classed among HOW THE CHARGE OF Lèse Majesté IS TO BE MEASURED

HADRIAN

[18] Anacharsis, quoted in Plutarch *Solon* V. 2, 3; Valerius Maximus VII. 2. 14.
[19] Cf. Plutarch *God Is Slow to Punish* 5.

the good princes, would never listen to a charge of *lèse-majesté*;[20] and not even that cruel monster Nero gave much

NERO heed to secret accusation on that charge.[21] There was another one [22] who paid no attention at all to charges of this sort and said, "In a free country, tongues likewise should be free." Therefore, there are no crimes which a good prince will pardon more readily or more gladly than those which affect him alone. Who can scorn such trivial things more easily than the prince? It is easy for him to take vengeance and therefore hateful and unbecoming. Vengeance is a proof of a small, weak character; and nothing is less appropriate in a prince, who should be generous and magnanimous.[23] It is not enough for the prince to be clear of all crime; he should be untainted by any suspicion or appearance of crime. For this reason he will not only carefully weigh the deserts of him who commits a crime against the prince but also the opinions of others concerning the prince, and out of respect for his own position he will sometimes pardon an unworthy man and with a thought for his own reputation will be lenient to those who deserve no clemency.

Do not let anyone cry out at once that this idea shows too

THE little thought for the majesty of princes which with the great-
MAJESTY est care should be kept sacrosanct and inviolate by the state.
OF THE
PRINCE There is no other way, on the contrary, by which to look out for the greatness of the prince than for the people to understand that he is so alert that nothing escapes him; so wise that he understands what things comprise the real majesty of a prince; so lenient that he avenges no injury to himself, unless the good of the state calls for it. The majesty of Caesar Augustus was enhanced and made safer by the clemency extended to Cinna, when so many punishments had gained nothing.[24] He is really guilty of injury to the prince's majesty who cuts down that in which the prince's true greatness lies. The

---

[20] *Scriptores historiae Augustae, Hadrian* 18. 4, 5.
[21] Suetonius *Nero* 39.
[22] Tiberius, in Suetonius *Tib.* 28.
[23] Cf. Seneca *De clementia* I. 5. 4; I. 20. 3.
[24] Seneca *De clementia* I. 9.

prince's greatness is in the quality of his character and in the affairs of his people that are prospering through his wisdom. Whoever destroys these factors is to be accused of *lèse-majesté*. They go far astray and have no real conception of the real majesty of the prince, who think that it is increased when the laws are reduced to a minimum of effectiveness and the liberty of the people is broken, [L 602] as if the prince and the state were two separate entities. But if a comparison is to be made between the things which nature has united, the king should not compare himself with anyone of his subjects that he pleases but with the whole body of the state; for thus he will see how much more important the latter is, embodying so many men and women, than the prince alone, who is the head. The state will be a state,[25] even if there be no prince. Even the greatest dominions prospered without a prince; for example, the republics of Rome and Athens. But a prince cannot exist without a state; in other words, a state carries with it the idea of a prince, but the reverse does not hold. What is that which alone makes a prince, if it is not the consent of his subjects? A man who is great because of his own good qualities, that is, his virtues, will be great even if his princely authority is stripped from him. It is perfectly plain, then, that they who measure the position of a prince by those things which are unworthy of the high position of a prince are very wrong in their judgment. He is called a "traitor" (for this is accepted to be the most hated epithet) who by his frank advice recalls the prince to a better course when he has swerved to those interests which are neither becoming nor safe for himself nor beneficial to the state (*patria*). Surely he is not looking out for the position of the prince, is he, who corrupts the prince with plebeian ideas, leads him into disgraceful worldly pleasures, into wild feasts, into gambling, and into other disgraceful diversions of that sort? It is called "loyalty" to flatter a stupid prince by ready obsequiousness, but "treason" to block any of these wicked plans. On the contrary, no one is

REAL TREASON AGAINST A PRINCE

REAL LOYALTY

[25] The Latin term here is *res publica*, as elsewhere; not *civitas*, the technical, "sovereign state."

[in reality] less a friend to the prince than the man who by base flattery deludes him and takes him from the course of right, who involves him in wars, who advocates robbery of his people, who teaches him the art of tyranny, who makes him hateful to every good man. Such conduct is real treason and deserves more than one punishment.

THE
GUARDIAN
OF THE LAWS

Plato [26] wanted his *gardiens des lois*, that is, those who were placed in charge of the laws, to be absolutely trustworthy. A good prince should punish none more severely than those who are corrupt in their administration of the laws, since the prince himself is the first guardian of the laws. It is advisable, then, that the laws be as few as possible, and secondly, that they be as just as possible, and [prepared] with a view to the welfare of the state; [B 466] in addition they should be very thoroughly familiar to the people. On this very account the ancients used to exhibit the laws publicly written in the records and on tablets so that they might be plainly discernible by all.[27] Some follow the abominable theory of using the law in place of nets with the one purpose of catching as many as they can, with no regard for the state, but just as if they were capturing spoils. Finally, let the laws be set forth in clear language with as few complexities as possible, so that there will be no urgent need for that most grasping type of man who calls himself "jurisconsult" and "advocate." This profession was once open only to men of the highest standing and carried with it a very high position and very little money. But now the lust for gold which has sapped everything has corrupted this field. Plato [28] says that there can be no enemy more blighting to the state than the person who subjects the laws to the human will. But the laws are at the peak under a good prince.

[26] *Rep.* VI. 484. The text of Erasmus reads νομοφύλακες.
[27] Cf. Plato *Laws* XI. 917.
[28] *Laws* IV. 715.

# VII

## ON MAGISTRATES AND THEIR FUNCTIONS

The prince should demand the same integrity which he him- THE
self exhibits, or at any rate the closest approximation to it, INTEGRITY
from his officials. He should not consider it enough to have OF OFFICIALS
appointed his magistrates, but it is a matter of prime importance how he appoints them. In the second place, he must be on
the watch to see that they perform their duties honorably.
Aristotle [1] wisely and with deliberation gives us the advice ARISTOTLE
that good laws are passed to no purpose unless they are defended by those who passed them. The very opposite sometimes has happened, and laws that were enacted with the
loftiest purpose were turned to the complete ruin of the state
through the vicious practices of the magistrates.

Although the magistrates should not be selected on the
basis of wealth or family or age, but rather on that of wisdom MAGISTRATES
and integrity, yet it is more appropriate that older men should ARE TO BE
be selected for those offices on which the safety of the state MAINLY
depends. This is not only because older men possess more FROM THE
prudence as a result of their experience and their personal OLDER MEN
feelings are more restrained but also because among the people
their advanced years give them some authority.[2] Accordingly
Plato [3] laid down the rule that no one who was less than BROKEN
fifty years old, or more than seventy, should be made a custo- OLD AGE
dian of the law. He would not have a priest less than sixty.
After the richest maturity of life there is a decline to which
is due a release and relaxation from all duties.

A chorus dance is a delightful spectacle if it is developed THE ORDER
in rhythm and harmony. On the other hand, it is a farce when OF THE CITY
the gestures and voices are a confused jumble. So a city OR KINGDOM
IS THE MOST
MAGNIFICENT
OBJECT

[1] *Pol.* IV. 8.
[2] Cf. Plato *Rep.* III. 409.          [3] *Laws* VI. 755.

(*civitas*) or a kingdom is a wonderful thing if each [citizen] has his own place, if each one performs his own peculiar duties, that is, if the prince conducts himself as he should, if the magistrates are faithful to their parts, and if the common folk yield obedience to good laws and honorable magistrates. But when the prince looks out for his own business and the magistrates do nothing but fleece the people, when the common people do not obey fair laws, but only flatter the prince and officials, whatever the matter may be, then there is sure to be a disgraceful lack of order in everything. The first and prime interest of the prince should be to see how he can be of most service to his state. There is no better way of showing this service than by being careful to see that the magistrates and offices are filled by men of the best character and with the greatest interest in the public welfare.

THE PRINCE IS THE PHYSICIAN OF THE STATE    What is the prince but the physician of the state? It is not enough for a physician to have skilled assistants if he himself is not most adept and alert. Likewise it is not enough for the prince to have trusted magistrates if he is not the most honorable of all, for through him the others are selected and corrected.

THE PRINCE IS THE CHIEF PART OF THE STATE    The parts of the mind are not all equal in importance: some control, others obey. The body only obeys. As the prince is the most important part of the state he ought to know most and be farthest divorced from all gross passions. Closest to him will be the magistrates, who obey in part and rule in part, for they obey the prince and rule over the common people. There-

THE MAGISTRATES SHOULD BE SELECTED HONESTLY    fore the prosperity of the state is closely associated with the honest creation of the magistrates and the honest apportionment of officers. Let there be in addition an action against malpractice in office, just as there was in antiquity an action against extortion. And finally, let there be the severest penalty inflicted on these men if they are convicted.

WHEN MAGISTRATES ARE HONESTLY SELECTED    The magistrates will be honestly created if the prince will select not those who pay the most nor those who bribe most disgracefully nor those who are closely related to him nor those who especially suit his habits, whims, and fancies but those who have the most reputable characters and are most adapted to the performance of the specific duties required. But when the prince does just one thing and that is to sell his offices to the highest bidders, what else can he expect from them except that they sell the offices over again, replenish their own loss by any means whatsoever and commercialize their administration just as they did their private businesses. And this practice should not seem less ruinous to the state, merely because by a lamentable custom it has been received by a great many nations, although it was considered a disgrace even among the pagans, and the laws of the Caesars directed those who presided over courts to have a princely salary so they would have no excuse for graft.[4]

[B 467] At one time it was a very serious crime to give a corrupt judgment, but on what basis can the prince punish a judge who, after a bribe, has given a judgment or has refused THE
to give one, when he himself sold the position on the bench CORRUPT
and taught the future judge his corrupt ways? The prince's JUDGE
relation to the magistrates should be that which he wishes them to have toward the common people.

Aristotle[5] gives us the prudent advice in his *Politics* that above all else we are to be on guard lest the magistrates gain THE
from the magistracies. Otherwise a double evil will result: the MAGISTRATE
first is that all the avaricious and dishonest men will bribe, or SHOULD
rather seize upon and literally take possession of, the office, INTERESTED
and [secondly] that the people will be wracked between the IN
two misfortunes of being not only shut out from [attainment GAIN
to] honor, but also robbed of their money.

[4] Cf. Dio Cassius LII. 23; LIII. 15.
[5] *Pol.* V. 8.

# VIII

## ON TREATIES

[L 604] In concluding treaties, as in everything else, the good prince should look to nothing but the advantage of his people. But when the opposite is done, when the prince considers it more to his advantage that the interests of his people have been reduced, then it is not a treaty, but a conspiracy. Whoever are of this opinion make two people out of one — the nobles and the commoners, one of whom profits by the other's loss. When that situation exists, there is no state. Among all Christian princes there is at once a very firm and holy bond because of the very fact that they are Christian. Why, then, is there a need to conclude so many treaties every day as if everyone were the enemy of everyone else and human agreements were essential to gain what Christ could not [accomplish]? When a matter is transacted through many written agreements, it is a proof that it is not done in the best faith and we often see it happen that many lawsuits arise as a result of these agreements which were prepared for the very purpose of preventing litigation. When good faith is a party and the business is between honest men, there is no need for many painstaking contracts. When the transaction is between dishonest men and not made in good faith, these very agreements produce grounds for suit. Likewise among good and wise princes, even if there is no treaty, there is an established friendship; but among stupid and wicked princes those very treaties into which they entered to prevent the outbreak of war are the causes of war, for some one complains that this or that clause among the countless articles has been violated. A treaty is usually prepared to set an end to war, but at the present time an agreement that starts a war is called a treaty.

WHAT
SHOULD BE
THE PURPOSE
OF TREATIES?

MANY
TREATIES,
LIKE MANY
AGREEMENTS,
ARE A SIGN
OF POOR
FAITH

DISADVAN-
TAGES OF
TREATIES

These alliances are nothing but war measures, and wherever the situation looks best, there treaties are arranged.

The good faith of princes is [shown by] their fulfillment of the duties they accepted, so that a mere promise from them is more sacred than an oath from anyone else. How base it is then not to live up to those agreements which they made in solemn treaty, with those ceremonies included in which are the most sacred of all among Christians? And yet we see this happen every day through somebody's fault. I do not know anything more about it, but it certainly cannot happen except by the fault of some one. If any portion of a treaty appears to have been broken, we should not at once conclude that the whole pact is invalidated, lest we seem to have pounced upon an excuse for breaking off friendly relations. On the contrary, we should rather strive to patch up the breach with the least trouble possible. It is advantageous sometimes even to overlook some points, since not even among private individuals do agreements long remain in effect, if they carry out everything to the letter, as the saying goes. You should not at once follow the dictates of anger but rather that for which the need of the state (*publica utilitas*) calls. A good and wise prince will make an effort to preserve peace with everyone but especially with his neighbors; for if they are wrought up they can do a great deal of harm, while if they are friendly they are a big help, and without their mutual business relations the state could not even exist.[1] Friendship easily arises and becomes fixed among those who have a common tongue, who are geographically close, and who have similar characteristics and traits. There is so great a difference in everything between some nations that it is far wiser to have refrained from relations with them than to be bound by even the stoutest treaties. Some are so far away that even if they were well inclined they could be of no assistance. Then there are some that are so surly, untrustworthy, and arrogant that even though they are close at hand yet they are worthless as friends. With them the wisest course will be neither to break in war nor to be bound to them in any

THE FAITH OF THE PRINCE IS VERY GREAT

FAITH MUST BE KEPT WITH THE NEIGHBORING STATES

[1] Cf. Aristotle *Pol.* VII. 14.

close ties of treaties or alliances, because war is always disastrous and the friendship of some peoples is hardly more bearable than war.

A part of the wisdom of a ruler lies in his knowledge of the traits and characters of all peoples. This he will gain partly from books, and partly from the memories of wise and experienced men. He need not think that it will be necessary for him to wander over all lands and seas as Ulysses did. For the other things, it is not easy to set down a definite rule. In general it may be said that the prince should not be too closely allied to those who differ from us in religion, as, for example, the heathens; or those whom the foresight of nature separated from us by mountains or seas, or those whom vast stretches of land cut off from us. These we should not ally with nor should we attack them. [B 468] Although there are many examples of this very point, yet one from close at hand will be enough. France is obviously by far the most prosperous of all countries, but it would be much more flourishing if it had refrained from attacking Italy.

THE PRINCE
SHOULD
UNDERSTAND
THE CHARAC-
TERISTICS OF
ALL PEOPLES
AND KNOW
THEIR
CUSTOMS

## IX

## ON THE MARRIAGE ALLIANCES OF PRINCES

For my part, I should think that it would be by far most beneficial to the state if the marriage alliances of princes were confined within the limits of their own kingdoms or, if they had to go beyond their boundaries, with only their nearest neighbors and then only those who warrant faithful friendship. But, they say, it is not right for the daughter of a king to marry anyone except a king or a king's son. Those are merely the fancies of individuals to raise their own kin to as high a position as they can, and the prince should have no sympathy with them at all. Suppose the sister of a king marries one who is less powerful? What of it if it is more felicitous to everyone? The disregard for the dignity of his sister's marriage will bring the prince more prestige than if he sacrificed the advantage of his people to the desires of a mere woman.

The marriage of princes is really a private matter of their own. It is called the greatest of human affairs, so that we too often have a recurrence of what happened to the Greeks and the Trojans because of Helen. But if you please to make a choice becoming a prince, your wife should be selected from all women for her integrity, modesty, and wisdom, and [she should be] one who would be an obedient wife to a good prince and would bear him children worthy both of their parents and the state (*patria*). She is honorable enough, whatever her birth, who will make a good wife for the good prince. It is admitted that nothing is so important to everyone as that a prince should warmly love his people and be loved by them in return. Common characteristics of body and mind, a sort of native essence which a deep affinity of character develops, is of major interest to the country; but a great part of this must of course be destroyed if marriages between different peoples confuse all these factors. It could hardly be expected that the state (*patria*) would whole-heartedly recognize children born of such alliances, or that such children would be lastingly devoted to the state (*patria*). Yet the common opinion is that these are the adamantine bonds of public harmony, although the very facts show that the greatest upheavals of human affairs spring from this source. One [prince] complains that something or other in the betrothal contract has been broken; another takes offense at something and withdraws the bride; a third changes his mind, renounces his first intention, and marries another. One thing or another is always making trouble. But what does the state get out of all this? If the mutual alliances of princes would give peace to the world, I should wish each of them to have six hundred wives. What was gained a few years ago by the alliance of King James of Scotland, since he invaded England with his hostile forces? It sometimes happens that after long violent wars, after countless disasters, a marriage is finally arranged and the matter settled, but only after both parties are worn out from misfortunes. Princes must strive to bring about a lasting peace among all peoples and direct their common plans to this end. Although marriages may secure peace, they certainly cannot make it perpetual; for as soon as one of the pair dies, the bond of accord is broken. If, however, peace is established on real grounds, then it will be fixed and lasting. Someone will say that the rearing of children will cement the bonds forever. Why, then, is there most fighting among those who are most closely related? [L 606] Why? From these children come the greatest changes of kingdoms, for the right to rule is passed from one to another: something is taken from one place and added to another. From these circumstances can come only the most serious and violent consequences; the result then, is not an absence of wars, but rather the cause of making wars more frequent and more atrocious; for while one kingdom is allied to another through marriage, whenever anyone is offended he uses his right of relationship to stir up the others. As a result, a great part of the Christian world is at once

THE EVILS THAT ARISE FROM ALLIANCES

PEACE FOR THE COUNTRY COMES FROM THE TRUE SOURCES OF HARMONY called to arms over a trivial offense, and the petty anger of a single individual is placated by a tremendous shedding of Christian blood. I shall advisedly refrain from example so as not to offend anyone.

In a word, by alliances of this sort the sway of princes is perhaps increased, but the affairs of their people are weakened and shattered. A good prince does not consider his own affairs prosperous unless he looks out for the welfare of the state. I shall not talk about the heartless effect (the result of these alliances) on the girls themselves, who are sometimes sent away into remote places to [marry] men who have no similarity of language, appearance, character, or habits, just as if they were being abandoned to exile. They would be happier if they could live among their own people, even though with less pompous display. Although I am aware that this custom is too long accepted for one to hope to be able to uproot it, yet I thought it best to give my advice in case things should turn out beyond my hopes.

## X

## ON THE OCCUPATIONS OF THE PRINCE IN PEACE

THE DUTIES OF THE PRINCE

[B 469] The prince who has been instructed in the teachings of Christ and in a protecting wisdom will consider nothing dearer (or rather, nothing dear at all) than the prosperity of his people, whom he ought to love and care for as king and member of one body. All his plans, all his efforts, all his interests will be turned to the one aim of ruling over the province entrusted to him in such a manner that when Christ makes the final reckoning he will win approval and leave a very honorable memory of himself among all his fellow men. Whether the prince be at home or traveling, let him imitate the famous and admirable Scipio,[1] who said he was never less alone than when he was by himself, or less idle than when at leisure, for whenever he was free from the cares of the state, he was always going over in his mind some plans for the welfare or position of the state. Let him imitate Vergil's Aeneas, whom the wise poet[2] depicts often turning over many problems in his mind during the night while others slept, so that he could better look out for their interests. And these verses from Homer,[3]

> These claim thy thoughts by day, thy watch by night,
> Rise, son of Tydeus! to the brave and strong
> Rest seems inglorious, and the nights too long.

(the general idea of which is that it is not becoming for him to whom the people are entrusted and upon whom there are so many responsibilities, to sleep the whole night through) should be inscribed on the walls of every palace, or better, in the minds of kings.

[1] Cicero *De off.* III. 1.
[2] *Aen.* I. 305.
[3] *Iliad* V. 490; *ibid.*, X. 159. Erasmus gives the Greek, followed by a Latin verse rendering. The translation is by Pope.

Whenever the prince travels in public he should be doing something for the common good; that is, he should nowhere be anything but a prince. It is more becoming a prince to appear at public functions than to remain secluded; but whenever he goes out, let him be careful that his looks, his carriage, and especially his speech be such as will better his people. He should always be mindful that whatever he does or says is observed and known by all. Wise men have not THE PERSIAN approved the custom of the Persian kings who spent their KINGS KEPT lives buried in their palaces.[4] They hoped to be acclaimed AWAY FROM THEIR PEOPLE highly by their subjects by this means alone, that they were not regularly seen and rarely appeared before their people [for state occasions]. Whenever they did go forth they merely displayed a barbaric arrogance and immoderate wealth in the face of the people's misfortunes. The rest of the time they spent in sports or in bad expeditions, just as if there were nothing for a good prince to do in times of peace, when there is waiting such a great harvest of wonderful deeds if only the prince has a spirit worthy of a prince.[5] There are some even today who think that the one thing which is most honorable for kings, that is, participation in public affairs, is unworthy of a king. There are likewise some bishops who think that there is nothing less their function than teaching the people (which, in fact, is the one duty for a bishop to perform), and who by some wondrous scheme delegate to others, as if unworthy of them, their especial functions and claim steadfastly for themselves the most debased. But Mithridates, who was a noble king no less for his learning than for his rule, was not MITHRIDATES ashamed to pronounce to the people the laws with his own lips and without an interpreter. In order to do this he is said to have thoroughly familiarized himself with twenty-two languages.[6] And Philip of Macedon did not deem it beneath the PHILIP position of a king to sit and listen to cases every day; nor did his son, Alexander the Great, although ambitious to the point ALEXANDER

[4] Xenophon *Agesilaus* IX. 1.
[5] Cf. *ibid.*, VIII. 8, 9.
[6] Cf. Aulus Gellius *N. A.* XVII. 17. 2; Valerius Maximus VIII. 7. 16; on p. 208 the number is given as 20.

of madness in other respects. He was said to have had a habit of covering one ear with his hand while trying a case, saying that he kept this ear unbiased for the other party.[7] The perverted praising of princes is to blame for the turning of some so far away from these things, for the old proverb [8] says that each one likes to employ the art he knows and avoids those things in which he realizes he has little ability. How, then, can you expect that anyone who has spent his first years among flatterers and frothy women, corrupted first by base opinions and then by sensual pleasures, and wasting these years engaged in gambling, dancing, and hunting, could later on be happy in those duties the fulfillment of which requires the most diligent thought? Homer [9] says the prince does not have enough leisure to sleep the whole night away, and yet such persons as I have in mind have only one desire and that is to while away the boredom of life by finding ever new pleasures just as if there were nothing at all which princes could do. A good *paterfamilias* is never at a loss for something to do in his own home. Is a prince without anything to do in so vast a domain?

THE PRINCE
IS NEVER
WITHOUT
SOMETHING
TO DO

Evil practices are to be checkmated by good laws, distorted laws are to be emended, evil ones are to be repealed, good magistrates are to be sought out, and corrupt ones are to be punished or corrected. The prince must seek out the means by which the poor common folk will be burdened as little as possible, by which his country is freed from robbery and criminals (and that with the least bloodshed), [B 470] and by which he may foster and strengthen lasting agreement among his people. There are some other things, less important than these but not unworthy of even the greatest prince, such as visiting his cities (*civitates*) with a mind to improving them. He should strengthen the places that are unsafe; adorn the city (*civitas*) with public buildings, bridges, colonnades, churches, river walls, and aqueducts. He should purify places

---

7 Cf. Plutarch *Alex.* XLII. 2.
8 Quoted in Cicero *Tusc. Disp.* I. 18. 41, and in other places.
9 *Iliad* V. 490.

filled with deadly pestilence either by changing the buildings or by draining the swamps. Streams that flow in places of no advantage he should change to other courses; he should let in or shut out the sea as the need of his people demands; he should see that abandoned fields are cultivated so that the food supply is increased and that fields which are being cultivated to little advantage are farmed in other ways — for example, by forbidding vineyards where the wine does not warrant the trouble of the farming but where grain could be grown. There are literally countless activities in which it would be honorable for a prince, and for a good prince even pleasant, to engage. Consequently, he never will have need to seek a war because of the tedium of idleness, or to waste the night in gambling. In those matters which pertain to public affairs (such as his public buildings or games) the prince should not be extravagant or lavish, but splendid; so, too, in receiving embassies that relate to the affairs of his people. In those matters which pertain to him as an individual, he should be more frugal and moderate, partly that he may not seem to be living at the public expense, and partly that he may not teach his subjects extravagance, which is the cause of many misfortunes.

I observe that many of the ancients fell into this error (I only wish it did not claim any [victim] today!) of turning all their efforts to one end, namely, to leave their kingdoms not better but greater. I have often seen it happen that while interested in extending their boundaries they have even lost what they already had. That much-praised statement of Theopompus [10] is not irrelevant here. He said that he was not interested in knowing how great a kingdom he should leave to his children but only how much better and more secure he should leave it. And I think the Laconic proverb,[11] "*Sparte t'est échue par le sort, orne-la,*" [L 608] that is, "Sparta is yours, adorn her," is worthy of being engraved on the devices

---

[10] Plutarch *Discourse to an Unlearned Prince* 1.

[11] *Diogenianus* 8. 16; 8. 46. Erasmus's text gives as the original Greek, Σπάρταν ἔλαχες, ταύτην κόσμει, but Diogenianus reads κείναν for ταύτην (as does Euripides, *Frag.* 723: κείνην).

of every prince. The good prince should be thoroughly convinced that he can do nothing more magnificent than to hand over more prosperous and in all ways more beautiful the kingdom — whatever it may be — which fortune assigned to him. The character of the general Epaminondas has been praised by the most learned men. When, because of envy, he had been assigned a magistracy that was lowly and commonly despised, he so conducted himself that after his term it was considered one of the most distinguished and was sought after by the greatest men; thus he proved that the office did not confer dignity on the man but the man on the office. If, as we have shown in part, the prince will see to those things especially which strengthen and beautify the state, it follows that he will likewise shut out and ward off those which reduce the condition of the state. It is helped by the example of the good prince, by his wisdom and his watchfulness; by the integrity of magistrates and officials; by the holiness of priests; by the choice of schoolmasters; by just laws; and by interests leading to good habits. All the attention of the good prince should be devoted to increasing and confirming these things. Harm is done by the opposite things, which will more easily be excluded from the state if we will first try to tear out the very roots and sources whence these things come. The philosophy of a good prince teaches him to be zealous and painstaking in matters of this sort. To make beneficial arrangements together for these things, and to compare all their plans for these ends is the one thing really worthy of Christian princes.

If the celestial bodies are thrown out of order only slightly, or wander from their true course, they do not do it without serious disasters to mankind, as we clearly see manifested in eclipses of the sun and moon. The same is true of the great princes. If they wander from the path of honor or do any wrong through ambition, anger, or stupidity, they cause a great deal of misfortune to the whole world. No eclipses ever brought so much harm upon the human race as the conflict between Pope Julius and Louis, king of France, which we have just witnessed and wept over.

EPAMINON-
DAS

HOW THE
KINGDOM
MAY BE
PASSED ON
MORE
PROSPEROUS

# XI

## ON BEGINNING WAR

Although a prince ought nowhere to be precipitate in his plans, there is no place for him to be more deliberate and circumspect than in the matter of going to war. Some evils come from one source and others from another, but from war comes the shipwreck of all that is good and from it the sea of all calamities pours out. Then, too, no other misfortune clings so steadfastly. War is sown from war; from the smallest comes the greatest; from one comes two; from a jesting one comes a fierce and bloody one, and the plague arising in one place, spreads to the nearest peoples and is even carried into the most distant places.

A good prince should never go to war at all unless, after trying every other means, he cannot possibly avoid it. If we were of this mind, there would hardly be a war. Finally, if so ruinous an occurrence cannot be avoided, then the prince's main care should be to wage the war with as little calamity to his own people and as little shedding of Christian blood as may be, and to conclude the struggle as soon as possible. [B 471] The really Christian prince will first weigh the great difference between man, who is an animal born for peace and good will, and beasts and monsters, who are born to predatory war; [he will weigh also] the difference between men and Christian men. Then let him think over how earnestly peace is to be sought and how honorable and wholesome it is; on the other hand [let him consider] how disastrous and criminal an affair war is and what a host of all evils it carries in its wake even if it is the most justifiable war — if there really is any war which can be called "just." Lastly, when the prince has put away all personal feelings, let him take a rational estimate long enough to reckon what the war will cost and whether the final end to be gained is worth that much — even if victory is certain, victory which does not always happen to favor the best causes. Weigh the worries, the expenditures, the trials, the long wearisome preparation. That barbaric flux of men in the last stages of depravity must be got together, and while you wish to appear more generous in favor than the other prince, in addition to paying out money you must coax and humor the mercenary soldiers, who are absolutely the most abject and execrable type of human being. Nothing is dearer to a good prince than to have the best possible subjects. But what greater or more ready ruin to moral character is there than war? There is nothing more to the wish of the prince than to see his people safe and prospering in every way. But while he is learning to campaign he is compelled to expose his young men to so many dangers, and often in a single hour to make many and many an orphan, widow, childless old man, beggar, and unhappy wretch.

The wisdom of princes will be too costly for the world if they persist in learning from experience how dreadful war is, so that when they are old men, they may say: "I did not believe that war was so utterly destructive!" But— and I call God to witness — with what countless afflictions on the whole world have you learned that idea! The prince will understand some day that it was useless to extend the territory of the kingdom and that what in the beginning seemed a gain was [in reality] tremendous loss, but in the meantime a great many thousands of men have been killed or impoverished. These things should better be learned from books, from the stories of old men, from the tribulations of neighbors: "For many years this or that prince has been fighting on for such and such a kingdom. How much more is his loss than his gain!" Let the good prince establish matters of the sort that will be of lasting worth. Those things which are begun out of a fancy are to our liking while the fancy lasts, but the things which are based on judgment and which delight the young man, will also afford pleasure to the old man. Nowhere is this truth more to be observed than in the beginning of war.

Plato [1] calls it sedition, not war, when Greeks war with Greeks; and if this should happen, he bids them fight with every restraint. What term should we apply, then, when Christians engage in battle with Christians, since they are united by so many bonds to each other? What shall we say when on account of a mere title, on account of a personal grievance, on account of a stupid and youthful ambition, a war is waged with every cruelty and carried on during many years?

WARS BETWEEN CHRISTIANS IS NOT WAR BUT SEDITION

Some princes deceive themselves that any war is certainly a just one and that they have a just cause for going to war. We will not attempt to discuss whether war is ever just; but who does not think his own cause just? Among such great and changing vicissitudes of human events, among so many treaties and agreements which are now entered into, now rescinded, who can lack a pretext — if there is any real excuse — for going to war? But the pontifical laws do not disapprove all war. Augustine [2] approves of it in some instances, and St. Bernard [3] praises some soldiers. But Christ [4] himself and Peter and Paul [5] everywhere teach the opposite. Why is their authority less with us than that of Augustine or Bernard? Augustine in one or two places does not disapprove of war, but the whole philosophy of Christ teaches against it. There is no place in which the apostles do not condemn it; and in how many places do those very holy fathers, by whom, to the satisfaction of some, war has been approved in one or two places, condemn and abhor it? [6] Why do we slur over all these matters and fasten upon that which helps our sins? Finally, if any one will investigate the matter more carefully, he will find that no one has approved the kind of wars in which we are now commonly involved.

CHRIST AND THE APOSTLES EVERYWHERE DECRY WAR

[1] *Rep.* V. 470; cf. also *Laws* I. 628.
[2] *Civ. Dei* IV. 15; see also XIX. 7.
[3] St. Bernard (1090-1153) favored the military orders of the church, and in 1129 wrote *De laudibus novae militiae* which he dedicated to Hugh de Payns, prior of Jerusalem; in 1146 he preached the Second Crusade. His *apologia* for its failure is contained in the second part of his *Book of Considerations.*
[4] *Matt.* 5:9; *Luke* 2:14; *John* 14:27; 16:33.
[5] I *Pet.* 3:11; II *Pet.* 3:14; *Hebrews* 12:14; II *Cor.* 13:11.
[6] Augustine *Civ. Dei* V. 17; see also III. 14; IV. 3 and 14; XII. 22.

Certain arts are not countenanced by the laws on the ground that they are too closely allied to imposture and are too frequently practiced by deceit; for example, astrology and the so-called "alchemy," even if someone happens to be employing them for an honorable purpose. This restriction will be made with far more justice in the case of wars, for even if there are some which might be called "just," yet as human affairs are now, I know not whether there could be found any of this sort — that is, the motive for which was not ambition, wrath, ferocity, lust, or greed. It too often happens that nobles, who are more lavish than their private means allow, when the opportunity is presented stir up war in order to replenish their resources at home even by the plunder of their peoples. [L 610] It happens sometimes that princes enter into mutual agreements and carry on a war on trumped-up grounds so as to reduce still more the power of the people and secure their own positions through disaster to their subjects. [B 472] Wherefore the good Christian prince should hold under suspicion every war, no matter how just.

People may lay down the doctrine that your rights must not be forsaken. In the first place those rights are connected to a large extent with the private affairs of the prince if he has acquired them through alliances. How unfair it would be to maintain them at the expense of such great suffering to the people; and while you are seeking some addition or other to your power, to plunder the whole kingdom and to plunge it into deadliest turmoil. If one prince offends another on some trivial matter (probably a personal one such as a marriage alliance or other like affair) what concern is this to the people as a whole? A good prince measures everything by the advantage of his people, otherwise he is not even a prince. He does not have the same right over men as over animals. A large part of the ruling authority is in the consent of the people, which is the factor that first created kings. If a disagreement arises between princes, why not go to arbiters? There are plenty of bishops, abbots, and learned men, or reliable magistrates, by whose judgment the matter could better be settled than by such slaughter, despoliation, and calamity to the world.[7]

The Christian prince should first question his own right, and then if it is established without a doubt he should carefully consider whether it should be maintained by means of catastrophes to the whole world. Those who are wise sometimes prefer to lose a thing rather than to gain it, because they realize that it will be less costly. Caesar, I think, would prefer to give up his rights rather than seek to attain the old monarchy and that right which the letter of the jurisconsults conferred on him. But what will be safe, they say, if no one maintains his rights? Let the prince insist by all means, if there is any advantage to the state, only do not let the right of the prince bear too hard on his subjects. But what is safe anywhere while everyone is maintaining his rights to the last ditch? We see wars arise from wars, wars following wars, and no end or limit to the upheaval! It is certainly obvious that nothing REMEDIES is accomplished by these means. Therefore other remedies AGAINST WAR should be given a trial. Not even between the best of friends will relations remain permanently harmonious unless sometimes one gives in to the other. A husband often makes some concession to his wife so as not to break their harmony. What does war cause but war? Courtesy, on the other hand, calls forth courtesy, and fairness, fairness. The fact that he can see, from the countless calamities which war always carries in its wake, that the greatest hardship falls on those to whom the war means nothing and who are in no way deserving of these catastrophes, will have an effect on the devoted and merciful prince.

After the prince has reckoned and added up the total of all the catastrophes [which would come] to the world (if that could ever be done), then he should think over in his own mind: "Shall I, one person, be the cause of so many calamities? Shall I alone be charged with such an outpouring of human blood; with causing so many widows; with filling so many

---

[7] Cf. *Deut.* 17:8-10. Arbitration, especially in a small way, was not a new idea; the authority of Erasmus must certainly have increased its standing.

homes with lamentation and mourning; with robbing so many old men of their sons; with impoverishing so many who do not deserve such a fate; and with such utter destruction of morals, laws, and practical religion? Must I account for all these things before Christ?" The prince cannot punish his enemy unless he first brings hostile activities upon his own subjects. He must fleece his people, and he must receive [into his realm] the soldier, who has been called ruthless (and not without justification) by Vergil.[8] He must cut off his subjects from those districts which they formerly enjoyed for their own advantage; [or else the reverse], he must shut up his subjects in order to hem in the enemy. And it frequently happens that we inflict worse sufferings upon our own people than upon the enemy. It is more difficult, as well as more desirable, to build

WAR IS MORE COSTLY THAN PEACE a fine city than to destroy it. But we see flourishing cities which are established by inexperienced and common people, demolished by the wrath of princes. Very often we destroy a town with greater labor and expense than that with which we could build a new one, and we carry on war at such great expense, such loss, such zeal, and pains, that peace could be maintained at one-tenth of these costs.

Let the good prince always lean toward that glory which is not steeped in blood nor linked with the misfortune of another. In war, however fortunately it turns out, the good fortune of one is always the ruin of the other. Many a time, too, the victor weeps over a victory bought too dearly.

If you are not moved by devotion, nor by the calamity of the world, surely you will be stirred by the honor of the term "Christian." What do we think the Turks and Saracens are saying about us when they see that for century after century there has been no harmony between Christian princes; that no treaties have secured peace; that there has been no end to bloodshed; and that there has been less disorder among the heathen than among those who profess the most complete accord in following the teachings of Christ?

How fleeting, short, and delicate is the life of man, and

[8] *Eclog.* I. 70; cf. *Georgics* I. 511. The Latin word is *impius*.

how exposed to calamities, with so many diseases and accidents which are continually happening such as the falling of buildings, shipwrecks, earthquakes, and lightning? There is no need, then, of wars to stir up misfortunes; and more calamities come from that source than from all else. It was the duty of the preachers to have uprooted completely the ideas of discord from the hearts of the common people. But now practically every Angle hates the Gaul, and every Gaul the Angle, for no other reason than that he is an Angle. [B 473] The Irishman, just because he is an Irishman, hates the Briton; the Italian hates the German; the Swabian, the Swiss; and so on throughout the list. District hates district, and city (*civitas*) hates city. Why do these stupid names do more to divide us than the common name of Christ does to unite us?

Although we may grant some war to be just, yet, since we see that all men go mad over this scourge, it is the part of wise priests to deflect the minds of commoners and princes into different channels. Now we see them often as the very firebrands of war. The bishops are not ashamed to go about in the camp, and there is the cross, and there the body of Christ, and they mix His heavenly sacraments with things that are more than Tartarean and in such bloody discord produce the symbols of the greatest charity. What is more ridiculous, Christ is in both camps, as if he were fighting against himself. It was not enough that war was tolerated among Christians, it must also be given the place of highest honor.

If the whole teachings of Christ do not everywhere inveigh against war, if a single instance of specific commendation of war can be brought forth in its favor, let us Christians fight. The Hebrews were allowed to engage in war, but only by consent of God. Our oracle, which we hear steadily in the Gospels, restrains us from war, and yet we wage war more madly than they. David was most pleasing to God for various good qualities, and yet He forbade His temple to be built by him on the one ground that he was tainted with blood; that is, he was a warrior. He chose the peaceful Solomon for this task.[9] If

---

[9] I *Chron.* 22:7-10.

these things were done among the Jews, what should be done among us Christians? They had a shadow of Solomon, we have the real Solomon, the Prince of Peace, Christ, who conciliates all things in heaven and earth.

WAR AGAINST THE TURKS

Not even against the Turks do I believe we should rashly go to war, first reflecting in my own mind that the kingdom of Christ was created, spread out, and firmly established by far different means. Perchance then it is not right that it should be maintained by means differing from those by which it was created and extended. We see how many times under pretexts of wars of this kind the Christian people have been plundered and nothing else has been accomplished. Now, if the matter has to do with faith, that has been increased and made famous by the suffering of martyrs and not by forces of soldiery; but if it is for ruling power, wealth, and possessions, we must continuously be on guard lest the cause have too little of Christianity in it. But on the contrary, to judge from some who are conducting wars of this kind, it may more readily happen that we degenerate into Turks than that they become Christians through our efforts. First let us see that we ourselves are genuine Christians, and then, if it seems best, let us attack the Turks.[10]

We have written elsewhere more extensively on the evils of war and should not repeat here. I will only urge princes of Christian faith to put aside all feigned excuses and all false pretexts and with wholehearted seriousness to work for the ending of that madness for war which has persisted so long and disgracefully among Christians, that among those whom so many ties unite there may arise a peace and concord. Let them develop their genius to this end, and for this let them

LET THE PRINCES BE EAGER FOR PEACE

show their strength, combine their plans, and strain every nerve. Whoever desires to appear great, let him prove himself great in this way. If any one accomplishes this, he will have done a deed far more magnificent than if he had subdued the whole of Africa by arms. It would not be so difficult to do, if everyone would cease to favor his own cause, if we could set

[10] Cf. *John* 8:7.

aside all personal feelings and carry out the common aim, if Christ, not the world, was in our plans. [L 612] Now, while everyone is looking out for his own interests, while popes and bishops are deeply concerned over power and wealth, while princes are driven headlong by ambition or anger, while all follow after them for the sake of their own gain, it is not surprising that we run straight into a whirlwind of affairs under the guidance of folly. But if, after common counsel, we should carry out our common task, even those things which are purely personal to each one would be more prosperous. Now even that for which alone we are fighting is lost.

I have no doubt, most illustrious of princes, but that you are of this mind; for you were born in that atmosphere and have been trained by the best and most honorable men along those lines. For the rest, I pray that Christ, who is all good and supreme, may continue to bless your worthy efforts. He gave you a kingdom untainted by blood; He would have it always so. He rejoices to be called the Prince of Peace; may you do the same, that by your goodness and your wisdom, at last there may be a respite from the maddest of mad wars. The memory of the misfortunes we have passed through will also commend peace to us, and the calamities of earlier times will render twofold the favor of your kindness.

# BIBLIOGRAPHY

# BIBLIOGRAPHY [1]

## ERASMUS

### Texts and Translations

ERASMUS, DESIDERIUS, Opera omnia. Basle, 1540.
———— Opera omnia. Leyden, 1703-6.

ALLEN, P. S., Opus epistularum Desiderii Erasmi. Oxford, 1906-.
BAILEY, N., The Colloquies of Erasmus. Edition of 1725 reprinted, 3 vols., London, 1900.
Complaint of Peace, The. First American edition, Boston, 1813.
CORBETT, P., Erasmus' Institutio principis Christiani. London, 1921. Grotius Society Publications. Texts for Students of International Relations, No. 1.
MACKAIL, J. W., Erasmus against War. Reprint of first English translation, 1533-34. Boston, 1907.
NICHOLS, F. M., The Epistles of Erasmus. London and New York, 1901-18.
WILSON, J., The Praise of Folly. Reprint of the English edition of 1668. London, 1913.

### Critical Literature

BAGDAT, E. C., La "Querela pacis" d'Érasme. Diss., Paris, 1924.
Bibliotheca Erasmiana, répertoire des œuvres d'Érasme; 1$^{re}$ série, liste sommaire et provisoire des diverses éditions de ses œuvres; 2$^{me}$ série, liste sommaire, auteurs publiés, traduits ou annotés par Érasme. Ghent, 1893.
BORN, L. K., Erasmus on Political Ethics: the Institutio principis Christiani, *Political Science Quarterly*, XLIII (1928), 520-43.
———— The Political Theories of Erasmus, *Journal of Modern History*, III (1930), 226-36.
Enthoven, L. K., Ueber die Institutio principis Christiani des Erasmus, *Neue Jahrbücher für das klassichen Altertum*, XXIV (1909), 312-29.
———— Erasmus Weltbürger oder Patriot?, *ibid.*, XXIX (1912), 205-15.

[1] This bibliography includes only those works which have been cited or from which quotations have been made in the Introduction and Text. Editions, and the number of volumes comprising a work are not given here unless special significance is attached to that information. In many cases it has been given in the original citation.

GELDNER, F., Die Staatsauffassung und Fürstenlehre des Erasmus von Rotterdam, *Historische Studien*, Heft 191 (Berlin, 1930).

IONGH, ADRIANA W. DE, Erasmus' denkbeelden over staat en regeering ... Diss., Amsterdam, 1927.

KNIGHT, A. M., The Sources of Erasmus's Institutio principis Christiani from the Fourth Century B. C. through the Fourth Century A. D. Master's Thesis, unpublished. Western Reserve University, 1931.

MANGAN, J. J., Life, Character and Influence of Desiderius Erasmus of Rotterdam. New York, 1927.

SCOTT, J. B., The Spanish Origin of International Law ... Oxford, 1934.

SMITH, P., The Age of the Reformation. New York, 1920.

―――― Erasmus. New York, 1923.

## GENERAL REFERENCES ON POLITICAL THEORY

ALLEN, J. W., A History of Political Thought in the Sixteenth Century. New York, 1928.

BRYCE, J., International Relations. New York, 1922.

DUNNING, W. A., History of Political Theories ... New York, 1902-20.

GETTELL, R. G., History of Political Thought. New York, 1924.

GHOSHAL, U., A History of Hindu Political Theories. London, 1923.

GUMPLOWITZ, L., Geschichte der Staatstheorien. Innsbruck, 1926.

HILLEBRANDT, A., Ueber die altindische Erziehung der Prinzen zu Politik, *Deutsche Revue*, XLI (1916), 196-202.

JANET, P. A. R., Histoire de la science politique dans ses rapports avec la morale. 4th ed., Paris, 1913.

LINDSAY, T. M., History of the Reformation. New York, 1906-07.

MÜNCH, WM., Gedanken über Fürstenerziehung aus alter und neuer Zeit. München, 1909.

SARKAR, B. K., Political Institutions and Theories of the Hindus. Leipzig, 1922.

SELIGMAN, E. R. A., Principles of Economics. New York, 1905.

THOMAS, E. D., Chinese Political Thought. New York, 1927.

WILLOUGHBY, W. W., An Examination of the Nature of the State. New York, 1896.

―――― The Political Theories of the Ancient World. New York, 1903.

WILSON, W., The State. Boston, 1908.

WU, K. C., Ancient Chinese Political Theories. Shanghai, 1928.

## CLASSICAL ANTIQUITY
### *General References*

Bibliotheca philologica classica. Leipzig, 1899-.

BLASS, F., Die attische Beredsamkeit. Leipzig, 1868-80.

CHRIST, WM., WM. SCHMID, and O. STÄHLIN, Geschichte der griechischen Literatur. 6th ed., München, 1912-24.

CROISET, A., and M. CROISET, Histoire de la littérature grecque. 5 vols., Paris, 1914-29.

HUDSON-WILLIAMS, T., King Bees and Queen Bees, *Classical Review*, XLIX (1935), 2-4.

Jahresbericht über die Fortschritte der klassischen Altertumswissenschaft. Berlin, 1875-98; Leipzig, 1899-.

JEBB, R. C., Attic Orators. London, 1876.

KÄRST, J., Studien zur Entwickelung und theoretischen Begründung der Monarchie in Altertum. München, 1898.

MAROUZEAU, J., ed., Dix années de bibliographie classique (1914-24). Paris, 1927-28.

——— ed., L'Année philologique. Paris, 1928-.

PÖHLMANN, R., Geschichte der sozialen Frage und des Sozialismus in der antiken Welt. 3d ed., München, 1925.

SCHANZ, M., Geschichte der römischen Literatur. 4th ed., München, 1927-.

### Texts and Translations [2]

BABBITT, F. C., Plutarch: Moralia. New York, 1927-. Loeb Classical Library.

BÄHRENS, W., XII panegyrici Latini. Leipzig, 1911.

BASORE, J. W., Seneca: Moral Essays. New York, 1928-. Loeb Classical Library.

BERNARDAKIS, G. N., Plutarchi moralia. Leipzig, 1888-96.

BOISSEVAIN, U. P., Cassii Dionis . . . opera quae supersunt. Leipzig, 1895-1926.

BUDÉ, G. DE., Dionis Chrysostomi orationes. Leipzig, 1916-19.

——— Dion Chrysostome traduit. Corbeil, 1927.

BÜTTNER-WOBST, TH., Polybii historiae. Leipzig, 1882-1904.

BURNET, J., Platonis opera. Oxford, 1900-1907.

BURY, R. G., Plato: The Laws. New York, 1926. Loeb Classical Library.

CARY, E., Dio Cassius: Roman History. New York, 1914-27. Loeb Classical Library.

COHOON, J. W., Dio Chrysostom. New York, 1932-. Loeb Classical Library.

DODS, M., St. Augustine's City of God. Edinburgh, 1872.

---

[2] In the notes to the translation references have been made to the Bible, Vergil, Pliny the Elder, Valerius Maximus, Pseudo-Seneca, Macrobius, Festus, Ambrosiaster, and Q. Curtius Rufus. These references can be found in any standard edition of the author.

DOMBART, B., Augustini de civitate Dei Libri XXII. 3d ed., Leipzig, 1909-1905.

DRERUP, E., Isocratis opera omnia. Leipzig, 1906-.

DRUON, H., Oeuvres de Synesius . . . Paris, 1878.

FITZGERALD, A., The Essays . . . of Synesius. London, 1930.

FRANÇOIS, L., Dion Chrysostome. . . . Paris, 1922.

GOODWIN, W. W., Plutarch's Miscellanies and Essays. . . . 6th ed., Boston, 1898.

GUMMERE, R. M., Seneca: Moral Epistles. New York, 1917-25. Loeb Classical Library.

HAINES, C. R., Marcus Aurelius Antoninus. New York, 1916. Loeb Classical Library.

HEALY, J., Augustine: The City of God. . . . New printing, London, 1931.

HENSE, O., L. Senecae epistulae morales. Leipzig, 1914.

HERMES, E., L. Senecae dialogorum libri XII. Leipzig, 1905.

HERTLEIN, F., Juliani opera. Leipzig, 1875-76.

HOHL, E., Scriptores historiae Augustae. Leipzig, 1927.

IHM, M., C. Suetoni Tranquilli de vita Caesarum libri VIII. Leipzig, 1925.

IMMISCH, O., Aristotelis opera omnia. 3d ed., Leipzig, 1929.

JOWETT, B., The Politics of Aristotle. Oxford, 1885.

———— The Dialogues of Plato. 3d ed., Oxford, 1892.

KEYES, C. W., Cicero: De republica and De Legibus. New York, 1928. Loeb Classical Library.

KRAUT, K., Dio Chrysostomus aus Prusa. Ulm, 1901.

KURFESS, A., C. Sallustii Crispi epistulae ad Caesarem. . . . 2d ed., Leipzig, 1930.

MAGIE, D., Scriptores historiae Augustae. New York, 1922-32. Loeb Classical Library.

MARCHANT, E. C., Xenophontis opera omnia. Oxford, 1900-.

———— Xenophon: Scripta minora. New York, 1925. Loeb Classical Library.

———— Xenophon: Oeconomicus. New York, 1923. Loeb Classical Library.

MILLER, W., Xenophon: Cyropaedia. New York, 1914. Loeb Classical Library.

———— Cicero: De officiis. New York, 1913. Loeb Classical Library.

NORLIN, G., Isocrates. New York, 1928-. Loeb Classical Library.

PATON, W. R., Polybius: Histories. New York, 1922-27. Loeb Classical Library.

RACKHAM, R., Aristotle: Politics. New York, 1932. Loeb Classical Library.

ROLFE, J. C., Sallust. New York, 1921. Loeb Classical Library.
────── Suetonius. New York, 1914. Loeb Classical Library.
ROSS, W. D., The Works of Aristotle. Oxford, 1908-31.
PRICKARD, A. O., Selected essays of Plutarch. Oxford, 1918.
SABINE, G. H., and S. B. SMITH, Cicero: on the Commonwealth. Co-
    lumbus, Ohio, 1929.
SCHENKEL, H., Marci Aureli imperatoris . . . libri XII. Leipzig, 1913.
SHOREY, P., Plato: The Republic. New York, 1930-35. Loeb Classical
    Library.
SICHIROLLO, G., M. T. Ciceronis leges. Padua, 1885.
SYNESIUS, Opera omnia, in Migne, "Patrologia Graeca," LXVI.
TUCKER, T. G., Selected Essays of Plutarch. Oxford, 1913.
WACHSMUTH, K., and O. HENSE, Stobaei anthologia. Leipzig, 1884-
    1912.
WAKEFIELD, G., Select Essays of Dio Chrysostom. London, 1800.
WELLDON, J. E. C., S. Aureli Augustini . . . de civitate dei. London, 1924.
WRIGHT, W. C., The Works of the Emperor Julian. New York, 1913-
    23. Loeb Classical Library.
ZIEGLER, K., Ciceronis respublica. Leipzig, 1915.

*Critical Literature*

ARNIM, H. VON, Leben und Werke des Dio von Prusa. Berlin, 1898.
BARKER, E., The Political Thought of Plato and Aristotle. London,
    1906.
BORN, L. K., Animate Law in the Republic and the Laws of Cicero,
    *Transactions of the American Philological Association*, LXIV
    (1933), 128-37.
────── The Perfect Prince according to the Latin Panegyrists, *Amer-
    ican Journal of Philology*, LV (1934), 20-35.
CAUER, F., Ciceros politisches Denken. Berlin, 1903.
CARLYLE, A. J., "St. Augustine and the City of God," in *The Social
    and Political Ideas of Great Mediaeval Thinkers*. New York, 1923.
COMBÈS, G., La Doctrine politique de Saint Augustin. Paris, 1927.
DAHLMANN, H., Sallusts politische Briefe, *Hermes*, LXIX (1934),
    380-89.
EDMAR, B., Studien zu den Epistulae ad Caesarem senem de re publica.
    Diss., Lund, 1931.
FIGGIS, J. N., The Political Aspects of St. Augustine's City of God.
    London, 1921.
GOODENOUGH, E. R., The Political Philosophy of Hellenistic Kingship,
    *Yale Classical Studies*, I (1928), 55-102.
HIRZEL, R., Plutarch. Leipzig, 1912.
LOOS, I. A., The Political Philosophy of Aristotle, *Annals of the Amer-
    ican Academy of Political and Social Sciences*, X (1897), 313-33.

MATHIEU, G., Les Idées politiques d'Isocrate. Diss., Paris, 1925.

PETERSSON, T., Cicero. Berkeley, 1920.

SCOTT, K., Plutarch and the Ruler Cult, *Transactions of the American Philological Association*, LX (1929), 117-35.

SIMPSON, W. D., Julian the Apostate. Aberdeen, 1930.

VALDENBERG, V., La Theorie monarchique de Dion Chrysostome, *Revue des études grecques*, XL (1927), 142-62.

────── Philosophie politique de Dion Chrysostome (in Russian), *Bulletin de l'Académie des sciences de l'U. R. S. S.*, 1926, pp. 943-75, 1281-1307, 1533-54; 1927, pp. 287-306.

──────Discours politiques de Themistius dans leurs rapports avec l'antiquité, *Byzantion*, I (1924), 557-80.

## THE MIDDLE AGES

### General References

BARTSCH, K., Das Fürstenideal des Mittelalters im Spiegel deutscher Dichtung, *Gesammelte Vorträge und Aufsätze*, pp. 185-222. Freiburg i. B., 1883.

BOOZ, E., Fürstenspiegel des Mittelalters bis zur Scholastik. Diss., Freiburg i. B., 1913.

BORN, L. K., The Perfect Prince: a Study in Thirteenth- and Fourteenth-Century ideals, *Speculum*, III (1928), 470-504.

────── The Specula principum of the Carolingian Renaissance, *Revue belge de philologie et d'histoire*, XII (1933), 583-612.

BUISSON, F., Dictionnaire de pédagogie et d'instruction primaire, Paris, 1882-87.

CARLYLE, A. J., and R. W. CARLYLE, A History of Medieval Political Theory in the West. New York, 1903-28.

FIETZ, CHR., Prinzenunterricht im 16. und 17. Jahrhundert . . ., Dresden, 1887. *Jahresbericht des neustädter Realgymnasium zu Dresden.*

FORTESCUE, SIR J., The Difference between an Absolute and a Limited Monarchy. Rev. text. Oxford, 1885.

GANEM, H., Éducation des princes ottoman. Bulle, 1895.

GILBERT, A. H., Notes on the Influence of the Secretum secretorum, *Speculum*, III (1928), 84-98.

JACOBIUS, H., Die Erziehung des Edelfräuleins im alten Frankreich nach Dictungen des XII., XIII., und XIV. Jahrhunderts, *Zeitschrift für romanische Philologie*, Beiheft XVI, Halle, 1908.

KRUMBACHER, K., Byzantinische Litteraturgeschichte. 2d ed., München, 1897.

KÜHNE, U., Das Herrscherideal des Mittelalters und Kaiser Friederich I, *Leipziger Studien auf dem Gebiet der Geschichte*, V (1898), 4 ff., 57 ff.

MANITIUS, M., Geschichte der lateinischen Literatur des Mittelalters. München, 1911-31.

—— Beiträge zur Geschichte des Ovidius und anderer römischen Schriftsteller im Mittelalter, *Philologus*, Suppl. Bd. VII (1899), 723-68.

—— Zu römischen Schriftsteller im Mittelalter, *Philologus*, LXI (1902), 455-72.

Mitteilung der Gesellschaft für deutsche Erziehung- und Schulgeschichte, XV (1905).

Monumenta Germaniae paedagogica, XIV (1892) and XIX (1899).

REIN, W., Encyclopädisches Handbuch der pädagogik. Langensalza, 1895-99.

ROLOFF, E. M., Lexicon der Pädagogik. Freiburg i. B., 1913.

SCHEVILL, R., Ovid and the Renascence in Spain. Berkeley, 1913.

SCHÖNHERR, F., Die Lehre von Reichsfürstenstande des Mittelalters. Leipzig, 1914.

SMITH, R. M., The Speculum principum in early Irish Literature, *Speculum*, II (1927), 411-45.

STROMER-REICHENBACH, F. VON, Der deutsche Fürstenspiegel. Dresden, 1925.

TOYNBEE, P., Dante Notes, *Modern Language Review*, XX (1925), 43-47.

WERMINGHOFF, A., Die Fürstenspiegel der Karolingerzeit, *Historische Zeitschrift*, LXXXIX (1902), 193-214.

—— Drei Fürstenspiegel der 14. und 15. Jahrhunderts, *Studien an A. Hauck zum 70. Geburtstage*. Leipzig, 1916.

WOODWARD, W. H., Studies in Education in the Age of the Renaissance. Cambridge, 1906 (reprinted, 1924).

## Texts and Translations

ALCUIN, Epistulae, in Migne, "Patrologia Latina", C.

ANSPACH, A. E., Isidori Hispalensis institutionum disciplinae, *Rheinisches Museum*, LXVII (1912), 556-68.

AQUINAS, THOMAS, Opera omnia. Parma, 1852-71.

ARMES, W. D., The Utopia of Sir Thomas More. New York, 1912.

De XII abusivis, in Migne, "Patrologia Latina," IV.

DICKINSON, J., The Statesman's Book of John of Salisbury. New York, 1927.

HELLMAN, S., Pseudo-Cyprian: De XII abusivis, in *Texte und Untersuchungen zur Geschichte der altchristlichen Literatur*, Vol. 34, Pt. 1 (1909).

HINCMAR OF RHEIMS, Opuscula, in Migne, "Patrologia Latina," CXXV.

ISIDORE OF SEVILLE, Opera, in Migne, "Patrologia Latina," LXXXII-IV.

MANDONNET, R. P., Opuscula omnia S. Thomasi Aquinatis, I (Paris, 1927), 312-487.

MARTIN OF BRACARA, Opera, in Migne, "Patrologia Latina," LXXII.

MOLENAER, S. P., Les Livres du governement des rois . . . New York, 1899.

PETER DAMIANI, Opera omnia, in Migne, "Patrologia Latina," CXLV.

SMARAGDUS OF ST. MIHIEL, Opera omnia, in Migne, "Patrologia Latina," CII.

WEBB, C. C. J., Ioannis Saresberiensis . . . policratici . . . libri VIII. Oxford, 1909.

WRIGHT, TH., Thomas Occleve: De regimine principum. London, 1860.

## Critical Literature

ASTER, H. F., Verhältniss des altenglischen Gedichtes, "De regimine principum" . . . zu seinen Quellen . . . Diss., Leipzig, 1888.

BAUMANN, J. J., Die Staatslehre des H. Thomas von Aquino. Leipzig, 1873.

BOSONE, C. A., Der Aufsatz, "De regimine principum" von Thomas von Aquino. Diss., Bonn, 1894.

DELARUELLE, L., Guillaume Budé: les origenes, les debuts, les idées mâitresses. Paris, 1907.

Histoire littéraire de la France, III (Paris, 1735), V (Paris, 1740).

SHERWIN, P. F., Some Sources of More's Utopia, Bulletin of the University of New Mexico, I (1917), 167-91.

TRIWUNATZ, M., Guillaume Budés De l'institution du prince. Erlangen, 1903.

# INDEX

# INDEX

If references to the same person or idea occur in both text and notes on the same page, only the page reference is given.

# RECORDS OF CIVILIZATION

## SOURCES AND STUDIES

*Edited under the auspices of the*

DEPARTMENT OF HISTORY, COLUMBIA UNIVERSITY

XVIII. TRACTS ON LIBERTY IN THE PURITAN REVOLUTION, 1638-1647. Edited, with a commentary, by William Haller. In three volumes. Vol. I, xiv + 197 pages; Vol. II, 339 pages; Vol. III, 405 pages. $12.50.

XIX. PAPAL REVENUES IN THE MIDDLE AGES. By W. E. Lunt. In two volumes. Vol. I, x + 341 pages; Vol. II, v + 665 pages. $12.50.

XX. THE EARLIEST NORWEGIAN LAWS. Translated, with introduction, annotations, and glossary, by Lawrence M. Larson. xi + 451 pages, maps. $5.00.

XXI. THE CHRONICLE OF THE SLAVS, by Helmold. Translated, with introductions and notes by Francis Joseph Tschan. vii + 321 pages, map. $4.00.

XXII. CONCERNING HERETICS; AN ANONYMOUS WORK ATTRIBUTED TO SEBASTIAN CASTELLO. Now first done into English by Roland H. Bainton. xiv + 342 pages. $4.00.

XXIII. THE CONQUEST OF CONSTANTINOPLE, FROM THE OLD FRENCH OF ROBERT OF CLARI. Translated by Edgar H. McNeal vii + 150 pages, map. $2.75.

XXIV. DE EXPUGNATIONE LYXBONENSI (THE CONQUEST OF LISBON). Edited from the unique manuscript in Corpus Christi College, Cambridge, with introduction, notes, and an English translation, by Charles Wendell David. xii + 201 pages, maps, illustrations. $3.75.

XXV. THE WARS OF FREDERICK II AGAINST THE IBELINS IN SYRIA AND CYPRUS, BY PHILIP DE NOVARE. Translated, with introduction and notes, by John L. La Monte, and with verse translation of the poems by Merton Jerome Hubert. xi + 230 pages, illustrations, maps, and table. $3.75.

XXVI. SEVEN BOOKS OF HISTORY AGAINST THE PAGANS; THE APOLOGY OF PAULUS OROSIUS. Translated, with introduction and notes, by Irving Woodworth Raymond. xi +436 pages, map. $4.50.

XXVII. THE EDUCATION OF A CHRISTIAN PRINCE, BY DESIDERIUS ERASMUS. Translated, with an introduction on Erasmus and on ancient and medieval political thought, by Lester K. Born. xiii + 275 pages. $3.75.

### FORTHCOMING VOLUMES

ABELARD: SIC ET NON. By Richard McKeon, Dean of the Division of the Humanities, University of Chicago, and Mary Sweet Bell.

CORRESPONDENCE OF BISHOP BONIFACE. By Ephraim Emerton, Late Professor Emeritus, Harvard University.

ENGLISH TRANSLATIONS FROM MEDIEVAL SOURCES; A BIBLIOGRAPHY. By Austin P. Evans, Professor of History, Judith Bernstein, and Clarissa P. Farrar, Columbia University.

EUDES OF ROUEN; THE DIARY OF A BISHOP. By Sidney M. Brown, Professor of History, Lehigh University.

MEDIEVAL HANDBOOKS OF PENANCE. By John T. McNeill, Professor of the History of European Christianity. University of Chicago, and Helena M. Gamer, Instructor in Latin, Mt. Holyoke College.

MEDIEVAL UNIVERSITIES AND INTELLECTUAL LIFE. By Lynn Thorndike, Professor of History, Columbia University.

PASCAL: ON THE EQUILIBRIUM OF FLUIDS. By A. G. H. Spiers, Professor of French, and Frederick Barry, Associate Professor of the History of Science, Columbia University.

SOURCES FOR THE EARLY HISTORY OF IRELAND, THE. Volume Two: Secular. By Dr. James F. Kenney.

WILLIAM OF TYRE: HISTORY OF THINGS DONE IN THE LANDS BEYOND THE SEA. By Mrs. Emily Atwater Babcock, Instructor in Latin, and A. C. Krey, Professor of History, University of Minnesota.

M